PET LIBRARY'S

Advanced Aquarist

Guide

PET LIBRARY'S

Advanced Aquarist
Guide

by Feroze N. Ghadially

England

THE PET LIBRARY LTD

The Pet Library Ltd.,
Subsidiary of Sternco In-
dustries Inc., 600 South
Fourth Street, Harrison,
N.J. Exclusive Canadian
Distributor: Hartz Moun-
tain Pet Supplies Limited,
1125 Talbot Street, St.
Thomas, Ontario, Canada.
Exclusive United King-
dom Distributor: The Pet
Library (London) Ltd.,
30 Borough High Street,
London S.E. 1.

© 1969
Feroze N. Ghadially, M.D.
(England)

Printed in the Netherlands

ISBN 0-87826-002-1

Table of Contents

Inheritance in Fishes – Recessive Inheritance of the Albino – The Intermediate Phenotype – Genetic Determination of Sex and Sex-linked Inheritance – Linkage – Gene Exchange – Mutation – Practical Aspects of Genetics in Fish Breeding

Cover picture: A. van den Nieuwenhuizen

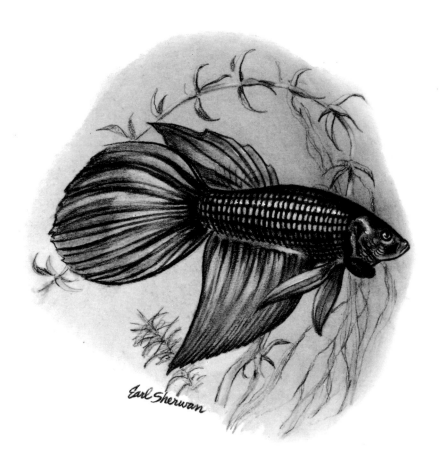

Preface

Many books have been written about the popular hobby of tropical fish keeping. There are large works devoted to cataloging, keeping, and breeding fishes and small elementary works dealing with the needs of the beginner. There is, however, a need for a book on aquarium biology and techniques aimed mainly at the man who has more than one tank at his disposal and is increasingly interested in the many scientific aspects of the hobby.

In order to be comprehensible one must start with elementary concepts and then proceed to a more detailed analysis of the situation. Such an approach is doubly useful for not only does it provide for the aquarist seeking further enlightenment but also enables the enthusiastic novice to partake in the exercise. It is for this reason that I have tried to begin with a straightforward review of the elementary facts, most of which the novice knows, and then proceed to a more detailed discussion of the subject.

Above all this book does not set out to be a catalog of all the fishes and plants known to the aquarist. Such books (e.g., Sterba, 1966; Roe, 1967) are already in existence. Here a few fishes from each family are chosen to help illustrate their needs, care under aquarium conditions, and breeding habits. The last point receives particular attention and analysis, for the person who has passed the novice stage is as a rule acutely interested in this aspect of our hobby.

I trust then that this book will be of interest to the novice and the advanced aquarist alike. Any excursions into the realms of science are carried out in the simplest of terms. Almost every word and argument in this book can be followed with ordinary common sense without referring to an extensive scientific training and background.

References
Sterba, G. *Freshwater Fishes of the World*. New York, 1966.
Roe, C. D. *A Manual of Aquarium Plants*. Birmingham, 1967.

I The History of Fish and Aquarium Keeping

One must at the onset distinguish between these two: the history of fish keeping and the history of aquarium keeping. When man first began to keep fish is lost in the aeons of time. The history of aquarium keeping is more recent and better documented. About the former one might speculate that not long after the hunter turned herdsman the possibility of domesticating fishes either for food or fun must have occurred to the human mind.

It is said (Atz, 1949) that as far back as 2500 BC the Sumerians kept food fish in ponds and that at about 100 BC, or earlier, the Chinese had begun to domesticate the carp, while the Romans kept Moray eels. The Goldfish was kept during the Sung Dynasty (AD 960-1278) and it is believed that in some instances this fish was brought indoors in porcelain bowls during the winter (Chen, 1925). Thus one could give the credit for being the first in aquarium keeping to the Chinese.

If, however, we insist that only a transparent-walled container should be called an aquarium then, since the Egyptians are credited with having made glass around 2000 BC, there is a strong possibility that they put some fishes in the glass bowls they made. If this reasonable speculation is correct, the Egyptians not only antedate the Chinese and Romans as aquarists but they could claim to be also the first tropical fish keepers using all-glass aquaria.

The first book on aquarium management was to come much later. It was in 1596 that Chang Chi'en-te wrote the "Book of Vermilion Fish" in which he described not only his beautiful Goldfish but also how he fed them, changed the water, and siphoned off the dirt and droppings (Hervey and Hems, 1963).

There are records of fish having been kept in glass bowls as early as 1566 in England and it is said that the transportation of exotic fish to England began in 1611. However, the French claim that the first exotic fish keeper in Europe was Madame Pompadour in 1750 (Fitchett, 1958).

An interesting record that has aroused speculation and controversy is by Samuel Pepys (1665), who wrote in his diary "...Thence home and to see my lady Pen where my wife and I were shown a fine variety of fishes kept in a glass of water, that will live so for ever; and finely marked they are being foreign." Coates, Atz, Hervey, and Hems consider that the fishes referred to were Paradise-fish and not Goldfish, as suggested by earlier editors of Pepys's Diary (Wheatley, 1904). Certainly by the latter years of the 18th century the "Goldfish globe" had well and truly arrived in Europe and many home-bred and imported fishes had become available.

At this stage, however, plants had not been introduced into the aquarium and maintenance was carried out by repeated changes of water, though the notion of the balanced aquarium was just around the corner; it was in 1819 that this theory was first clearly proclaimed by W. T. Brande, who wrote, "Fishes breathe the air which is dissolved in water; they therefore soon deprive it of its oxygen, the place of which is supplied by carbonic acid; this is in many instances decomposed by aquatic vegetables, which restore oxygen and absorb the carbon."

This report stimulated experiments by Robert Warrington (1851), who succeeded in keeping Goldfish in a tank planted with *Vallisneria* without changing the water for many months. He not only described the gaseous cycle in the tank but also began to appreciate the existence of the nitrogen or food cycle both of which we shall study in detail in later chapters. Although much criticism has been levied against these theories and their relevance to the home aquarium, the practical value of the results obtained at this stage by Warrington and others can hardly be underestimated. Gone were the days when one *had* to park the Goldfish on the draining board while its glass globe was washed out at the sink, a procedure unfortunately not entirely unknown even today. The aquarium which, with its growing plants and fish, did not become polluted every few days, had at last arrived.

In 1853, owing mainly to the efforts of Gosse, the first public aquarium was built at the London Zoological Gardens. Such was the interest aroused that dozens of public aquaria were built within the next five years all over Europe.

The beginning of the tropical fish hobby as we know it started with the introduction of the Paradisefish *(Macropodus opercularis)* by M. Simon in 1868. He brought them from China to Paris and gave them to P. Carbonnier, who succeeded in breeding them on July 21, 1869 (Buckland, 1880). Adolph Busch of St. Louis introduced these fish to America in 1876.

Since then tropical fish keeping has grown at an amazing pace. Hundreds of species have been kept and bred and many wonderful new strains of aquarium fishes have been developed. Outstanding in this respect is the work that has been done on the Siamese Fighting Fish (*Betta splendens*) and the many live-bearing fishes such as the Guppy (*Poecilia reticulata*). Today tropical fish keeping has become big business, catered for by thousands of importers, dealers, and breeders.

A vast amount of literature has also accumulated on the subject, yet there is still much to learn and discover about many species. Aquarium keeping has had a long and venerable history; there is little doubt that it has also a long and exciting future.

References

Atz, J. W. (1949). *The Aquarist and Pondkeeper, 14,* 159-160; 179-182.

Brand, W. T. (1819). *A Manual of Chemistry,* p. 467. London.

Buckland, F. (1880). *The Natural History of British Fishes,* p. 366. London.

Fitchett, W. O. (1958). *The Aquarium, 27,* 252-253.

Hervey, G. F., and Hems, J. (1963). *Freshwater Tropical Aquarium Fishes.* Spring Books, London.

Warrington, R. (1851). *Quart. J. Chem. Soc., 3,* 52-54.

Wheatley, H. B. (1904). *The Diary of Samuel Pepys, iv,* 425.

II   Gaseous Exchanges

The first important thing that the aquarist has to learn is that fishes, like other animals, need oxygen, and that an adequate amount of this gas must be available, dissolved in the water. Three potential sources of oxygen (O_2) are available: (1) that taken in by the water from the atmosphere via the water surface; (2) that produced by plants with the aid of light; (3) that provided (indirectly) from the atmosphere by aeration. We shall consider the relative importance of these and the way they fit into the scheme of things.

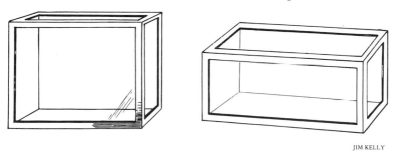

(Left) A tall narrow tank will support fewer fishes than will a long low one (Right), even though both contain the same amount of water.

The Water Surface

The water surface, or what is sometimes called the air-water interface, is the zone at which gases can enter or leave the water. It might be called the door of the aquarium. The larger this door the quicker and more efficiently can the gaseous exchanges occur. Since fishes in the water are using up oxygen and this oxygen is arriving via the water surface it does not need great logic to deduce that the larger the surface area the better.

Indeed under average conditions the limiting factor as to how many fishes a tank can hold is its water surface. Within reason it has nothing to do with the actual volume of water present. Thus one can state that a tank with a surface area of $24 \times 12''$ will hold almost the same number and size of fish whether it be 12 or 18" deep. The larger volume in the 18"-deep tank does not mean that more fish can be kept in this tank. There is no way of accurately calculating the size of the surface area needed per inch or per gram of fish. There are just too many variables to permit this to be done even reasonably accurately. Further, a surface area adequate for a given species or size of fish at the moment may be inadequate for another species or prevent growth to its full size and capacity. Some books on aquarium keeping indulge in elaborate calculations which to my mind are rather nonsensical. As in so many instances the advice given by W. T. Innes (1948) can hardly be improved upon. He recommends an area of 3 square inches of water surface for fully grown Guppies, 18 square inches for Swordtails and Platies, and 20 square inches for Barbs and similar fishes of 3½ inch size. This may appear to be a crude sort of measurement but it will give the beginner an approximation as to the number and size of

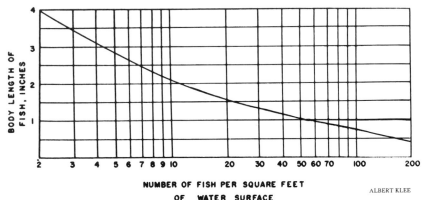

NUMBER OF FISH PER SQUARE FEET
OF WATER SURFACE

ALBERT KLEE

Another way to determine the number of fishes which your aquarium can safely support is by using this graph. Measure the surface area (length x width) of your aquarium in feet. The sloping line indicates the number of fishes of various body sizes which may be kept for each square foot.

fish he can put in his tank. The advanced aquarist must realize that the only rule here is that he should provide the maximum possible surface area per fish if he is seeking optimum growth and development. While we are including a graph of the fish-supporting abilities of a given quantity of water, it is not accurate under all circumstances and is presented only as a starting reference.

Technically speaking, there are three forms of oxygen: O_1, O_2, and O_3. We are concerned here with O_2 which is molecular oxygen such as we find in the atmosphere. O_1 is nascent oxygen and extremely active, combining readily with other elements to form new compounds. O_3 is ozone which is used as a sterilizing agent and like O_1 is not stable. Let us now examine how oxygen enters the water at the air-water interface. Oxygen is a gas sparingly soluble in water. The solubility of a gas decreases with temperature increase, therefore the warmer we keep tanks the less oxygen they will contain. At a given temperature the amount that will be dissolved will depend on the partial pressure of oxygen. Since oxygen comprises one fifth of our atmosphere the partial pressure of oxygen will be one fifth atmospheric pressure. This factor may be of interest to a few aquarists living at high altitudes but it need not concern us further.

Solution of gas at the surface is one thing; its diffusion throughout all the layers of the water is quite another point. Diffusion can in fact be a very slow process in static waters. An aerator can significantly alter this situation by moving the water about, bringing the poorly oxygenated water in the deeper layers to the surface where it can pick up oxygen.

Gaseous Exchanges in Animals and Plants

Both terrestrial and aquatic animals use oxygen to carry out the metabolic processes (in their tissues) necessary to maintain life and produce heat and energy. Terrestrial animals obtain oxygen from the air via their lungs while the fishes take up oxygen dissolved in the water via their gills. As one result of this process carbon dioxide (CO_2) is produced, which in the case of the fishes is released into the surrounding water. This physiological process is called respiration.

Plants, too, respire, i.e., they take in oxygen and give out CO_2 throughout the 24 hours of the day. However, they carry on another vital process called photosynthesis during the hours of daylight, by which they synthesize sugars and starches with the help of their green coloring matter called chlorophyll. For this process they take in carbon dioxide and give out oxygen. Since far more oxygen is given out by the photosynthetic process than is used by the plant for respiration, it follows that during the daytime plants add oxygen to their environment.

During the hours of darkness, however, when only the respiratory but not the photosynthetic process is going on, plants, like animals, add carbon dioxide to the environment.

Pros and Cons of the Balanced Aquarium

It has long been accepted that virtually all the oxygen we and other animals breathe is derived by the photosynthetic action of the plants, carried out with the help of sunlight. We in turn provide the plants with some carbon dioxide via our respiratory process. There is thus a gaseous cycle between the plants and animals on this planet; this is obviously well balanced, for no overt changes in the amount of oxygen and carbon dioxide have occurred in the atmosphere over many years. (Pollution of air over cities may make local changes. This should be considered when pumping air through tanks so that no pollution is pumped in too).

When people began to keep fish and plants together in aquaria, they tried to apply this model of the gaseous interdependence of plants and animals seen in the world at large (macrocosm) to the little world (microcosm) within the glass walls of the aquarium. With this the notion of the balanced aquarium was born (see Chapter I). But such a doctrine, attractive though it is, soon ran into trouble. The fact that fishes can live in water devoid of plants and algae clearly showed that the situation is much more complex than this and that the water can derive its oxygen from another source.

Factors Affecting Oxygen Content of Water

To consider the tank as an isolated microcosm is romantic nonsense; in fact it is part of the macrocosm and communicates with it via the water surface. Here oxygen from the atmosphere can dissolve and enter the water and excess carbon dioxide can make its exit. This in fact must of necessity go on in a tank where fishes are present, but no plant life. However, current thought as expressed in aquarium literature goes further; it considers that the surface exchange of gases is the important and vital process in both planted and unplanted tanks. Thus Atz (1949) states: "As soon as the slightest deficiency in oxygen exists in the tank, oxygen from the atmosphere passes into solution to make it up." The idea propounded is that since the water is in contact with the air it will always be *saturated* with oxygen and as such the plants will not, indeed cannot, affect the oxygen content to any extent.

Nevertheless this view is incorrect as witnessed by actual measurement of oxygen concentration in water samples collected from different levels in stagnant natural waters (e.g., ponds) or in unplanted, unaerated, aquaria. Only the surface layer is usually saturated with oxygen from the atmosphere and a diminishing gradient of oxygen is found as we go to the bottom where frequently little or no oxygen is present (Fry, 1957). We can also demonstrate this experimentally in a quantity of water from which oxygen has been driven out by boiling. If after cooling rapidly to room temperature we study the concentrations of oxygen in different layers over a period of time, we will find that it will be many many hours before the oxygen has penetrated to the depths of the water (Van Duijn, 1952).

All this is readily explained by the slow rate of diffusion of oxygen through the water. If aeration or any other suitable manner of circulating the water is employed, then the entire body of water is easily saturated with atmospheric oxygen; for in such a system the effect of slow diffusion of oxygen is no longer relevant. The poorly oxygenated deeper layers are mechanically raised to the surface and brought into contact with atmospheric oxygen.

Thus it would appear that oxygen diffusion from the air is in fact a slow process which may not keep pace with oxygen consumption by the fish (and by plants during the night) when the water is static. Further, it has been shown that the abundant oxygen produced by the plants in strong light can supersaturate the water with oxygen (i.e., the concentration rises beyond the theoretical maximum possible by simple solution of the gas from the atmosphere) and that even on dull days high local concentrations of oxygen can be produced.

This in no way belittles that vital factor in successful fish keeping: the surface area of water. The important point is that at night both fish and plants are using up oxygen and concentrating carbon dioxide in the water and that, unless adequate surface area is provided, a serious oxygen deficiency and carbon dioxide excess may develop. Aeration under these circumstances would be an indubitable asset for it would assist the uptake of oxygen and the removal of carbon dioxide. During the daytime aeration of a well-lighted, well-planted tank assists in the removal of oxygen from the supersaturated water to the atmosphere.

Factors Affecting Carbon Dioxide Content of Water

Carbon dioxide is more soluble in water than oxygen. Nevertheless since there is far less of it in the air (0.03 per cent) its partial pressure will be low and the amount that will dissolve in this manner will be small. Its solubility is then of little importance. In fact the amount of carbon dioxide taken up by a quantity of aquarium water largely depends upon the amount and balance of carbonate/bicarbonate present in the water. There is an equilibrium established between these as shown by the following equation:

$$CaCO_3 + CO_2 + H_2O \rightleftharpoons Ca(H CO_3)_2$$
(calcium carbonate)   (calcium bicarbonate)

If more carbon dioxide is added to the system by the respiratory processes of the fishes some of the existing carbonate will be converted to bicarbonate. If carbon dioxide is removed (e.g., by the action of plants in sunlight) some of the bicarbonate will be converted into carbonate. Such changes will obviously affect the pH of the water. It is said (Van Duijn, 1952) that in a tank crowded with fishes and plants the pH can sink to dangerously low levels (pH 5) during the nighttime when both fishes and plants are adding carbon dioxide to the water. Conversely during the daytime in strong light the pH can rise to 9 (pH values above this are dangerous to many fishes).

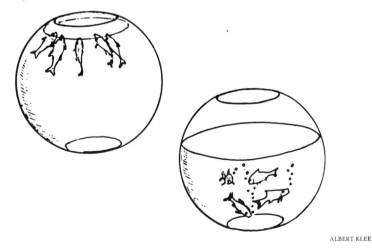

ALBERT KLEE

By reducing the amount of water in this globe, we actually increase its capacity to support fish by enlarging the surface area.

Signs of Oxygen Lack and Carbon Dioxide Excess

In overcrowded tanks where there is an inadequate amount of water surface per fish, one finds that the fishes swim about at the surface, and their respiratory rate (as evidenced by the rapid movement of their gill covers) is increased. If this is not remedied the fishes may die. Much argument has raged over whether this phenomenon is due to a lack of oxygen or excess of carbon dioxide. The fact that either an excess of carbon dioxide or a lack of oxygen can be injurious or even lethal is not doubted, but it is the relative importance of these two factors in actual aquarium practice that is difficult to assess.

No clear-cut answer is possible, for experimental evidence on this point is scanty. Some interesting points may, however, be noted: (1) In some species (perhaps in only a few species) excess of carbon dioxide leads to a decrease in the power to utilize oxygen. (2) Only the free (or noncarbonate) carbon dioxide causes respiratory distress; that combined as carbonate or bicarbonate is not relevant to the question. Therefore in any but very soft waters much carbon dioxide will be absorbed by the buffer system and little will be left to distress the fish. (3) In an experimentally created situation where there is a lack of oxygen without carbon dioxide excess, fishes come to the surface and behave as they do in crowded aquaria, but when there is an excess of carbon dioxide but no oxygen lack they may not behave in this fashion. In fact they appear drowsy, rest on the bottom and rock from side to side.

Thus the bulk of evidence goes against the widely accepted notion that when fishes come to the top of a crowded or polluted tank they do so to escape the noxious effects of excess carbon dioxide and not to seek life-giving oxygen.

References

Innes, W. T. *Exotic Aquarium Fishes*, pp. 7, 9. Innes Publishing Co., 1948.

Atz, J. W. (1949). "The Balanced Aquarium Myth," *The Aquarist*, *14*, Oct. and Nov.

C. Van Duijn (1952). *Water Life, 7,* 231-233, 289-290.

Fry, F. E. J. (1957). "The Aquatic Respiration of Fish" in *Physiology of Fishes,* ed. M. E. Brown, pp. 2, 3. Academic Press, London and New York.

III Hardness and pH of Water

Natural Waters

Water is such a powerful solvent that it does not occur in the pure state in nature. Even rainwater, the purest form of natural water, takes up the normal atmospheric gases in solution or chemical combination as it descends to the earth. In towns and industrial areas it picks up other gases (e.g., hydrogen sulphide, H_2S, and sulphur dioxide, SO_2) and also much particulate matter. On reaching earth in its passage on and through the soil to form springs, streams, and pools it picks up further amounts of carbon dioxide, CO_2, and many other substances in solution and suspension as well.

The CO_2 now combines with water to form a weak acid called carbonic acid (H_2CO_3). The reaction that occurs is as follows:

$$H_2O + CO_2 \rightleftharpoons H_2CO_3$$

(The arrows pointing in either direction indicate that the acid can also dissociate to form H_2O and CO_2).

Now limestone and calcareous matter in the ground is largely made up of calcium carbonate ($CaCO_3$) and a variable amount of magnesium carbonate ($MgCO_3$). These compounds are feebly soluble in pure water but in carbonic acid-containing water they are turned to bicarbonates, which are much more soluble. The reaction that occurs is as follows:

$$CaCO_3 + H_2CO_3 \rightleftharpoons Ca(HCO_3)_2$$
$$MgCO_3 + H_2CO_3 \rightleftharpoons Mg(HCO_3)_2$$

The ratio of calcium to magnesium varies in different waters from approximately 10 to 1 to 10 to 3 (Sterba, 1967). However, carbonates and bicarbonates are not the only calcium and magnesium salts dissolved in the water in its passage through the ground. Sulphates, chlorides, and nitrates of calcium and magnesium when and where available are also dissolved and incorporated in the water.

Hard and Soft Waters

Popularly waters are described as hard or soft, depending upon how *hard* or easy it is to wash with such waters and soap. In soft water (low content of calcium and magnesium salts) soap dissolves and lathers quickly and freely. If the water is hard, i.e., contains a lot of calcium and magnesium salts, a lather is obtained only slowly and with some difficulty.

Temporary and Permanent Hardness

As we have seen, the actual salts responsible for the hard state of the water are the bicarbonates, chlorides, and sulphates of calcium and magnesium. Now if such water is brought to a boil the bicarbonates are readily decomposed as follows:

$$Ca\,(HCO_3)_2 \rightarrow CaCO_3 + H_2O + CO_2$$
$$Mg\,(HCO_3)_2 \rightarrow MgCO_3 + CO_2 + H_2O$$

The result of such decomposition will be:
1. Carbon dioxide gas (which will be driven out of the water by the boiling).
2. Calcium and magnesium carbonate. (Poorly soluble, it will precipitate out of the water. This is the stuff which forms the coating popularly known as "fur" in kettles and boilers used in districts with hard water.)
3. The water itself becomes softer because the amount of calcium and magnesium salts in solution is reduced.

This hardness which can be removed by boiling is spoken of as *temporary hardness* or carbonate hardness. Boiling, however, does not decompose the salts of strong mineral acids such as sulphates, chlorides, or nitrates. Hence these remain in solution and constitute what is known as the *permanent hardness* or mineral acid hardness of the water.

Total hardness is the sum of the temporary and permanent hardness and is an indication of the total amount of calcium and magnesium salts present in the water. There are many ways of expressing this quantitatively and various countries have evolved their own systems of stating the degree of hardness. It is therefore important to study these and see how one system relates to the other. This is particularly essential since at times even well-known books on fish keeping have published completely erroneous facts and figures. The main systems for expressing water hardness are as follows:

A. 1 French degree = 1 part of $CaCO_3$ in 100,000 parts of water

B. 1 ppm (parts per million = 1 part of $CaCO_3$ in 1,000,000 parts of water.

C. 1 English or Clark degree = 1 grain of $CaCO_3$ in one imperial gallon of water

D. 1 American degree = 1 grain of $CaCO_3$ in one U.S gallon of water

E. 1 German degree (°D.H.) = 1 part of CaO in 100,000 parts of water

For converting values expressed in one system into another the following information should prove useful. It covers all the above mentioned systems for expressing hardness.

1 French degree = 10 ppm = 0.7 English (Clark) degrees = 0.585 U.S. degrees = 0.56 °D.H.

However, our interest as aquarists lies mainly in the German system (°D.H.), the ppm system frequently used in the U.S.A. and the U.K., and the British or Clark system, of which we have to take note because Clark's soap solution has been universally employed for measuring hardness, and this keeps cropping up in the aquatic literature.

To assist in conversions between these three main systems and to reduce the possibility of error the following table has been prepared.

	ppm	°Clark	°D.H.
1 ppm =	1	0.07	0.056
1 °Clark =	14.3	1	0.8
1 °D.H. =	17.9	1.25	1

The use of the table can be illustrated by a simple example. Suppose we are reading a German article and wish to know what °D.H. 10 means in terms of ppm. We look up °D.H. in the left-hand vertical column and ppm in the horizontal column; the two intersect in a square containing the figure 17.9. This shows that 1 °D.H. = 17.9 ppm. We multiply by ten and find that 10 °D.H. = 179 ppm.

Methods of Measuring Hardness

There are many methods of measuring hardness. The principles involved and the accuracy and limitations of these should be noted.

The Soap Method

Here we take advantage of the fact that soap combines with the hardness-producing salts in the water to form a scummy precipitate, and only when these salts have been so removed from solution does a good lather appear. The amount of soap used up can obviously be used to estimate the amount of such salts that were present in the water. To do this we titrate the sample of water against a standard soap solution called Clark's soap solution (obtained from chemists). The object of the exercise is to determine the minimum amount of soap solution needed to produce a "permanent lather." This is quite simply done and the equipment required is fairly cheap. We require a 20- or 25-ml.* burette, a burette stand, a well-stoppered bottle or flask capable of holding about 200 ml. of water, and a 50-ml. measuring cylinder or graduated pipette.

Now hold the burette in the burette stand, fill up with Clark's solution, and adjust level by means of the tap to zero. Next measure out 50 ml. of test water and place it in the 200-ml. flask. Add one ml. of soap from the burette to the water in the flask, cork, and shake vigorously. Carry on, adding one ml. at a time and shaking till a permanent lather is obtained. This is defined as a lather which persists upon the surface in an unbroken layer even when the shaken bottle is laid aside for 5 minutes. An extra vigorous shake should be given before the final 5-minute test is performed.

Next read off the amount used. Suppose the reading is 10 ml. of soap solution; if the test has been properly performed it means that the correct end point lies between 9 and 10 ml. Now we must repeat the test but this time we can get to the 8 or 9 ml. mark fairly quickly by adding the soap solution in two or three large doses and shaking in between; after that we go slowly, adding only small amounts of soap solution so as to determine the end point of our titration more precisely. From the number of ml. of soap used to produce a permanent lather we can find out the hardness in ppm from the following table. Thus if in our example the burette reading stands at 9.8 ml. it means that the water has a hardness of 130 ppm.

* ml. – abbreviation for milliliter. One millliter is equivalent to 1 c.c. or cubic centimeter. There are 5 c.c. in a teaspoon.

As you will see, the table does not go beyond 15.5 ml. or 220 ppm. For waters harder than this, 25 or 10 ml. of the test sample must be diluted with distilled water to make up a total volume of 50 ml. Determine the hardness as before and multiply the result by 2 or 5.

ml. of soap	ppm of $CaCO_3$	ml. of soap	ppm of $CaCO_3$
1.35	10	9.15	120
2.05	20	9.8	130
2.85	30	10.5	140
3.6	40	11.1	150
4.3	50	11.75	160
5.0	60	12.4	170
5.7	70	13.0	180
6.4	80	13.65	190
7.1	90	14.25	200
7.8	100	14.9	210
8.45	110	15.5	220

The above method, of course, gives the total hardness. Both calcium and magnesium salts are estimated by this method, the latter being expressed in terms of the equivalent amount of $CaCO_3$.

To determine temporary and permanent hardness a measured volume of water is placed in a flask and boiled for a few minutes, any loss in volume being made up by the addition of distilled water. Next the water is filtered through fine filter paper; 50 ml. of the filtrate is then titrated with Clark's soap in the manner described previously. This gives us the permanent hardness. The difference between the total and permanent hardness gives the temporary hardness.

Unfortunately hardness tests employing soap solution have many snags and are somewhat crude if for no reason other than that the end point is not very sharp. Very hard waters, waters containing much magnesium, can also be troublesome but much of this can be eliminated by diluting the initial test sample with distilled water. This is discussed in greater detail later.

Other Methods

Two other methods are commonly employed to measure water hardness. (1) The acid titration method using N/10 HCl, which gives the carbonate or temporary hardness and (2) the EDTA (Schwarzenbach) method, which is a modern accurate way of determining total hardness.

There are several modifications of this technique and at least one of these is available to the aquarist in kit form with very simple instructions to carry out the hardness test. Those who wish to do this in a more sophisticated manner and who like dabbling in a little chemistry can obtain a professional kit (necessary chemicals only, you provide your own glassware) which is supplied by manufacturing chemists. In one such kit you receive an ampoule of concentrated EDTA (ethylene-diamine-tetra-acetic acid), an ampoule of ammonia buffer solution, and a bottle of indicator tablets. The actual test involves performing a simple titration with a clear-cut color change as the end point.

Methods of Softening Water

Perhaps the simplest way to soften a sample of water is to add distilled water or rainwater to it. If one volume of water with a hardness of 100 ppm is mixed with an equal volume of distilled water we now have two volumes of water with a hardness of 50 ppm.

Ion exchange resins such as zeolite or Permutit S take up calcium and magnesium ions from the water and replace them with sodium ions, leaving a softened but more alkaline water.

Other ion exchange resins are available which can remove the calcium and substitute hydrogen. This leaves behind a softened but more acidic water. Techniques are available to remove all salts and leave behind a water of greater purity than thrice distilled water.

The actual process of softening is carried out by allowing the water to run through a quantity of resin.

Peat is often used by aquarists to acidify and soften water. How this is accomplished is described elsewhere (Chapter III).

pH of Water

pH is an abbreviation of the term *pondus Hydrogenii* which means the weight of hydrogen. A detailed study of pH is not relevant to the needs of the aquarist but a brief explanation of what this term stands for is necessary. It has been found that in a given quantity of water most of it occurs as H_2O but a small amount is dissociated into what is known as ions. This can be expressed as follows:

$$H_2O \rightarrow H^+ + OH^-$$

A water is considered neutral when it has equal amounts of H^+ ions and OH^- ions, acidic if it has an excess of H^+ ions, and alkaline if it has an excess of OH^- ions or, to put it in another way, a relative deficiency of H^+ ions. Thus one can evolve a system of stating the acidity, neutrality, or alkalinity of the water on the basis of the amount of H^+ ions in the water. The simplest way to do this would be to state the concentration of H^+ ions directly but this would give us some rather awkward figures to handle. S. P. L. Sörensen therefore introduced the hydrogen ion exponent pH to express matters more simply. The formula for converting H^+ ion concentration to pH is as follows:

$$pH = -\log_{10} [H^+] \text{ or } = \log_{10} \frac{1}{[H^+]}$$

To put it in words, this means that pH is equal to the logarithm of the hydrogen ion concentration with a negative sign or it is equal to the logarithm of the reciprocal of the hydrogen ion concentration. Now 1 liter of very pure water at approximately 25 °C contains $\frac{1}{10,000,000}$ grams of H^+. The logarithm of the reciprocal of this value is 7. Thus neutral water has a pH value of 7. All values under 7 (0 to 7) represent a state of acidity and all values above 7 (7-14) represent a state of alkalinity. Thus the pH system permits us to express all states from strongest acid to strongest base by a series of positive numbers ranging from 0 to 14. In normal solutions dissociations producing H^+ beyond this range are not possible. A point to note and remember is that acidity increases as the figures decline. For example, pH 4 denotes a stronger acid than pH 5; but alkalinity rises with the numbers so that pH 9 is more alkaline than pH8. A further point to note is that since this is a logarithmic scale apparently small differences mean a large change in acidity or alkalinity. Thus a solution at pH 4 is ten times more acid than one at pH 5.

Methods of Determining pH

There are many ways of doing this and suitable kits are available from aquarist shops or manufacturing chemists.

Test Papers

Strips of paper (impregnated with suitable indicator dyes) and bound in little booklets are available for testing the pH of water. The principle here is that the color of the dye is affected by the pH of the solution. All that is necessary to test the pH is to dip one end of the paper in the test water and then compare the color with a color chart provided. The chart then tells us the pH value for that particular color. Simple though this method is, matching colors in this way is not at all easy and the result can be rather ambiguous.

Determination of pH by Bromothymol Blue

This is a simple, cheap way of rapidly determining the pH of water in our fish tank. What we need is (1) a drop bottle containing a solution of bromothymol blue. (This is a standard indicator solution which is easily purchased from chemists.) (2) A test tube. In the test tube we place about 5 to 10 ml. of the water to be tested, add one to three drops of the bromothymol blue solution, and note the color.

If it is a strong blue unadulterated with any greenish shade then the pH is 7.6 or over. If it is dull blue or greenish blue then the pH is around 7.3. If it is green the pH is 7, if it is a rather pale green or yellowish green the pH is 6.5. If it is yellow the pH is around 6 or under. The test *must* be done in daylight. This may sound a rather crude method but in fact after a little practice in judging the colors it can be reasonably accurate. Ranges of pH below 6 or above 8 are of little interest to aquarists, so this method is adequate for all except those keenly interested in this problem. One other point that must always be remembered when testing pH by this or other methods described later is never to add too much indicator solution to the water, or else the pH of the indicator solution may materially alter the pH of the test solution, and thus give a false answer.

Comparator Methods

Here the color of the test water with added indicator is compared with a set of colored standards. These comprise a set of sealed glass tubes containing buffer solutions of known pH with indicator added. On each tube, or the stand carrying the tubes, the correct pH for that particular color is indicated. This indicates the pH of our test water.

This is an excellent method but it faces two difficulties. (1) In time the standards fade and alter color. (2) If the test water is turbid or tinted (e.g., peat water) matching the color with the standards becomes difficult.

These defects can be remedied by the use of the Lovibond comparator, or better still the Lovibond Nessleriser where disks of permanent colored glass are used as standards. To compensate for turbidity or extraneous color in the test sample, provision is made to accommodate a tube containing another sample of the test water (without added indicator) in front of the color disk. The Lovibond Nessleriser is one of the finest pieces of equipment available for the colorimetric determination of pH, and as such is highly suitable for the aquarist wishing to study small changes of pH.

Electrical Measurement of pH

The equipment for doing this is not only expensive but fairly complicated to set up and maintain and as such not of much use to aquarists. The cheapest instrument of this type is a little over $ 100.

Altering the pH of Water

The pH can be lowered by the addition of dilute acids or acidic substances (e.g., hydrochloric acid, phosphoric acid, tannins or sodium biphosphate). It can be raised by adding dilute solutions of alkali or alkaline salts (e.g., sodium hydroxide or sodium bicarbonate). The pH can also be lowered by allowing the water to stand or filter through peat (p. 33).

Buffers and Their Action

Certain substances when in solution act as chemical buffers. One way of looking upon a chemical buffer system is that it can soak up acids or alkalies and thus *resist* a change in pH, just as a mechanical buffer *resists* the forces of rapid deceleration that would otherwise wreck a vehicle. In natural waters the buffering system is largely made up of a balance between the carbonates and bicarbonates of calcium. How this resists changes of pH when the CO_2 level and hence the carbonic acid level fluctuates in the water during night and day in a planted aquarium has already been discussed (Chapter II).

Here then is a point of some importance to aquarists. Suppose you are trying to alter the pH in the tank by the addition of small amounts of acid. At first you will probably find on adding a little dilute solution of acid that nothing happens, that is to say you cannot detect any change in pH. You add the same amount again and again, checking the pH each time, but if the water is hard the probability is that nothing much will happen. Exasperated by this, you add some more and suddenly there is a marked change in pH – probably far more than you had bargained for. What has happened is that the first additions of acid were soaked up by the buffer system in the tank and when the system was exhausted only a small amount of acid was quite enough to produce a very dramatic change in the pH.

This is one of the reasons why it is so dangerous to make adjustments of the pH in tanks containing fishes. Unless we are very patient and know what we are up to we can easily injure or kill the fishes. In any case such changes must be brought about very slowly over a period of many days or weeks, not in minutes or hours. A change of pH amounting to 0.2 to 0.5 is the maximum permissible for one day and this should not be done repeatedly on successive days. Certainly many fishes will perish with an abrupt change of pH exceeding 1.

Importance of pH and Hardness

All living creatures show considerable tolerance of and adaptation to their environment. Fishes continually amaze us by their temperature tolerance, power to survive overcrowding, variations in diet, light, and many other factors. It would therefore be foolish to imagine that each species survives or thrives at one small specific point or range on the pH and hardness scale. Nevertheless most species do show certain broad preferences. Thus livebearers and many Catfishes are unhappy in soft acid peat water, a condition which suits some Characins and egg-laying Tooth Carps. Certain plants do well in soft acid waters. others in hard alkaline waters (see Chapter IX). As one would expect, almost all species of plants and fish adjust fairly well to waters in between these two extremes. Therefore decorative community tanks housing mixed populations of plants and fish fare best when the pH lies between 6.8 and 7.5 and hardness between 100 and 200 ppm. If the water becomes too hard and alkaline, profuse algae growth may be encouraged. If it is made too soft and acid many plants will waste away and so will some fishes.

In the majority of aquaria the water tends to go harder and more alkaline with the passage of time. This is believed to be largely due to the solution of calcium salts from the gravel. However, even when "lime-free" gravel is used this change still occurs, the calcium being derived from the food added to the tank, disintegrating snail shells, and also perhaps from certain glazing compounds. Indeed this gradual shift toward increased alkalinity and hardness occurs (to a lesser degree) even in all-glass aquaria. Partial changes of water and *occasional* use of peat filtration help to keep the pH and hardness within optimum limits.

It is said that although adult fishes can adjust to life in waters of a pH and hardness different from their natural environment, eggs and young fry have only a limited capacity to do this and so greater care has to be exercised to provide the right kind of water, when breeding fishes.

Such arguments are based largely on our experience with breeding problem fishes such as Lyretails (*Aphyosemion australe*), Glowlights (*Hemigrammus erythrozonus*), and Neons (*Hyphessobrycon innesi*), which are reputed to breed best, or only, in soft acid peat water. Although the value of peat water in breeding these fishes can hardly be denied, it must be pointed out that all the above mentioned species have at times been successfully bred in alkaline waters of moderate hardness (Ghadially, 1957). Further, such successful results are rarely obtained when the pH and hardness of the water are adjusted to the soft acid state by the addition of mineral acids and rainwater. Thus it would appear that the undoubted value of peat may be in properties other than the alterations of pH and hardness it accomplishes. For instance, its bacteriostatic effect and the tanning effect it is likely to have on the egg membrane may be more relevant to the successful results obtained. The pH and hardness would then become incidental factors which would be useful as an index of the suitability of the water but not directly responsible for the successful results obtained in keeping or breeding certain problem species.

Throughout this book, particularly in chapters dealing with the various species of plants and fish, we have indicated the sort of pH and hardness at which that particular species is known to do well. But let it be clearly understood that this is just a rough guide. A large number of species seem to be quite unconcerned about this point while some others will adjust readily to water conditions different from that prescribed, as long as they are not diametrically opposite to what is recommended. In the text we use various descriptive terms such as soft, moderately soft, slightly acid, etc., but these mean different things to different persons. The following table should help to clarify this point for it indicates precisely what is meant by these terms as used in this book.

Range of Hardness and pH in Aquaria

	ppm		pH
very soft	0-20	very acidic	4 -5
soft	20-50	acidic	5 -6
moderately or slightly soft	50-100	moderately or slightly acidic	6 -6.8
		near neutral	6-8-7.2
moderately or slightly hard	100-200	moderately or slightly alkaline	7.2-8
hard	200-300	alkaline	8 -9
very hard	over 300	very alkaline	over 9

Peat Water

Reference has frequently been made in the last few pages regarding the use of peat for acidifying and softening the water. In a later section dealing with fishes we will again refer to the same topic, so at this point it would be convenient to examine the subject in some detail.

Peat is the incompletely decomposed remnants of plant life. It is humus that has lain for centuries in damp anaerobic conditions. Obviously, the type of peat will vary tremendously from one region to the next, depending upon the type of vegetation primarily involved and the details of processing that nature has given it, not to mention the processing it might receive to make it look elegant in the shops.

The ideal peat for our purpose is that derived from sphagnum moss and collected from moorlands. Such peat is rich in humic acids and tannins and poor in calcium content. Unfortunately, to make it suitable for gardening it is sometimes treated with lime, which makes it quite useless for our purpose. It is not too difficult to spot whether you have the right sort of peat or not. Stand some for a few days in a quantity of rainwater. If the water goes alkaline and hard you know that it has either naturally or artificially acquired a high calcium content and is useless for aquaria.

The correct kind will make the rainwater go amber color or brown and reduce the pH hardness. (Rainwater collected from greenhouse roofs picks up some calcium from the putty used for glazing.) The acidity is due to the release of organic acids (e.g., humic and tannic) and the reduction of hardness probably is due to the peat acting as an ion exchange resin.

Some peats collected from the surface are contaminated with a little soil or other extraneous matter. This is best washed away before the peat is used. To do this pour some boiling water on a sample of peat, stir until well mixed, then pour it out on a large fine-meshed sieve. This gets rid of clay, fine particles of peat, and dirt. The peat is now collected from the sieve by the handful, the water squeezed out, and the peat laid aside for further use. If the sample is too dirty a second wash is advisable. Such prepared peat is referred to in this book as scalded peat.

It can be used to form a layer at the bottom of the tank for bottom spawners and annual fishes (see Chapter XIII). It is also used for making peat water for breeding Characins. For this an all-glass tank or a polyethylene tub should be used. This is filled with rainwater, distilled water, or very soft tap water if that is available in your district. Now add the scalded peat in quantities sufficient to form a layer two or three inches thick when it sinks. The correct amount cannot be accurately specified as the acid content of different peats varies greatly.

In time the water should become soft and acid and when the requisite readings are reached it can be used for breeding problem fishes such as some Characins and Aphyosemions.

Peat can also be used in filters to acidify and softens aquarium water. Details of this are dealt with under Filtration (Chapter VI).

References
Ghadially, F. N. (1957). "pH Water Hardness and Fish Breeding." *Aquarist*, 22, 26-28.
Sterba, G. (1967). *Aquarium Care*, p. 32. Studio Vista, London.

IV Biological Cycles

The Nitrogen or Food Cycle

Although most aquarists seem deeply interested in the intricacies of gaseous balance and the O_2/CO_2 cycle, few seem to bother much about the biological cycles going on in a body of water. Intelligent control of algae or water pollution is hardly possible without such knowledge. Application of the principles involved has also led to a sophisticated method of fish keeping (Hughes, 1951 and Ghadially, 1953) by what is known as the circulating range system, which I shall briefly describe later.

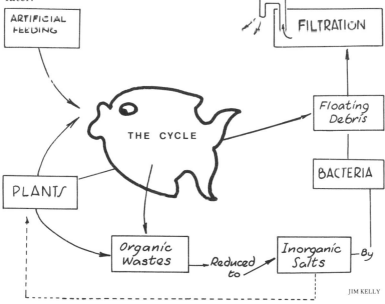

The food and the plants which the fish eat are returned to the water as organic wastes. These are reduced to inorganic salts by the action of microscopic organisms in the aquarium, such as bacteria and protozoans, which in turn convert them to fine debris. In nature, this debris would be further broken down by natural methods and to a certain extent absorbed by the plant life as fertilizer. In an aquarium we do not have the time nor the space to depend wholly on the natural cycle, so we filter the water. The plants in the aquarium also contribute debris to be removed by the filter.

Let us then begin by examining the food cycle in a natural body of water such as a small pond. Our starting point is organic waste, also sometimes called nitrogenous waste material. Land drainage and the action of winds bring into the pond much exogenous organic matter such as animal excreta, tree leaves, and small dead animals. Endogenous organic waste is provided by the tissues of dead fishes and aquatic plants, supplemented also by the excreta of fishes and other creatures such as snails, which inhabit the pond.

On this organic waste thrives a population of aerobic and anaerobic bacteria. The activity of these organisms breaks down organic waste into inorganic salts. The activity of snails mechanically assists this process for larger masses of material like dead plant leaves or dead fish, which are converted into feces that provide food for the bacteria.

Thus the net result of this process is the formation of colonies of bacteria and inorganic salts (nitrates, nitrites, and ammonia compounds). These soluble salts provide food for plants. For our purpose here we must divide plant life into three sorts: (1) Large fixed plants such as ones we use in our aquaria; (2) Fixed algae such as those that annoy us by growing on the plants, rockwork, and glass of our tanks; and (3) Free-floating microscope algae, the sort that makes our aquarium water turn into something resembling pea soup.

The fixed plants and algae provide food for snails and certain fishes. The free-floating algae and the bacteria serve as food objects for many small crustaceans (e.g., *Daphnia* and *Cyclops*).

On the colonies of (aerobic) bacteria thus produced thrive a vast number of protozoans (the infusoria of aquarists). These in turn are also consumed by various small crustaceans. Mosquito larvae will also feed on the protozoans and free algae. The anaerobic bacteria provide sustenance for many tubificids (*Tubifex* worms).

Finally tubificids, crustaceans, insect larvae, and the fixed plants and algae will form the diet of our fishes. All this has, as we have seen, been derived from the organic waste with which we commenced our description.

It only remains to point out that when the fish dies it will in turn add to the organic waste and thus complete the food cycle in the pond.

There are, as noted (see illustration), many subcycles and certain overlaps in the links of the chain that forms this food cycle. It will also be evident that for the functioning of this cycle there has to be some sort of balance between the numbers of each type of organism within a given body of water. This balance is maintained

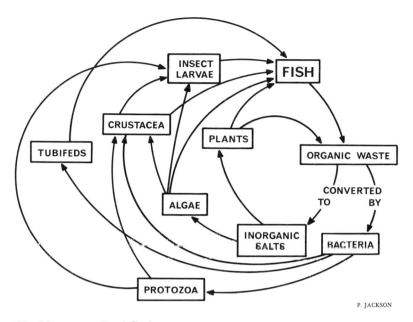

P. JACKSON

The Nitrogen or Food Cycle.

by two basic factors: (1) Adequate shelter so that the predatory organism does not wipe out its food organism completely, e.g., *Daphnia* and insect larvae hiding in shallow overgrown parts of the water where the fishes cannot pursue them (*Daphnia*, however, and some other similar creatures are attracted to the lightest part of the tank); (2) Population controlled by food availability, for obviously no animal can outgrow its food supply.

Thus if there were too many fishes the stores of *Daphnia* and insect larvae would run low, a state of famine would arise, and many of the weaker fishes would die. The death of the excess fishes would automatically relieve the strain on the food organisms and also the dead fishes would have a beneficial effect on the situation by adding nitrogenous waste to the pool.

Let us now return to the aquarium and see how the biological balance operates. Here of course the conditions are rather different. The average density of fish per gallon maintained in a tank is far higher than that occurring in natural waters. Obviously then one cannot rely on the fertility of the small volume of water to feed our fishes, and hence it becomes necessary for the aquarist to provide food.

The large density of fish also means a larger amount of organic waste in the form of excreta. The danger of piling up this waste is of course constantly in the minds of aquarists. This is why we add limited amounts of dried food to the tank, remove any large dead fish or rotting vegetation, and siphon off the mulm that collects at the bottom. Obviously such precautions are more important in a small than a large tank. Filtration is another method by which particulate organic waste is removed from the tank. However, whatever organic waste does remain behind is broken up by bacteria. The resulting salts are utilized by healthy growing plants, If these are not present or if the salts are being produced at an excessive rate, fixed and/or free forms of algae will develop. Although these may be a nuisance to the aquarist they do perform a useful function, for a buildup of such inorganic salts (particularly ammonia) would be detrimental to the health of fishes. This is where partial changes of water become useful. The changing of part of the aquarium water once or twice a week helps to remove these soluble substances with which ordinary mechanical filters cannot deal.

If too much nitrogenous waste is allowed to break down in the tank, we reach a state of affairs known as pollution. The excessive amount of waste breeds and supports a large population. The water now has a turbid, cloudy, or milky appearance. Further, as the bacteria use up oxygen this gas may become severely depleted unless aeration is employed. Some bacteria, particularly anaerobes, also produce poisonous, foul-smelling gases, like hydrogen sulphide (H_2S), which further makes life impossible for the fishes. (This is the same gas that gives rotten eggs their characteristic odor. In this case also it is due to anaerobic bacterial activity.)

Another characteristic sign of pollution or impending pollution is well known to most aquarists. The aquarium gravel goes black in color.

The "black gravel" gets its color from a coating of iron sulphite formed by the interaction of H_2S (produced by the anaerobic bacteria) and iron compounds present in the gravel.

Let us now return to the mainstream of our narrative and see what happens in a healthy tank with its modest bacterial content. As in the pond, this leads to a culture of infusoria. In some tanks we can see these organisms as a small cloud floating at the surface, collecting at spots where the light is the strongest.

This is where we reach the end of the cycle in most tanks for neither

Daphnia nor insect larvae are present to continue the cycle further. The population of fish in our tanks is so great that small crustaceans have no chance of surviving and breeding. The food chain is thus broken, and as we have seen we get by only because we feed sparingly but sufficiently, change the water occasionally, and perform the numerous other exercises called good aquarium management.

The Circulating Range System

We have seen that the biological cycle in the aquarium is interrupted and that this is because the fishes wipe out the unprotected crustaceans.

A simple way to combat this is to connect two or more tanks together by a system of siphons and airlifts so as to circulate the water between them. In such a circulating range of tanks one tank is reserved for *Daphnia*. A small light kept switched on day and night over the *Daphnia* tank, away from the outflowing siphons, prevents these crustaceans from being swept away into the other tank containing the fishes. The bacteria and infusoria developed in the tanks containing fish in time arrive with the circulating water to the *Daphnia* tank where they provide food for the *Daphnia*. *Daphnia* soon grow and multiply under such conditions and occasionally a few may be netted out and fed to the fishes, or the light above the *Daphnia* tank can be switched off briefly. This scatters the *Daphnia* and sends them sweeping down the siphons into the fish tanks.

With the fish eating the *Daphnia* the biological cycle is now complete. The water attains a state of naturalness which no system of filtration or aeration can provide. In sizable ranges (500-1000 gallons) like those I operated in my fish house it is virtually impossible to pollute the water. Not only can one forget about removing even large dead fishes but it is at times useful to throw organic waste (banana peel, potatoes, and yeast are my favorites) into the range so as to increase the organic waste and produce a few extra *Daphnia*. Needless to say, a much larger population of fish can be maintained when this system is employed.

The system, however, is not self-supporting; the small amounts of *Daphnia* produced cannot feed the large numbers of fish in the range. External feeding is needed and heavy, almost reckless, feeding can be indulged in for a state of pollution is extremely unlikely to develop.

This is a sound system. I have used it for many years. There are,

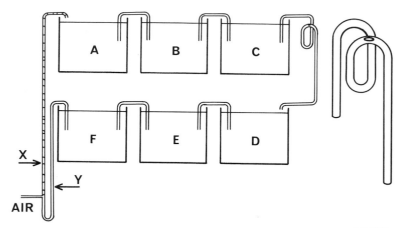

P. JACKSON

Details of the mechanical arrangements of the circulating range system, utilizing the constant level or automatic leveling siphon. This can be constructed of plastic tubing. The water will remain at the level of the hole at the top of the loop.

however, a few snags. The siphons have to be cleaned and maintained. In fact I like to duplicate each siphon so as to prevent a mechanical breakdown. The siphons may become airbound by an air bubble lodging at the high point.

Another snag is *Hydra.* The beautiful water conditions that result in the range are frequently followed by the arrival of this pest which of course soon destroys every *Daphnia* in the range. This pest, however, can be easily eliminated, as described in Chapter XV, and the range restocked with *Daphnia.*

Still another would be the spread of disease should one have the misfortune to introduce inadvertently a sick or weak fish.

Mechanical Arrangements of the Circulating Range

There are two theoretically possible ways of linking tanks together in a circulating range although many intermediate variations can be devised. Given tanks A, B, C, D, E, and F, of which A is the *Daphnia* tank and the others contain fishes, we can have what one might call a series arrangement where water flows from A to B, B to C, C to D, D to E, E to F, and finally back from F to A, or we can have a parallel arrangement where water circulates between A and B, A and C, A and D, etc. The latter is theoretically sounder but it involves laying out the tanks on a large flat surface or the siphon connections would be too long and inconvenient in use (Hughes, 1951). In the usual sort of fish house with its rows of tanks the series system is mechanically sounder and it is this which I employ in my fish house (Ghadially, 1953). Here (see illustration) two rows of tanks placed one above the other are connected together. Water from tank F is lifted by an air-lift to tank A and it flows via a set of leveling siphons through tanks B and C. An automatic leveling siphon in tank C permits surplus water from tank C to drop into tank D, which is then conveyed by a further set of leveling siphons to tanks E and F, from where it is returned to tank A. Any one of these tanks can be the *Daphnia* tank, the rest fish tanks set up in the usual manner. In tanks containing small fry which might get carried away via the siphons, small strainers made of perforated plastic tubing are fitted. The flow of water through the system need not be very fast; a movement of about one or two gallons per hour is quite adequate and this can be easily achieved by the simplest air pump and airlift pump.

References

Ghadially, F. N. (1953). "Adaptations to the Circulating System for Fish Culture." *Water Life, 8, 312-313.*

Hughes, C. D. (1951). "Modern Technique for Tropical Fish Culture." *Water Life, 6, 247-249.*

V   Temperature and Light

Body Temperature

All animals produce heat mainly as a result of the biochemical reactions going on within them. The main reaction involved in heat production is the oxidation of sugars (glucose) derived from the food. This process is akin to combustion and a popular way of saying it is that we burn foodstuffs to produce heat and mechanical energy. Since part of the energy is expended in motion, it follows that it is in the muscles that much of the heat is generated. It also follows that an animal moving actively is producing more heat than one at rest. All this applies to both man and fish, but now we come to a fundamental difference.

In cold-blooded animals (poikilothermic) such as fish the heat produced is quickly dissipated to the environment with the result that the inside temperature of the fish is virtually the same (actually a little higher) as the environment in which it finds itself.

In warm-blooded animals (homoiothermic), however, there is an elaborate thermo-regulatory mechanism, which keeps the internal temperature fairly constant. We cannot go too deeply into this here, but you all know that if we get "too hot" during exercise or on a hot day, the blood vessels of the skin dilate and we sweat. Both these increase the heat loss and help to hold our internal temperature stable. On a cold day the skin vessels contract, thus cutting down the heat loss; we may also start shivering, a muscular activity that will add to the heat needed to maintain a constant internal temperature.

The biochemical reactions going on in animals are largely mediated by substances called enzymes. These as a rule operate efficiently over only a fairly narrow temperature range, so if the internal temperature of an animal drops, the metabolic processes are first slowed down and then come to a halt and the animal dies. It is for this reason that we have to maintain our fishes within a fairly narrow temperature range (70-82°F.). Sudden drops or increases in temperature of 5°F. to 10°F. cause a state of shock and may even kill some of them. It can also lessen their resistance to various infections.

Aquarists have frequently tried gradually to acclimatize their charges to low temperatures. I have witnessed one such experiment where a variety of tropicals which should have been kept at 78°F.

were kept at 65° for six months. Those that survived had virtually ceased to grow.

Temperature Requirement of Fishes

In a way it is unfortunate that the fishes we keep are called "tropical fishes" for this creates the notion that they revel in water at a constant high ambient temperature. In fact our fishes come from far-flung places with widely varying temperatures. Therefore it is not surprising that some of them can stand low temperatures (65°F.-70°F.) while others prefer much higher temperatures (78°F.-82°F.).

A further point to note is that in their native waters there is a marked diurnal variation of temperature. In small bodies of water the night temperature can fall 20°F. or more below that reached in the noonday sun. At any given time there may also be a similar large gradient of temperature in the pool, the top layers being much warmer than the bottom ones.

It would therefore be wrong to assume, as is sometimes done, that tropical fishes have to be maintained at 80°F. ± ½°F. by an accurately adjusted thermostat. Indeed, many aquarists purposely set the differential of their thermostats so that the thermostat switches in at approximately 74°F. and switches off at 78°F.

This appears to be a satisfactory situation for almost all the "tropicals" we keep. There are, however, some hot water fans who like to run tanks at 80°F. to 85°F. Such excessively high temperatures do not accelerate growth, probably because at this stage the relative paucity of dissolved oxygen begins to make its effect felt over any metabolic acceleration one might expect from the increased temperature. In the section dealing with fishes the temperature requirements of each species is indicated. This is based on the accumulated experience of many aquarists. Nevertheless this figure can only be an approximation and a few degrees above or below the stated value is unlikely to have a deleterious effect.

Light

The quantity, quality, and duration of light an aquarium receives is a decisive factor in its success or failure. To provide the correct conditions many factors have to be considered.

The needs of plants for light vary from those of the fishes, the former as a rule needing more light to carry out photosynthesis. Most fishes do not like a strong light; a dimly lit tank is bright enough for their needs of vision and the seeking of food. Certain plants such as *Cryptocoryne* do well in far less light than is needed by such fastgrowing green plants as *Cabomba* or *Vallisneria*. Yet another factor is the depth of the tank. Since the level of illumination falls rapidly from surface to bottom, a deep tank needs more light than a shallower one if low-growing vegetation is to flourish.

These and other factors such as whether the tank is sparsely or densely planted, whether floating plants are present or not, the color of the gravel and hence the amount of light it reflects, etc., make it impossible to state exactly the amount and duration of light that should be provided for a given tank. A rough guide, however, will be given. For a 2 × 1' tank 12 to 15″ deep, situated in a room away from windows and direct sunlight but receiving some diffuse daylight, not too densely planted with a mixed variety of plants and the usual population of fishes, two 40- or 60-watt (each) electric light bulbs in a reflector should be adequate. These will need to be switched on for 8 to 10 hours a day. The exact length of time will vary. This has to be discovered by experiment. If algae begin to appear and show signs of getting out of hand the lights are probably being left on too long. If the plants are not thriving, the period of illumination can be increased. Thus by careful observation, which in time becomes second nature, the skilled aquarist regulates the illumination in his tank.

The quality of light is the next question we should examine. Some consider daylight or even direct sunlight to be the best form of illumination and indeed in the old aquatic literature it was sometimes recommended that aquaria should be established under a window. Today few would subscribe to such a view. Daylight is difficult to control and in any but skilled hands the water is almost certain to turn into something resembling pea soup.

Most aquarists rely heavily on artificial illumination and indeed very satisfactory aquaria have been housed in basements where no daylight enters. Electric illumination can be provided in one of two ways: with incandescent lamps or with fluorescent tubes. Regarding the former we have had long experience and their adequacy in respect to the quality of light they produce is no longer in doubt. First-class plant growth can be achieved with these but the running and replacement costs are high, for most of the electricity is lost in producing heat rather than light. When fluorescent lights were first introduced to illuminate aquaria it rapidly became apparent that plant growth was rather disappointing. The reason for this was that the light they produce was lacking the red end of the spectrum. Incandescent lamps are not lacking in this respect. Soon, however, tubes called "warm white" were produced where this defect was apparently remedied. The plants certainly did better than before but some oldtimers maintain that they are not quite as good as incandescent light for growing aquarium plants. Actually, the source of light is so large, relatively, that they do not have the "punch" to penetrate far into the water.

In recent years fluorescent light manufacturers have developed new tubes, sold under the name of Gro-Lux (Sylvania) and Plant-Gro (Westinghouse). These are rich in both the red and blue ends of the spectrum and, as far as one can gather from the available reports, are superb for growing aquatic plants. At one time much controversy raged on whether plants needed red or blue light. The fact is that they need both for normal growth. The middle part of the spectrum does not appear to be quite as important. Fluorescent tubes have one further advantage: they do not radiate as much heat as incandescent lamps, and thus avoid stratification in the water.

No discussion on aquarium lighting would be complete without some consideration of the aesthetics of illumination. If the main reason we keep fishes is that they are beautiful and we like to see them, then it is obvious that some attention should be paid to the illumination from this point of view.

A most elementary requirement for satisfactory viewing is that the object to be viewed be adequately illuminated and that light from the lamp not shine directly into the eye of the observer. This is achieved by housing the lamp in some form of hood, cover, or strip light. The lights should be situated as far forward as is reasonably possible. If they are placed in the middle or further back the fishes will be silhouetted against the light rather than illuminated by it. A very light-colored aquarium gravel must be avoided for the light reflecting from this can be distracting. Bright lights or brightly lit objects in the room reflecting from the front glass of the tank cause glare and spoil the aquatic picture. Due attention should be paid when siting the tank to see that this will not happen.

VI   Aquarium Equipment

The fish-keeping hobby is catered to by an amazing range and variety of equipment to suit all purses. We shall concentrate on major items of equipment with discussion on how they work and what to look for when purchasing them.

Fish Tanks

Tanks to hold fishes have been made from all sorts of materials, but the angle-iron-framed aquarium offers so many advantages that it is extremely popular with most aquarists. Such aquaria can be purchased ready-made at competitive prices and it is doubtful whether one could save money building one at home.

If you are purchasing, say, a two- or three-foot aquarium, here are the points to watch for. The angle iron should be at least ⅛ inch thick and one inch wide for a two-foot tank. These dimensions should become progressively larger as the size of the tank increases. The bottom of the tank should be perfectly square so that it can rest without rocking on a level surface. The glazing should be reasonably even throughout, that is to say, there should be approximately ⅛ inch thickness of glazing compound showing between the glass and the angle iron all along the frame on every face of the tank. If the compound is too thick at one spot and too thin at another it indicates either a bad glazing technique or a twisted frame.

The thickness of glass used varies with the size of tank we purchase and also the price we are prepared to pay. Doublethick window glass, or 32-ounce glass is quite satisfactory for the usual two foot tank and smaller, but larger tanks should be glazed with at least ¼ inch thick polished plate (see below, Thickness of Glass). If one has to economize, the sides and bottom can be made out of ¼ inch rough cast glass, only the front being made of plate glass.

Today the top quality commercially available tanks are pretreated with one of the many processes available for inhibiting rusting. These include hot dip galvanizing, electro-galvanizing, metal spraying, cold galvanizing, and other modern methods, many attempting to protect and decorate at the same time in such ways as coating the angle iron with nylon or other plastics.

Stainless steel frames probably provide the final answer for the man who wants nothing but the best. Unfortunately this is an expensive metal difficult to work or weld; nevertheless first-class tanks are now available at competitive prices, and have become quite popular.

Size and Shape

It can be argued that since the fish-holding capacity of a body of water is largely dependent on the area of the water surface, a shallow tank is preferable to a deep one. Actual practice has, however, shown that shallow tanks rarely make good decorative aquaria, though they may be useful in the fish house for rearing baby fishes.

A shallow tank is not only aesthetically displeasing but is also unsuitable for cultivating even the commoner aquatic plants. It is generally agreed that a depth of 12″ is the minimum necessary and that 15″ to 18″ is preferable. Tanks are frequently made to fit certain room arrangements. As a general rule, an effort should be made to keep the tank at least as wide as the depth of water.

Thickness of Glass

The thickness of glass needed for glazing a given tank is primarily dependent on the depth of water it holds, this being the factor that determines the pressure to which the glass is subjected.

Nevertheless this is not the only factor which will determine whether the glass will break or not. In fact the mechanical rigidity of the angle iron frame will also have a bearing on this point. As a general rule, the more rigid the frame, the safer the glass for if the frame bends or bows unduly the glass will be severely stressed and will probably break at the least further provocation. Obviously the length of the tank, the thickness of the angle iron used, how well and over what area the glass is supported on the frame will be relevant to this aspect of the problem. Thus the longer the tank and glass the greater the chance of bowing and breaking. We can counteract this in various ways: (1) make the frame more rigid by the use of cross ties; (2) use more substantial angle iron; (3) use a thicker glass.

An intelligent assessment of these factors is particularly necessary when designing large aquaria. Assuming a rigid frame of reasonable proportion, one can relate the thickness of glass needed to the depth of water. The empirical figures generally accepted are depth between

12 and 15 inches, ¼ inch thick glass; between 15 and 18 inches, 3/8 inch thick; 18 and 30 inches, ½ inch thick.

Cover Glass

It is worthwhile covering the top of an aquarium with a sheet of glass or a rigid sheet of clear plastic (e.g., Perspex or Lucite). This prevents fishes from jumping out, cuts down loss of water by evaporation and heat by convection and evaporation, for when water vapor condenses on the undersurface of the cover both water and some heat are returned to the aquarium.

The disadvantages of a cover glass are that it soon scratches the paint on the top angle iron frame. This combined with the perennially present condensed water causes rusting and crumbling of the top angle iron frame. Various clips are available either to hold the cover off the frame or, better still, within the frame. In the latter case the cover is allowed to slope slightly so that the condensed water drains away without touching the top frame of the tank.

A plastic cover is better than glass for it can be rested directly on the frame. It does not scratch the paint work and in time the plastic sags a little in the center, permitting water to drain off without touching the frame. In the long run such covers prove to be an economy for they are better insulators of heat and do not break as easily as glass covers do.

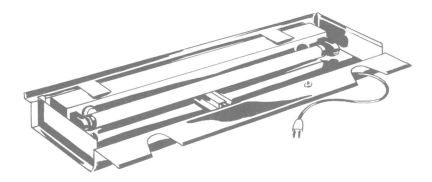

Underside of hood. This is a fluorescent hood. The Gro Lux bulb which enhances the colors of the fishes is the type most frequently used.

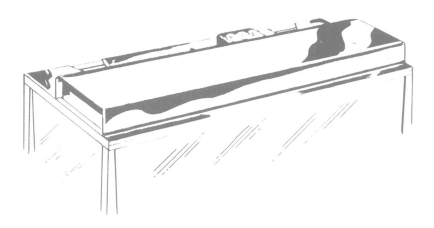

Tank hood. Used to illuminate and also cover the aquarium. A hood may contain either a fluorescent or incandescent bulb or both. The cutouts in the rear are for the installation of equipment: heater, filter, etc.

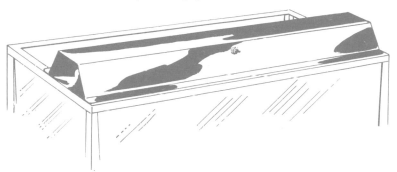

Aquarium reflector. The reflector should be positioned in the front of the aquarium where it can best reflect the colors of the fishes. The rear open portion should be covered with a sheet of glass or plastic.

Aquarium Hood and Strip Lights

A decorative aquarium needs some form of artificial light on top of it (see also Chapter V). This is best incorporated in some sort of canopy or hood which covers the entire top of the tank, or in a narrow strip-light which rests on the top near the front end. Many elegantly finished striplights and hoods are available commercially at very modest prices (see illustration).

It is bad practice to place a hood directly on the frame of a tank; a glass or plastic sheet should intervene between the two, or else condensation will soon play havoc with the electrical fittings and there is also the chance that undesirable metallic salts may be washed into the tank with the condensed water.

Electrical Heaters and Thermostats

To maintain a tropical fish tank at a temperature above that of the room we need a heater and a thermostat. These can be purchased as separate items or as one unit enclosed in a single glass tube. Most commercial heaters are made of coiled nichrome wire wound on a ceramic former; when a current flows through this, electrical energy is converted into heat.

A thermostat is a temperature-operated switch. The heart of the device is a bimetallic strip composed of two metals with differing coefficients of expansion. On heating, such a strip will bend. This

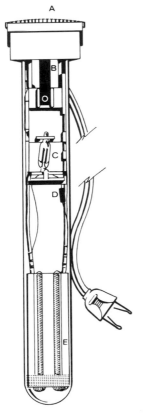

Parts of an aquarium heater-thermostat combination.

(A) Temperature adjustment.

(B) Bi-metal thermostat.

(C) Pilot light.

(D) Condenser (to eliminate static).

(E) Heating coil.

movement is employed to open a pair of electrical contacts (which switches the heater off) when the temperature rises beyond a set value and to make contact (switch heater on) when the temperature falls.

Many different varieties of separate heaters and thermostats are available, details of which can be obtained from dealers. Such devices are now being superseded by the combined heater-thermostat. In this elegant device the heater is housed in the bottom part of a large Pyrex test tube. The thermostat is housed in the top part, the two being separated from each other by an asbestos partition. A knob to adjust the temperature setting is provided on top of this device. The unit is installed in a corner of the tank with only the glass part submerged in the water. The main advantage of this device is that it eliminates trailing wires within the tank and extra connections outside.

Air Pumps

A large number and variety of pumps capable of delivering a few cubic milliliters to a few thousand cubic milliliters of air are commercially available. The simplest and cheapest are operated by a buzzer-like arrangement that vibrates a rubber diaphragm. This combined with a chamber and intake and outlet valves pumps the air forward along the air delivery tube. Such pumps are inherently noisy and the rubber diaphragm perishes in time and needs replacing. Nevertheless some excellent, fairly quiet, pumps of this type are available.

Larger pumps are usually driven by a fractional horsepower motor which actuates one or more piston and cylinder arrangements. Such pumps cost a little more but are worth the extra expense, particularly if one has more than two or three tanks.

Finally, for those who need really large volumes of air (as in a fish house) the best idea is to have a small compressor of the type that spray painters use. Here a motor and compressor are used to fill a metal cylinder. When a fairly high pressure is reached the motor cuts out. The pressure of the compressed air in the cylinder is reduced via a suitable valve and then fed to the air lines of the fish house. When air pressure in the metal cylinder drops below a certain point the motor and compressor cut in again, and the cycle is repeated.

A line filter should be introduced when piston and cylinder type pumps are used so that oil is not pumped into the fish tanks along with the air.

Airlifts

Air delivered from a pump can be used to lift or move water around for filtration, circulation, or other purposes. An example of this is the illustration on p. 40, where water is being raised from tank F to tank A. Air is pumped via a side tube into a tube containing a column of water. Soon the column of water is fragmented by a number of rising air bubbles, which reduce the weight of this column of water. Now the system begins to function as an inverted siphon, water moving from a zone of higher to lower weight. In this manner, the weight of the water in the longer arm (x) of the inverted siphon is reduced by the presence of air bubbles. The weight of the uninterrupted column of water in the shorter arm (y) of the siphon will move water from limb y to x and hence ultimately from tank F to tank A.

The lifting capacity of such an arrangement can be considerably enhanced by lengthening the limbs of the siphon by allowing them to dip downward as shown in the illustration. With such arrangements water can be lifted quite easily to a height of two or three feet, even when using only a cheap vibrator-type pump. This is a high lift and needs careful sizing of the water tubes. A little experimental trial and error is usually required.

Circulating Pumps

Although water can be circulated by means of an air pump and air lift, the amount that can be moved in this manner is rather limited. When larger quantities of water have to be moved about, some form of centrifugal pump is needed. Essentially this consists of an electric motor-driven paddle or impeller enclosed in a suitable housing. Water is led by a pipe to the center or hub of this arrangement from whence it is driven by centrifugal force to the periphery of the chamber. An exit tube located in this situation will lead the water away to where it is needed. Such an arrangement will obviously work only when the pump chamber is full of water, hence these pumps need priming, i.e., filling with water before they can commence to operate.

Until recently only metal pumps of this type were available but plastic pumps much more suitable for use by aquarists have been introduced. Further, in the older metal pumps the impeller within the chamber was driven directly by the shaft of the motor, so a "gland" had to be introduced. This is now eliminated by the use of a magnetic drive.

The recent development of such plastic pumps has permitted the evolution of some very potent filter systems, which can shift many gallons of water per hour. These systems are useful in maintaining very large tropical and marine aquaria.

Filters

Although it is possible to maintain perfectly clean and healthy aquaria without the aid of aeration or filtration, there is no doubt that life is made a lot easier with the help of these aids.

The basic idea behind filtration is to circulate the tank water past a prepared medium, which can remove suspended particulate matter and if deemed necessary even change the chemistry of the water by removing some substances in solution or adding others. The various mechanical means employed to achieve this and the different filter media that can be employed makes this one of the most complex and fascinating subjects for the aquarist.

The means by which water can be moved about or circulated through a filter have already been indicated (Chapter IV). Briefly, there are two ways of achieving this, either by means of an airlift operated by an air pump or by a centrifugal pump. Filters employing both these methods are now available but the former are much cheaper and all that is needed in most instances.

From the mechanical point of view filters can be divided into (1), Internal filters; (2), External filters; (3), Subgravel filters. These are large groups with numerous commercially available variants. We shall examine the main varieties of these and see how they work and what they have to offer.

Internal or Inside Filters

A cheap but highly effective variety of this is shown (see illustration). It consists of a box, which holds the filter medium, and a simple air lift, which raises the water from the bottom of the box to the surface of the tank. Thus water enters through the slots in the top of the box, passes through the filter medium, and then goes up the airlift. Particulate matter is deposited and collected within the box, which has to be cleaned out regularly. Such filters are ideal for the novice, for

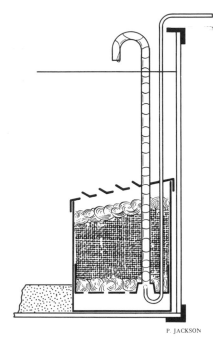

Details of an inside (internal) filter. Water is drawn through the holes in the cover, passes through the upper and lower layers of glass wool as well as the charcoal in the center, and emerges through the holes in the bottom plate into the clear water reservoir. The air lift tube then returns the water to the aquarium to start the cycle again.

P. JACKSON

plumbing failure does not create the disasters that sometimes occur with external filters.

External or Outside Filters

Here the box holding the filter medium is suspended by means of brackets or other devices outside the tank. An example of such a filter frequently constructed by the author (with many variations) is illustrated. This is a double box arrangement made out of clear plastic. The inner box holds the filter medium and a simple leveling siphon brings water from the tank to this inner box. After it has percolated through the medium the water escapes via fine slots to the larger box outside. From here the clean water is returned to the tank by an air-lift. The reason for having two boxes is simply that it facilitates cleaning. Only the inner box containing the filter medium needs to be removed for servicing; all else remains in place, undisturbed.

Note that the water is pumped out of the filter. This is important for it eliminates the risk of overflow.

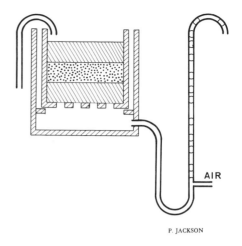

Details of an outside (external) filter. The tubing which supplies the air to the airlift tube should be looped above the level of the filter, to avoid the possibility of backflow of water should the air supply stop.

P. JACKSON

Under Gravel Filters

In this type of filter the gravel at the bottom of the tank serves as the filter medium. A perforated platform or a series of perforated tubes (see illustration) is located under the gravel. One or more airlifts are now used to draw water from this site and the net result is that the aquarium water is drawn through the gravel, where particles of debris are trapped and clean water returns to the top of the tank. The advantages claimed for this method are that the mulm is drawn to the roots and thus helps plant growth, and that there is no need for filter media that need constant replacement. As to the former it can be pointed out that only substances in solution are of any use to plants and regarding the latter it has been found that in time the gravel at the bottom of the tank does get silted up and the whole tank has to be reset if the filter is to start working again. This method does, however, largely prevent the development of anaerobic bacteria colonies.

Filter Media

All but the subgravel filters need some sort of extra filter medium to be provided by the aquarist. What material is in fact used depends upon the job we wish the filter to perform. If, as is usually the case, we wish to remove suspended matter from the water, some form of inert filter material will be sufficient. Glass wool, nylon staple, and aquarium gravel are examples of this kind of material. These operate by trapping particles of suspended matter but in time a growth of bacteria, infusoria, and other organisms develops on the surface of

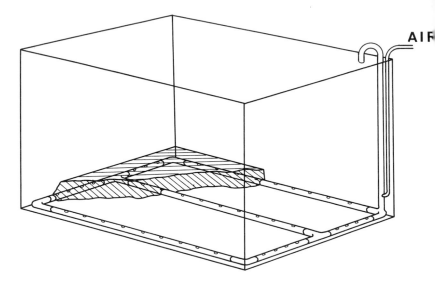

AIR

P. JACKSON

One type of under or sub-gravel filter. This arrangement of a series of interconnected tubes has largely been replaced by a system which uses a perforated plate covering the entire bottom of the aquarium. For larger aquaria, this plate is made in two parts, with an air lift tube in each.

the filter bed. This is called the zoogleal layer and it acts as a most potent biological filter medium. Thus the simplest and most economical way to charge one's filter box is to fill it up with the same sort of gravel as used in the bottom of the tank. (This is what I usually use.) To be effective the water through such filters must be permitted to flow fairly slowly. Gravel filters are labor-saving for they need to be cleaned infrequently. They are also very economical for the same gravel can be used repeatedly after washing.

Granulated charcoal of various types is the preferred medium, either alone or in combination with various other materials such as nylon wool, to construct filter beds. It is useful for removing bad gases and some organic materials by adsorption.

A recent innovation is the introduction of ion exchange resins to construct filter beds. Available resins will remove both organic and inorganic soluble nitrogenous compounds. Used with discretion, they could be of use to control algae. Resins that could change the pH and hardness of the water are also available but it is doubtful if these will be of great practical value to aquarists.

A simpler and cheaper way to make the water softer and more acid is to charge the filter box with some peat (see Chapter III). Frequent pH readings should be taken and a sharp eye kept on the behavior of the fish, for a quick and sometimes even lethal change of pH can be produced in a few hours by working such a filter.

Nets

Small and large nets in variety are available to the aquarist. When catching fishes the net should be able to move freely through the water, hence one made of wide-meshed material is preferable. Chasing fishes with a small net is an irritating and frustrating experience so always use the largest net that can be conveniently employed in the tank. After use the net should be hung up so that it dries rapidly. Larger nets of finer mesh (nylon organdy) are employed for collecting *Daphnia* from ponds. Such nets should be mounted on a five foot long or longer aluminum or wooden pole.

Aquarium Scrapers

Various methods are available for keeping the inside face of the front glass of an aquarium clean. One of the most efficient is a razor blade mounted in a holder at the end of a long stick. Such scrapers are available very cheaply or can be easily made at home. The scraper should be worked systematically over the glass with the blade flat against the glass. Care should be taken to see that the sharp edge is not scraped over the glass as would happen if the scraper is held at a tilt. Fine scratches can be made on the glass in this way. The use of steel wool to clean the front glass also carries with it the same hazard. Nylon scouring pads are much more suitable, but be careful they do not pick up grains of sand or gravel which will scratch the glass.

Diffusers or Air-Stones

In order to obtain the maximum beneficial effect from aeration it is essential to break up the air stream delivered by an air pump into a stream of fine bubbles. This is achieved by a variety of commercially available diffusers. Of these those made of porous stone are the best. Others made of metal are, in my view, less desirable. Diffusers tend to clog up after a time; they can be revived by scrubbing and heating in an oven.

Thermometers

Various thermometers are available. Some are designed to attach by a suction pad to the front glass of the tank, others float freely in the water. (The latter variety seem to float away into the most inaccessible corners whenever one wishes to check the temperature). My favorite is the small dial-type thermometer which sticks to the front glass. The larger mercury or alcohol types with a plastic plate are conspicuous and detract from the beauty of the aquascape. Thermometers can be inaccurate so those in use should be checked against a good one. The serious hobbyist should keep a high quality mercury thermometer (obtained from laboratory equipment suppliers) which is known to be accurate to within $\pm$ 0.1°F. Less expensive and new thermometers can be checked against this before purchase.

Feeding Rings

Ingenious devices for preventing the scattering of dried and other foods such as *Tubifex* and whiteworms over the whole of the aquarium are available. In its simplest form this is no more than a plastic ring, which floats on the surface of the water. Various small plastic boxes with holes in the side and bottom are used to dispense worms gradually so that the fishes eat them before they fall to the bottom and disappear in the gravel.

Selecting and Making Rockwork

While it is possible to set up small decorative aquaria without any rockwork, most larger ones should have arrangements of natural or artificial stones.

When natural rocks are selected for introduction in the tank one must make sure that they are not unduly soluble or likely to crumble in the water. Marble and some other limestones do just that and in the process make the water very hard. Granite, flint, and sandstone do not suffer from this defect and if collected near or from a stream or pond have the added advantage that they look more natural, and any readily soluble matter has long been removed from them.

The difficulty of finding the exact sort of natural stone needed to create the aquatic picture they envisioned has led aquarists to find ways of making artificial rockwork. Further, certain decorative schemes such as covering the back wall of a tank need a fairly large but thin section of stone. Pieces that fit so exactly to our needs may rarely be found in nature so they have to be made. Perhaps the easiest and cheapest way to achieve this is to make artificial rockwork out of concrete with or without added natural stone.

Let us now examine how we can build an artificial rock face to hide the back wall of, say, a 24 × 15 × 15″ tank. Since a tight fit is neither needed nor desirable, it will be apparent that a finished screen about 22 × 13″ will be adequate. The next stage is to make a light wooden frame of one inch square timber so that it encloses the required area. This is laid on some flat working surface such as a sheet of plywood which is first covered with one or two layers of newspaper (see illustration). Next a mixture of one part of portland cement

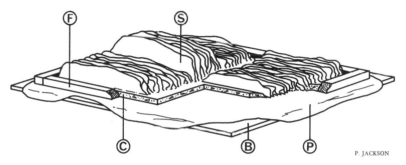

P. JACKSON

A method of making artificial rockwork. (B) wooden board – (P) sheet of paper – (F) wooden frame – (C) a layer of the concrete mixture – (S) thin pieces of slate. For further details see text.

and three parts of sand is made and sufficient water added to make an easily workable plastic mixture. Structural strength will be added if a piece of half inch wire mesh, about one inch smaller in both dimensions than the wood frame, is put in the frame before the cement mix is placed. The wire should be supported on bits of gravel about ¼″ above the newspaper.

Handfuls of the mixture (advisable to wear gloves) are taken and placed in the frame. Each handful is carefully placed and worked so as to fill all the corners of the frame and also so that the adjacent handfuls fuse together to form a compact whole.

When the wooden frame is just over three-fourths filled with the mixture, modeling of the rock face begins. It is at this stage that the artistic part of the exercise commences. The aim now is to build up and cut away material so that the finished surface looks like a natural rock face in miniature. Try to create fairly large rising and falling masses for it is only this sort of sculptured effect that will come through in the final setup. However, care must be exercised to see that not too much is cut away or a weak product will result. Similarly, building up must not be too enthusiastic. For instance, the maximum thickness need not go beyond $1\frac{1}{4}$ to $2''$. The aim should be to create the maximum relief within the very restricted limits of the total thickness one is forced to work in.

An important point is the creation of strata in our rockwork. These can be drawn in by a small piece of wood or even the edge of a screwdriver, but boxwood modeling tools from an artists' shop do the job much better.

Some people like to introduce pieces of natural stone in the design. Flat strips of slate or thin standstone are ideal for this purpose.

In my home tank (which I describe in Chapter VII) the rockwork screen covering the back of the tank and the artificial rockwork holding the gravel in place was supplemented by strips of roofing slate varying in width from $\frac{1}{2}$ to $3''$ and in length from 2 to $12''$ with the edges set in concrete. These make tiers and galleries for rooting plants.

When the work is completed it must be covered with a damp piece of cloth and the whole covered with a sheet of plastic wrap. Concrete must not be allowed to dry out quickly. It should be kept damp as long as possible, at least for four or five days, otherwise a weak product will result. At the end of this period the wooden frame can be easily removed, particularly if it was lightly oiled before use. The newspaper too should peel off easily from the back but sometimes it adheres fairly strongly and may require rubbing off with a flat piece of sandstone or a wire brush. The paper too may be lightly oiled before use so that it will not stick to the concrete.

Freshly made concrete rockwork placed in a tank will kill the fishes. This is because concrete contains alkaline substances which dissolve in the water and cause a sudden serious shift in pH. However, the amount of such substances present in the concrete is limited and once these are eliminated by repeated washing and/or neutralization the concrete object is rendered safe forever.

The quickest way to cure concrete rockwork is as follows. Place the object in a plastic container and cover it with water. Add a little dilute mineral acid until the water shows an acid reaction (red) with a strip of litmus paper. Dilute hydrochloric or acetic acid is best for this purpose. (Vinegar is too weak to treat economically any but the smallest pieces.) In time the alkali coming out of the rockwork will neutralize the acid and a blue reaction to litmus will develop. Add more acid to maintain the acidic state. When the water stays acidic for a few (3 or 4) days it means that no more alkali is released.

The excess acid is now removed by soaking and rinsing in fresh water. The whole process usually takes about a week to ten days for large pieces of rockwork.

The rockwork may now be placed in the tank. Unless you have experience of this technique it is best to check the pH of the tank regularly for a few days to see that the pH is not shifting toward the alkaline side. If a tendency toward this is noticed, partial replacement of the tank water should remedy the condition.

Spawning Media

Various artificial spawning media have been known to aquarists for a long time. Their use presents distinct advantages over the usual method of using fine-leafed plants when spawning egglayers. At one time it was commonly accepted, and even today it is sometimes argued, that a large, well-established tank is the ideal place in which to spawn a pair of fish. The reasons given are that the water in such an aquarium is mature and that there are already some infusoria present for the fry to feed on once they become free-swimming. All that is needed according to this doctrine is the introduction of some fine-leafed plants and the removal of snails, and the stage is set for spawning.

Superficially this appears to be a good idea but in actual practice many snags are encountered. Any hypothetical advantage derived from the "few infusoria" and the "mature water" are often offset by the fact that removing snails is easier said than done and that the tank may also contain other egg- and fry-destroying creatures, e.g., *Hydra* and planarians which seem to have a peculiar habit of making their presence felt only when the spawning is accomplished. Further, the water in old tanks is frequently very hard and alkaline.

It may therefore be desirable to set up a fresh clean tank for spawning and use some artificial spawning medium which, in contrast to plants, can be adequately cleaned and sterilized.

The choice here is very large. The medium with which I have had most success is cleaned and boiled willow root, large quantities of which can be readily collected from willow trees growing on the banks of rivers and streams, where they send masses of roots into the water.

The collected root has to be cleaned very thoroughly by repeated rinsing and boiling over a period of days. This is a long and tiring process but it must not be skimped for poorly prepared root can kill the fishes (Ghadially, 1953).

Once a quantity of root has been cleaned it can be stored indefinitely in the dry state. A small quantity is needed for each spawning. It can be used again and again hundreds of times by cleaning and boiling after each spawning. In my experience fishes *prefer* to spawn on this rather than on plants when both are provided in a breeding tank.

Other spawning media not requiring such strenuous effort in procuring or cleaning are available (Ghadially, 1955) but they are, in my view, somewhat inferior. The commonest of these are nylon fiber preparations of one sort or another. Roughly these can be grouped into three, (1) Nylon staple; (2) Coarser nylon fibers obtained by unraveling nylon scouring pads; (3) Nylon wool, prepared from nylon staple. The last seems to be most popular with the majority of aquarists.

Prior to use the wool has to be prepared into mops. To do this the skein of wool is first tied off firmly with short lengths of nylon wool at intervals of about 3 to 4 inches. By cutting approximately ½ inch to one side of each knot a series of mops is produced.

Nylon spawn-receiving mops supported on a glass rod frame.

F. N. GHADIALLY

For most of the egglayers 2 or 3 of these mops laid in the bottom of the tank will suffice. For surface spawners the mops can be floated by threading them through cork, by hanging them astride strings, or by supporting them on a glass rod frame.

Breeding Traps

Breeding traps are used to protect the newly born fry of livebearers from the cannibalistic tendencies of the mother. The trap consists of a box or cage with perforations or apertures on the bottom and/or the sides. Many varieties of these are commercially available. In one the base is made of glass rods. In another the entire trap is made of $\frac{1}{4}''$ mesh plastic material. Still a third method is to make the bottom in the shape of a V with the lower angle open along its length. The babies, which do not swim for the first few minutes, roll down the sloping sides and out the bottom.

The pregnant female is moved to the trap a week or two before delivery. When the babies are born they escape via the apertures into the fish tank in which the trap is suspended (see also Chapter XIII, Genera *Poecilia* and *Xiphophorus*, Breeding Methods). Needless to say there should be no fishes with carnivorous capabilities in the tank which receives the babies.

References
Ghadially, F. N. (1953). "Willow Root as a Spawning Medium," *Water Life, 8, 27.*
Ghadially, F. N. (1955). "Using Nylon for a Spawning Medium," *Water Life, 10, 276-277.*

VII   Decorative Aquaria

Virtually every aquarist maintains at least one decorative aquarium in his home. Indeed the first tank assembled by the beginner falls into this category. However, for many of us this is just the beginning; as the years pass and experience accumulates we make bigger and more elaborate aquascapes which reflect our tastes and abilities.

Here we shall first examine how a simple decorative tank can be set up by a novice; later we shall deal with the problems involved in larger, more ambitious aquascapes.

Locating and Setting Up a Simple Decorative Aquarium

There are two approaches to the problem of locating a tank. (1) You may have a space in the hallway or a niche in a wall where you feel a fish tank would look attractive. (2) You wish to set up a standard two- or three-foot tank and wonder which would be the best place to put it.

In the first instance a specially shaped tank may be necessary. As long as it is not too deep or of inadequate width you can make a success of the venture without auxiliary apparatus or deviating from standard methods. If the tank is too deep aeration will become a virtual necessity and probably tall-growing plants as well.

The chosen site for the tank must have substantial underpinning for a furnished aquarium is very heavy. A $36'' \times 15'' \times 15''$ tank with water, gravel and rockwork weighs at least 300 pounds. If the support shifts, yields, or vibrates, leaks may develop and the glass may crack.

The next question to consider is that of available light. Aquaria can be maintained in dark corners or even in cellars, with suitable artificial illumination (see Chapter V), but it is almost impossible to maintain an algae-free tank under a window receiving strong daylight. This is about the worst place to locate a decorative aquarium. The ideal lies between these two extremes for if the tank receives a reasonable amount of diffused daylight an economical use of the artificial light during the evening is all that will be needed. The tank should be placed as close as possible to an electric outlet, which should be devoted to supplying only the fish tank. If other devices are attached they may cause an accidental interruption of current to the tank.

Finally, the tank must be easily accessible so that the hood and coverglass may be raised for cleaning the front glass, and there should be room available for maneuvering buckets and pipes when siphoning the bottom and changing part of the water.

Setting Up the Tank

A new aquarium should first be cleaned and tested for leaks. This is done by standing it on a firm flat support and filling up with water. Most small leaks are self-healing but larger leaks may necessitate reglazing the tank. All leaks should be stopped before setting in its final position.

The cleaned and tested tank should be emptied and moved to its permanent site. To move a tank with water in it is to invite trouble. The tank should sit firmly without rocking on the corners. Slight irregularities may be accommodated by packing with thin strips of aluminum under one or two corners.

Gravel

The medium placed on the bottom of the tank is frequently referred to as gravel or sand. Fine sand like that found on sea beaches is unsuitable for it packs too closely and as a rule plants do not thrive in it. On the other hand coarse pebbles or stone chips are no good either, for they trap food which soon rots and sets up pollution. The ideal is gravel of particle size 1/16 inch to 1/8 inch in diameter. About ten pounds of gravel per square foot of aquarium floor will be needed. The gravel must be first washed thoroughly. This can only be done if small quantities at a time are washed in a plastic bucket or similar container. The cleaned gravel is spread out on the bottom of the tank. When the process is completed the tank should have a gently sloping layer of gravel ranging from 2½ inches deep at the back to about one inch at the front.

Rocks and Rockwork

Rocks are not absolutely essential for setting up a tank, and indeed many beginners' tanks contain no rockwork. However, there is no doubt that the addition of suitable rockwork considerably enhances the appearance of the decorative tank. How and where to lay the

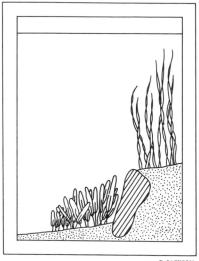

Method of building tiers and galleries using rockwork.

rocks is largely dictated by the artistic mind of the aquarist concerned.

The haphazard placing of pieces of nondescript rock is hardly likely to prove satisfactory. Rockwork is perhaps most effective when it is used to form tiers that extend along the tank at different elevations. This is shown diagrammatically in the figure.

Introduction of Water

In most districts it is quite safe to fill the tank with tap water. Since copper salts are poisonous to fish and plants (see Chapter XIV) it is best not to draw water from the hot water faucet for the boiler is likely to be made of copper. If the plumbing in the house is copper, the cold faucet should be allowed to run to waste for a few minutes before the aquarium is filled with water. Such precautions are doubly important in a newly built house.

An experienced aquarist can easily fill a tank with a hose turned down to a thin trickle directed against a suitable point on the glass side of a tank so that the gravel is not churned up and the tiers and galleries destroyed in the process, but beginners are advised to stand a small jar on a saucer and place this on a flat part of the gravel bottom. The stream of water is directed into the jar, which fills up and overflows onto the saucer and gently finds its way into the tank. At this stage the tank should be made about four-fifths full of water.

Heating

I like to introduce the heater and thermostat to the tank at this stage and leave the tank for a few hours to warm up. This allows the water to mature a bit, gets rid of excess chlorine, clears most of the turbidity, and allows the aquarist to work comfortably in warm rather than cold water. There are others who prefer to plant in cold water and introduce the heater and thermostat at a later stage. In any case, in the interest of safety, it is important to check that the heating equipment is completely disconnected from the electric outlet while planting is in progress.

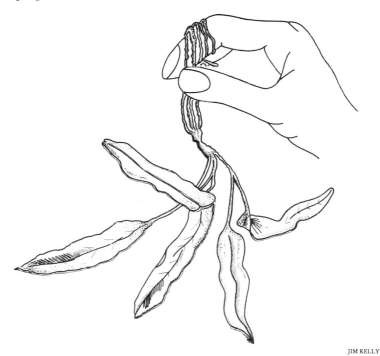

JIM KELLY

Twist the long roots around your finger before planting.

Planting

The bulk of the planting is best carried out by hand and not by planting sticks. These are useful for deep tanks and for introducing plants

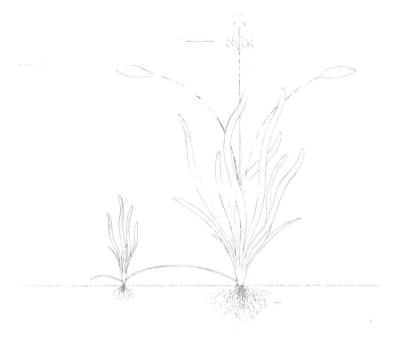

For optimum results, the crown of the plant should be level with the surface of the gravel.

in awkward spots, such as between rockwork or to plant an odd specimen without disturbing other neighboring plants.

To plant by hand, hold the roots and the crown of the plant between the extended thumb and first two fingers. Now push straight into the gravel; it is the fingers that should make the hole in the gravel while the roots are sheathed and protected by them. The thumb and the middle finger are now retracted while the index finger fixes the roots in the depths of the gravel. The thumb and middle finger hold the green part of the plant while the index finger is retracted. Finally the height of the plant is adjusted and the gravel firmed and tidied up against the plant. Be sure that the crown of the plant is always above the gravel or the plant is likely to rot away (see illustration).

When planting with a planting stick the roots are driven into the gravel after trapping into the V at the end of the stick. Needless to say, roots are usually damaged when this method is used, so the stick should be used only when absolutely necessary.

68

Topping Up and Adjusting Temperature

The tank should now be topped up with water until the surface just disappears from view behind the top angle iron. A thermometer is introduced and the cover glass and hood are placed in position. The current can now be switched on and the knob on the thermostat adjusted so that the heater switches on. After the temperature has risen a bit the thermostat will switch off. Note the temperature; if it is below that required then turn the knob once more to bring the heater on. Continue this process until the required temperature is attained. Watch the tank for a day or two to see that the desired temperature is maintained or make suitable adjustments to the thermostat.

It is useful to spend a few days on this process for it gives the plants a chance to settle and the water to mature before the fishes are introduced.

Introducing the Fishes

This is the moment for which the aquarist has been impatiently waiting. Having set up the tank as described, the aquarist now visits his dealer to purchase the fishes. The novice would be well advised to make a modest start by acquiring only a half a dozen or so inexpensive fishes, for there is much to learn and should anything go wrong no great financial loss is entailed. After a few weeks, when he is familiar with the principles of feeding and aquarium management, he can more confidently add to his collection.

A most important point to note at this stage is that the fishes should come from a reputable source, free from disease. Once a colony of fishes has been established he must always quarantine new animals before introducing them to the existing collection. How this is done is described in Chapter XIV. Failure to observe this is bound to lead to trouble sooner or later.

Advanced Decorative Aquaria

We have just described how a simple aquarium can be set up by a beginner. As in all things, with experience we learn to do things better. Great advances have been made in creating aquascapes of outstanding beauty, the best examples of which are in every sense of the word a living picture of no small artistic merit. Such achievements demand both artistic talent and an understanding of the technical problems involved.

The latter can be acquired and it is the purpose of this part of the book to help you to do so. About the former one can indicate the artistic principles involved and study how others have tackled the problem in the past. This is best done at shows where decorative aquaria are exhibited. There is just one further point to note before we start. At a show we set up a decorative tank which, if it looks all right for a few days, will have served its purpose, but the home decorative aquarium to be considered successful must look immaculate day after day, year after year, with the minimum of care and maintenance. The problem can be divided into two parts. A negative one, the hiding or camouflaging of all mechanical objects which do not belong to an aquascape and hence look incongruous and out of place, and a positive one, the introduction of attractive objects (plants, fishes, rocks, etc.) to create a good over-all composition.

Tank and Tank Frame

Strange as it may appear, the very first thing that detracts from the aesthetic pleasure of the tropical aquarium is the tank itself. The common glazed angle iron aquarium has many undoubted merits but few would consider it a pretty object in its own right. The chief objection is the angle iron frame; even when painted in pretty colors, it is virtually impossible to make it harmonize with the decor of a well-appointed modern home. Stainless steel tanks fare a bit better but ideally one would like to make the tank frame disappear from view so that nothing detracts from the interior of the tank, which should of course be the main point of interest. Many ingenious schemes have been evolved to achieve this. One such is to house decorative aquaria in alcoves on either side of a fireplace. A false wall may be built of timber framing covered with hard board, plywood, or other material, perforated with apertures that reveal just the glass front of the tanks, but hide the frame and other equipment from view. The apertures themselves can be made attractive by covering with suitable plastic or picture frame molding. Feeding and maintenance are carried out through hinged or otherwise suspended flaps placed just above the tanks, running along the length of the new wall.

Bookshelves and decorative niches can be incorporated into the design and an otherwise prosaic room converted into something that is attractive and reflects the ability and character of its owner.

Other ways to hide the frame of the tank are to build some sort of wooden box around the tank so that it can be made to blend with the furniture in the room, or to incorporate the tank into an existing piece of furniture such as a row of bookcases.

All these can be satisfactory solutions indeed but if you are about to build a new house you might consider incorporating the tank into a wall of the house.

Losing the Box Effect

One would imagine that aquarists at least would accept a tank as a tank and love it for what it is, but this is not so. Much ingenuity and effort have been exerted to remove not only the frame but the walls of the tank too from the final visual picture. According to this school of thought, the less you see or even feel the presence of the tank the better.

It is argued that the final picture should reveal only plants, fish, rockwork, and gravel but not the rectangular glass-sided box containing these objects. The final effect aimed at is that of a cross section through a body of water.

Having removed the frame from sight, what methods are available to undo the boxy look of the average aquarium? The bottom of the tank covered by gravel and rockwork is out of sight and causes us no concern. The water surface, preferably with a few floating plants added, again is quite pleasant and natural and does not constitute a problem. What makes an aquarium look like a glass box is the back and two sides. Steps must be taken to obliterate them from view. Let us take the back first.

One way of removing the back from sight would be to build a very wide tank so that the sheer distance of the back glass from the front renders it invisible or almost invisible even when the water is crystal clear. This of course is only a theoretical concept as far as the average aquarist is concerned for few could find room for a tank many feet wide. Nevertheless it is true that a tank of ample width (say about two feet or more) makes a far more impressive final picture than the 12″ wide tank usually employed. Further, it must be remembered that refraction of light through the water makes the tank look even less wide from front to back than it really is.

One good way to give added depth to the aquatic scene is to build

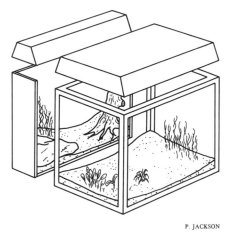

This is one way of adding the appearance of depth to your aquarium.

P. JACKSON

a box behind the aquarium containing rockwork and some plants (terrestrial or plastic). Such a box has only three sides and a bottom. The glass back of the tank forms its front. If this box is now illuminated by an overhead light and the back glass of the aquarium kept clean and free from algae, then the desired look of a deep body of water is obtained. Some quite attractive effects can be produced this way (see illustration). Nevertheless, this idea is not worth serious consideration where a permanent, easily maintained setup is required. The snag in the system is keeping the back glass spotlessly clean; otherwise the illusion of depth is quickly destroyed.

A simple and practical way of hiding the back glass would be by a thick growth of plants. One can also build up an artificial rock face so that the back is hidden by a screen of rockwork or, better still, a combination of plants and rockwork can be used to cover the back glass. Since the rockwork screen is bound to be fairly thick, it is obvious that such an exercise can only be effectively executed in a fairly wide tank. The manner in which such rockwork can be built up has been described (Chapter VI).

Let us now see how the ends of the tank can be removed from sight. This is a difficult problem for simply masking them with rockwork and/or a plant screen, or both, will accentuate rather than destroy the boxlike effect. Fortunately, in recent years a system of doing this has been evolved. I believe that such tanks were first exhibited at the Monaco Aquarium and hence they are sometimes referred to as the Monaco-type tanks.

Monaco-Type Aquaria

The basic idea here is to build a tank with sloping sides (see illustration). It will be appreciated that if the ends are sloping enough they will disappear from sight. The only objection one could raise is that this arrangement reduces the apparent size of the tank, for a tank is judged by the size of the front glass. Nevertheless, this is a very worthwhile proposition, for it completely destroys the boxlike look of the interior and permits some really fine aquatic scenes to be constructed. An added advantage is that the corners of the tank provide generous accommodation for all the heaters, wires, and plumbing one could wish to introduce in the tank. As you no doubt already know, camouflaging these in an ordinary tank is no mean feat.

Incidentally the original Monaco-type aquarium had a curved blue transparent plastic back, which was illuminated from outside. The result when viewed from the front gave the impression of looking into a great depth of blue water. Tanks of this type can be seen in some public aquaria. Such tanks, however, are not limited just to public aquaria; they can be modified to produce some very attractive aquaria for the home. To illustrate this point let me tell you how I built such a tank a few years ago.

A Built-In Design

The chance to build such a tank arose a few years ago when I was about to build a new house. The tank was designed as an integral part

An angle-iron frame built by the author for a special tank. The method of construction is described in the text.

F. N. GHADIALLY

of the house. The illustration shows the shape and size of the angle iron frame that was constructed. Its over-all length is seven feet six inches but the front glass is only four feet six inches long. The tank frame is two feet high and 20 inches wide. The back frame is not straight as in the conventional tank but has been broken, thus creating an irregularly pentagonal tank. A conventional straight back would have reduced the width of the tank and a long straight wall of rock-work covering it would not have looked very attractive. Breaking the back off center solves these problems.

The manner in which the finished tank is located in the house is shown in the illustration.

F. N. GHADIALLY

This is a decorative aquarium in the entrance hall of the author's home. The stone wall, figures, and plantings all contribute to the light and pleasant appearance.

As can be seen, the tank is housed in a stone enclosure measuring 11′ × 4′ × 8′6″ high. The front of the tank fits into an aperture in the stone wall facing the entrance hall. The margins of the stone aperture are covered by a timber frame covered with mosaics. The tank is supported on brick piers, which rest directly on the concrete floor of the stone enclosure.

The opposite wall of the stone enclosure facing the lounge accommodates a remote-controlled television set and two Hi-Fi stereo speakers. Also accommodated on this wall is an electrically operated projection screen (not shown in the sketch). The amplifiers and other electrical and electronic equipment to drive these speakers are accommodated elsewhere in the lounge and do not concern us here.

During the design stages I had grave doubts about the advisability of housing expensive electronic equipment with a large fish tank. It seemed possible that the sound emerging from the system might upset the fish and the high humidity might play havoc with the electronic equipment.

However, these systems have been in operation now for some six years and it seems that all these worries were totally unfounded. The stone enclosure is entered by a door which opens onto the garden. Feeding the fishes and servicing the tank are carried out at the back of the aquarium, reached through this door.

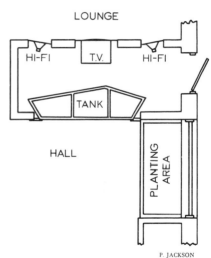

A floor plan of a portion of the author's home, showing the planting area and the stone enclosure which houses the decorative aquarium as described in the text. The door at the right leads directly to the garden.

P. JACKSON

To one side of the stone enclosure is a planting area. This is in fact a sunken rectangular trough in the timber floor of the hall and is lined with asphalt. It is filled with pebbles on and in which stand many potted plants. One of these, a creeper (*Rhoicissus rhomboidae*), has been trained over the stone wall of the tank enclosure and now forms an attractive surround to the front of the aquarium. The planting area receives light from a large glass panel forming the back wall to the area to one side of the hall.

The concept of the stone enclosure with its adjacent planting area has decorative and functional merits. It provides a setting for the fish tank, and readers who are Hi-Fi enthusiasts will already have realized that here we have one form of a theoretically ideal speaker enclosure of the infinite baffle type.

Tank Interior

Let us now turn to the interior of the tank and examine the special problems involved in setting up a large aquarium; the approach is somewhat different from that employed in equipping a conventional $2' \times 1' \times 1'$ tank.

The first point we have to note is that most aquarium plants under ordinary conditions grow to a height of approximately 8 to 12". If such plants are planted at the bottom of a tank 2 ft. deep then a foot or more of the top half of the tank will be virtually plantless. This unacceptable situation can be remedied by using special plants (e.g., giant *Hygrophila*) that grow high and/or by planting the smaller growing plants on raised platforms created by banking up the gravel with rockwork.

The second point concerns the viewing distance of a tank. The problem here is similar to that of viewing any feature such as a painting. We tend to view a large painting or a large tank from a greater distance than a smaller painting or a smaller tank. A large tank, like a large painting, must impress us from a fair distance, a distance at which unfortunately most of our little one-inch Characins will be barely visible. Thus a large tank needs not only larger plants but also a fair number of large fishes.

Here of course the aquarist's personal preferences step in. For me the answer is provided by large Angels; I think they are the supreme aquarium fish. It does not follow, however, that small fishes have no place in such a setup. When this distant view has been taken in, the observer will quite naturally move forward. Then in my aquarium medium-sized fishes such as colorful livebearers and Barbs come into view and finally, as the observer moves still closer, shoals of Cardinals, Glowlights, and other small fishes provide interest and material for endless conversation. In fact a fair amount of time and persuasion is needed to make visitors leave the hall and proceed to the lounge. Of course, one must take into account the compatability factor; otherwise he will end up with a tankful of only large fishes.

The right-hand corner of the author's decorative aquarium, showing how artificial rockwork has been used to form ledges and tiers.

The Rockwork

In this large aquarium the back rockwork screen had to be made in three sections. The manner in which this can be made is described in Chapter VI. Placed end to end they would cover a distance longer than the back wall of the aquarium. In the tank the front panel, which has irregular edges, overlaps the side panels. This arrangement eliminates ugly joints which would be difficult to hide, and in fact adds to the relief effect of the final assembly. Other small pieces of such rockwork are used to bank up the gravel and the final effect is shown in the picture. The size and scale of the project can be appreciated by the Angels in the picture, which have a 3″ body size.

Equipment in Large Tanks

A two-foot-deep tank like the one described presents some other technical problems to which attention must be given. Perhaps the most important is thermal stratification. If the water alone is heated with the usual short type of submersible heaters hanging from the top of the tank, the bottom layers of water can be some 15°F. cooler than the top layers. Such a large gradient may be all right in nature but not in an aquarium, for under such conditions fishes will keep to the top layers. Not only is this unattractive but it can also become dangerous because they are reluctant to go down and pick up bits of food that fall on the aquarium floor. The situation can be remedied completely by placing a heater under the gravel, by aeration and filtration. All these will circulate the water and tend to make the temperature more uniform. The tank discussed is provided with an under-gravel heater, aerators, and two external filters, one containing peat, the other ordinary mechanical filtering media. Thus the clarity and chemistry of the water are easily controlled.

VIII   Foods and Feeding

Perhaps no single fact about an animal we intend to domesticate is more important than a knowledge of its feeding habits. Given adequate temperature and water conditions, the health and growth of our fishes will depend almost entirely on what and how we feed them.

Dietetic and Nutritional Requirements

One way to gain an insight into the dietetic needs of an animal is to examine, macroscopically, microscopically, and chemically, the stomach contents of specimens caught in the wild. Results of such studies and observations on feeding fishes permit us to make certain broad generalizations regarding the nutritional and dietetic requirements of the small fishes kept in aquaria (Ghadially, 1957).

1.   Almost half of what a fish eats in the wild consists of indigestible material. This roughage, as it is called, is not absorbed from the gut into the blood stream, and has hence no nutritive value. It has, however, some physiological importance for without it gut movement would be impaired and the animal would become constipated.

2.   Most of the digestible matter in the majority of our fishes' diet comes from animal sources (e.g., insect larvae, smaller fishes, *Daphnia*, *Cyclops*, etc.). We must therefore regard them as predominantly carnivorous or omnivorous. Some of our aquarium fishes will eat a fair amount of algae and other plant life but they too will accept some animal foods. These are predominantly herbivorous. A few fishes, however, will accept only live or meaty foods; these are the true carnivores.

3.   Since most of the food eaten by the fishes is of animal origin and tissues are rich in protein, it follows that fishes live on a protein-rich diet. This fact can be expressed more precisely by stating the ratio of protein to that of fat plus carbohydrate in the diet of an animal. In the case of fishes this would be about 1 : 1, i.e., almost half the digestible material is protein. They have a poor tolerance for fats, so fat should be omitted as much as possible. This is in sharp contrast to such animals as man, dog, horse, or cow, who live on a carbohydrate-rich diet. Here the ratio of protein to carbohydrate plus fat lies between 1 : 3 and 1 : 10.

4.   Fishes hunt and feed more or less continuously throughout their

period of activity; thus they are accustomed to small and frequent meals. This is a point worth noting for such animals are unlikely to do well in captivity if they are fed just once a day. However, since they do not always find food, and since animals in captivity are less active than animals in the wild, many captive fishes thrive very well in public aquaria, where they may receive only three meals a week.

5. We have little knowledge of the vitamin, mineral, and trace element requirements of our fishes. Some vitamins are destroyed by drying and heating, as in the preparation of dried foods, but this should cause little concern if the diet also contains a reasonable amount of live and fresh foods.

6. Since many of our fishes have small mouths and few or no effective teeth, it behooves the aquarist to provide food of correct particle size. Food of a too fine size is likely to be ignored and may set up pollution.

Classification of Foods

The foods that we give our fishes can be divided into three main groups: dried foods, fresh foods, and live foods. All foods commence as live foods. In the dead or killed state they constitute fresh foods. These can be fed immediately or preserved for later use by freezing or bottling. Such food can also be dehydrated by heating or freeze drying and then we speak of them as dried foods.

Dried Foods

Water is the major component of all fresh foods. Its presence facilitates bacterial growth, which breaks down the foodstuff and makes it go rotten or unfit for consumption. Obviously then drying, which means removal of a major portion of the water, would permit us to preserve and easily store many items of food for considerable periods of time. Drying foods is thus just a convenience; there is no intrinsic value in drying foods. In fact, many changes can occur during the drying process that may adversely affect the taste, vitamin content, and nutritional value of the food. Nevertheless, with care and suitable techniques very satisfactory dried food products are produced today. A recent innovation, which eliminates the hazards arising out of heat-drying the food, is freeze-drying.

Here the fresh food is frozen quickly and then subjected to a very high vacuum. The water vaporizes and is removed. Since the food is frozen rapidly it is preserved straightaway before any deterioration can occur. Many freeze-dried foods are available but the two most popular with most pet fishes are freeze-dried brine shrimps and freeze-dried *Tubifex* worms.

The majority of dried foods available are, however, heat-dried foods. The best plan here is to buy a variety of well-known brands in the hope that some deficiency in one will be counteracted by a sufficiency in another. Dried foods are best fed in small quantities at frequent intervals. A golden rule which must not be abused is, "Never administer more dried food than will be completely cleared up by the fishes in under five minutes." Failure to observe this rule is the commonest cause of pollution or excessive algae growth. A feeding ring should be used so that the food is not scattered all over the tank. Snails and Catfish should be included in a tank where the diet comprises mainly dried foods. These will help to scavenge particles that fall on the bottom of the aquarium.

Making Your Own Dried Food

Two approaches are open to the hobbyist who wishes to make his own dried food.

The first and simplest method comprises sifting and mixing together various dried and pulverized food items such as fish meal, meat meal, shrimp meal, with some cereal preparation such as Pablum. Some brands of dog biscuits containing a high protein content, when ground down to the required size, are ideal for compounding food mixtures. The thing to aim for is a fairly high protein content and a final particle size suitable for the fishes one intends to feed.

The second method, though a bit more time-consuming, offers many advantages. Here various food items, fresh or dried, minced or pulverized are made into a thick doughlike mass by mixing with some oatmeal, egg, and water. Small amounts of salt and baking powder are worked in, the mass is spread out into thin layers in baking tins, and cooked in the oven. The resulting biscuit is pulverized in a coffee grinder or by other means and sifted and stored for use.

Fresh Food

Many items of human diet provide a quick and easy supply of food items for our fishes. These may be administered cooked or uncooked. The tastes of different species vary considerably and the aquarist must experiment to find out what his fishes will accept. Most tropicals will accept shredded shrimp, prawn, and lobster with great relish. Raw scraped lean beef and fish, crisp-cooked bacon, and chicken liver are also moderately popular with most fishes. Other items which can be tried are herring roe (cod roe is rarely accepted by my fishes), hard cooked egg (very little for it rapidly clouds the water), and some varieties of grated hard cheese. Oatmeal cooked until it is stiff is acceptable to Goldfish and some Barbs, especially if a little chopped liver is added. Spinach, lettuce, and other vegetable matter is accepted by Mollies and other livebearers. The list in fact is endless and only personal experiment can establish what the fishes will or will not take. A small amount of the test food should be added to the tank when the fishes are hungry, and their reaction noted. Any uneaten fresh foods should not be allowed to remain in the tank for more than eight to ten hours.

Equipment for bottling fish food: a pressure cooker and some universal containers.

F. N. GHADIALLY

Preserved Fresh Foods

Fresh foods and food preparations can be bottled or frozen for convenience. For bottling small amounts of food it is best to obtain small containers or bottles from a firm dealing in laboratory supplies. About $3 \times 1''$ thick-walled glass bottles with metal caps lined with $\frac{1}{8}''$ thick rubber disks are suitable. The method of bottling is similar to that used by housewives. The food is placed in the bottles and the caps lightly screwed on. The bottles are then heated in a pressure cooker containing some water in the bottom; 20 minutes at 15 pounds pressure will kill off all bacteria and spores. As the bottles come out of the cooker the caps are screwed on tight to prevent bacteria from entering the containers and spoiling the food later. Minced meat, or liver, either singly or mixed with proprietary cereal preparations, are ideal for storing in this fashion. Food can also be preserved for limited periods by freezing. The food is first placed in small plastic containers and then frozen by placing in a deep freeze or the cold compartment of a refrigerator. Some frozen foods such as frozen brine shrimps are available commercially.

Live Foods

These comprise many collected or cultured live organisms suitable for feeding fishes. Live foods are considered superior to dried or fresh foods. The live foods in this section are arranged on the basis of size. We begin with the small ones suitable only for fry and progress gradually to the larger ones suitable for adult fishes.

Infusoria

This name has been given to a heterogeneous collection of organisms (mainly protozoans), which develop in an infusion of hay or other suitable organic matter. These minute organisms constitute an ideal first food for the fry of many egg-laying fishes. The commonest infusorian is *Paramecium*, which measures about a quarter to half a millimeter in length. Since it is well-nigh impossible to rear large numbers of fry without a good infusoria culture, it is important to study in detail the principles involved in making such a culture.

Infusorians are organisms which live in water, feed on bacteria, utilize oxygen, and thrive at temperatures between 60°F. and 70°F.

The first task then is to provide a culture medium where some organic material is allowed to rot, for this will produce the bacteria needed by the infusoria. This should be carried out in a fairly large container with a good air-water surface so that plenty of oxygen is available.

The manner in which this culture is made is quite simple. A whole large lettuce is broken into small pieces and placed in a fish tank or a plastic bowl of about 10- to 15-gallon capacity. A gallon or so of boiling water is added and the whole allowed to stand for a few hours, after which about six gallons of tap water are added. Aquarium water should not be used for this purpose for if it contains some *Cyclops* or *Daphnia* they will feed on the infusoria and soon you will have a culture of these organisms and no infusoria.

It is worthwhile to stir the contents of the tank two or three times a day and observe the changes that occur. By about the third day the water will have become turbid and will have a distinct odor. This is due to the growth of millions of bacteria in the culture medium. Spores of infusoria occur in the air and soon alight in the medium. They hatch and begin to multiply in the medium. The infusoria feed on the bacteria and multiply at a rapid rate. As a result of this the population of bacteria declines and by about the 10th day the culture becomes quite clear, and virtually odorless. By about the 20th day the culture will be really thick with infusoria and suitable for feeding fry. For small installations a little hay or a banana peel covered with boiling water in a quart glass jar will also produce infusoria.

Some aquarists harbor the fallacious notion that a culture of infusoria is a foul-smelling turbid mass of water. From what I have said earlier you will appreciate that this is not so: turbidity indicates a high bacterial content, in fact a state of pollution. If such water is poured into a tank containing fry there will be little for them to feed on and they will perish either from starvation or the pollution that will be created by such a procedure.

A foul smell in a culture indicates that anaerobic conditions prevail, favoring the growth of anaerobic bacteria which produce hydrogen sulphide. If this is noted, the culture should be stirred more frequently or mild aeration applied for a while. Remember that infusoria need oxygen and anaerobic conditions will impede their growth and multiplication. Many infusoria cultures fail because of too low a temperature, so this point should be checked also. Successful fish breeding commences with learning to produce good thick cultures of infusoria. The final product should be virtually as clear as aquarium water and teeming with thousands of organisms. The trained eye can see them clearly if a glass jar full of culture is held so that light strikes from one side. A hand lens giving about five power magnification is useful but the magnification given by even a low power microscope is too high to enable one to assess the strength of the culture.

Rotifers

This is undoubtedly one of the finest fry foods but usually difficult to come by when it is most needed. Rotifers are two or three times bigger than *Paramecium*. The rotating wheel effect produced by the hairlike processes (cilia) around the mouth gives this group of organisms its name.

A few rotifers occur in almost any pond, but finding enough to feed fishes is another matter. Sometimes, however, large numbers occur in *Daphnia* ponds, either free or riding on the backs of *Daphnia*. A fine nylon net is best suited for collecting these organisms.

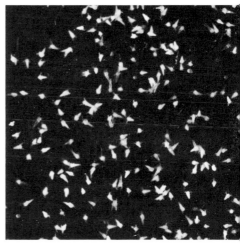

Newly hatched brine shrimp – an ideal food for both fry and small-mouthed fishes.

F. N. GHADIALLY

Brine Shrimps

Newly hatched brine shrimps are readily produced from the small brown eggs of *Artemia salina*, which can be purchased in most aquarist shops. It is the ideal first food for the fry of livebearers, Cichlids, and other fishes (e.g., some Barbs) which produce fair-sized fry. It is

85

also the ideal second food for fry that have passed the infusoria stage.

The method of culture depends largely upon the amount of newly hatched brine shrimps required per day. The basic principles, however, are the same. A quantity of brine to hatch the eggs in is needed and an adequate supply of air should be supplied to keep the hatched shrimps alive, until they are needed. Three methods of culture are in common use. These are (1) The jar method; (2) The pan method; (3) The inverted cone method. The brine used in all these methods is prepared by dissolving six tablespoonfuls of sea salt to each gallon of water.

In the first method a half-gallon glass jar is about three quarters filled with brine, and enough brine shrimp eggs are sprinkled to cover about three fourths of the surface of the brine. If more eggs are added there is a danger that the newly hatched shrimps will be overcrowded and suffocate. Here, as in the case of fishes, the importance of the surface area for gaseous exchange must be kept in mind. At 75°F. to 80°F. the culture should be ready for harvesting after 36 hours. This is done by filtering the entire contents of the jar through a handkerchief or piece of nylon cloth.

In the second method a shallow (2″ or so deep) rectangular enamel or plastic tray is used. This is divided across the middle by a thin strip of wood or plastic which fits tightly at the sides but leaves a space of about ¼″ at the bottom. Eggs are sprinkled in feeding rings floating in one half of the dish (see illustration). The shrimps hatch and escape under the dividing strip to the other compartment from

Brine shrimp hatcher (pan method).

F. N. GHADIALLY

whence they can be collected by means of a large pipette fitted with a rubber bulb similar to that used for car batteries. The fact that newly hatched shrimps go toward the light is used to facilitate migration from the egg-containing compartment to the next. This is done by placing the tray correctly oriented to a source of light such as a window and/or covering the egg-containing compartment. This method yields a more or less continuous supply of shrimps, fresh egg being added as the old ones hatch out. The yield, however, is small; hence this method is useful only when a few fry are being fed with brine shrimps.

To produce really large quantities of shrimps in a limited space, aeration has to be employed to keep the shrimps alive. Strong aeration of a culture in an ordinary jar will make the eggs sink and collect in a heap on the bottom of a container; under such conditions the eggs are more likely to rot than hatch. To circumvent this in our third method, a conical or pyramidal vessel made of plastic is employed. The vessel, point down, is filled with brine and a large number of eggs added. Air is forced through the apex of the cone. The falling eggs cannot settle; they are swirled away by the rising current. Such an apparatus, constructed by me out of plastic, is shown in the picture. It holds a gallon and a half of brine and carries a heater and thermostat to maintain the brine at 80°F. A tube is provided to draw off the shrimp-containing brine when hatching is accomplished.

A few queries frequently raised regarding the feeding of shrimps may be considered. The first relates to the salt introduced into the fry tank with the shrimps. Some believe that the shrimps should be rinsed with fresh water before being offered to the fry. This to my mind is an unnecessary rule, for quantities of salt introduced are very

F. N. GHADIALLY

Cone-shaped brine shrimp hatcher as described in the text.

modest. You will have observed that in some of the methods described above the technique was such that both hatched shrimp egg shells and unhatched eggs will be introduced into the fry tank. Tidy-minded aquarists may find this distressing but the fry will come to no harm from this practice. Once the fry have grown beyond the brine shrimp stage, they will need moving to larger tanks. At this stage the spawning tank can be cleaned out and the egg shells and other debris removed.

Brine shrimps can be grown to adult size in an all-glass aquarium. Allow the tank to go green by standing it in the light. The algae and other organisms will provide food for the shrimps. This can be supplemented by the addition of a very dilute suspension of yeast. Sufficient should be added to make the brine slightly turbid; excess will kill the shrimps.

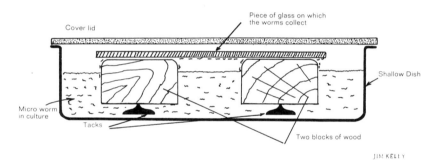

JIM KELLY

Microworm incubator. While commonly used, the blocks and piece of glass are not really necessary. The worms may be collected from the sides.

Microworms

This food is only slightly larger than brine shrimps. It can substitute for the shrimps or better still can be used in conjunction with the shrimps, for a varied diet is more conducive to speedy growth.

To culture this food obtain a small plastic dish and roughen the sides slightly by rubbing with a very fine grade of emery or sandpaper. Now place in it a one-inch-deep layer of fairly stiff, well-cooked oatmeal. Smear the surface liberally with a culture of microworms obtained from a pet store, cover the dish to cut down the light reaching the culture and to prevent it from drying out. Stand in a warm place (70°F. to 75°F.). If in two or three days the culture is held up to the light, you will see the whole surface shimmering with the movement of enormous numbers of worms inhabiting the surface. In a week or so the worms will migrate as a sheet from the culture up the sides of the container. It is customary to remove them from here by wiping them off with a finger, which is then dipped into the fry tank to release the worms. I have recently found that a much better way of doing this is to use the edge of a small piece of suitably shaped polystyrene foam.

There is rarely any difficulty in culturing these worms for they are most prolific breeders; sometimes, however, they refuse to climb up the wall. In such instances the surface of the culture should be sprinkled with a little yeast. In a few hours large numbers of the worms will leave the culture and thus become available. I now use this as a routine method for harvesting cultures.

Grindal Worms

A prolific, easily cultured worm measuring approximately ⅛ to ¼" in length, it was first isolated by Mrs. M. Grindal of Sweden from a white worm culture. It is best cultured in small shallow wooden boxes measuring about 12 × 6 × 2" deep. The box is filled (1½" deep) with a mixture of two parts peat to one part of sand. This should be maintained in a damp but not wet state all the time. A culture of Grindal worms is obtained and located in two or three foci on the surface. The wormbearing areas are now sprinkled with a small amount of precooked cereal baby food. Each worm colony is covered by a square of clear plastic or a piece of glass. The entire box is covered with a piece of hardboard or similar material to exclude light. The cultures will produce masses of worms if maintained between 70°F. and 75°F.

White Worms

This is the prime cultured food for adult fishes and every aquarist should make an attempt to culture it although it is by no means an easy or reliable food to cultivate. The adult worms are about ½ to ¾" in length. The setup for culture is essentially similar to that of Grindal worms, except that a somewhat deeper box is more suitable.

Harvesting from a thriving culture is easy. A mass of clean worms can be quickly picked up with a forceps and fed to the fishes. If several

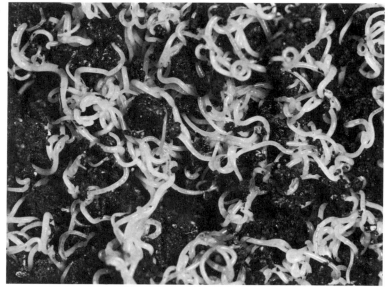

White worms on the surface of the culture.

layers of moist burlap are spread over the surface, a good many of the worms will secrete themselves between the sheets and can easily be removed for feeding. Many pests can infest the culture: fruit flies, mites, fungi, and chromogenic bacteria to mention but a few; none of them completely ruin the culture but they all reduce the yield of worms. Should the infection become too heavy, remove enough worms to inoculate a new culture, clean them by rinsing in water and then set up a fresh culture.

Earthworms

Considered by many to be the best fish food, ideal for conditioning breeding pairs. Worms can be fed entire to large fishes such as Cichlids and Goldfish or chopped up for smaller fishes. They can be purchased or collected while digging in the garden. Watering a lawn with a large volume of a fairly strong solution of ammonia (not domestic cleaning fluid) often brings hundreds of worms to the surface. Compost heaps enriched by potato peelings and tea leaves also can provide masses of worms when needed.

Snails

Most aquarists sooner or later complain that they have too many snails in a tank. An ideal way of getting rid of the excess is to crush them against the glass wall of the tank. A little care is needed for the broken shell can cut the finger. The soft part of the snail will be readily eaten by most fishes.

Tubifex

These worms, which live on the banks and flats of sewage ponds and streams, can be purchased at aquarist shops. To cleanse them and keep them alive, they must be placed in a pan of water and left under a very gently running stream of cold water. At least twice a day and preferably more frequently, the ball of worms is unscrambled by shaking. Excreta and dead worms are then washed away and the healthy ones will once more collect in a mass. Most fishes will readily accept limited quantities of these worms. Any that escape capture soon establish themselves in the gravel, where they create an unsightly spectacle. However, small Catfish will help control them.

Tubifex does not enjoy the unequivocal popularity of other live foods. There are many aquarists who believe that it is unclean food, which leads to diseases and wasting. How much of this is fact and how much plain superstition is difficult to assess. If you decide to use this food do so after thorough cleaning and feed only modest quantities.

A small freshwater Puffer, *Tetraodon fluviatilis*, feasting from a mass of *Tubifex* worms.

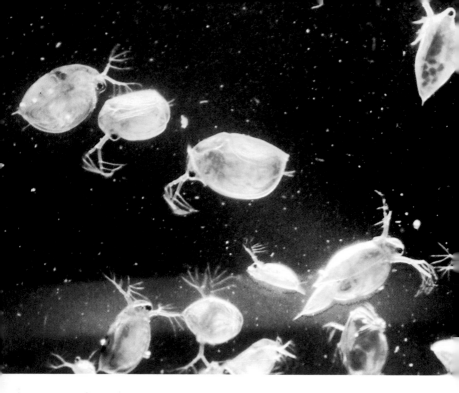

Daphnia – Considered by many to be the ideal fish food.

Daphnia (Water Fleas)

This little crustacean delights the aquarist and his charges, more than almost any other creature. There are many species of *Daphnia* varying in size from about 1/16 to 1/8" long. Their hopping movements and shape are responsible for their popular name, water flea. Almost all fishes love this food and will gorge incessantly on it. The chitinous shell of these creatures provides much roughage; hence this food is believed to have a laxative effect.

Daphnia are widely distributed in nature but adequate amounts are found only in stagnant, foul-smelling cattle or duck ponds, not in clean ponds with fishes or in fastmoving streams.

An organdy or nylon net about 10" in diameter fitted to a sectional pole made of aluminum tubing is ideal for catching these crustaceans. The process of collecting is called sweep netting, the object being to move the net in the water in such a manner that the water is swept or filtered through the net. This is an art that is best learned at the pond side. Surface clouds can be readily lifted off by simple straight strokes while *Daphnia* form the depths can be raised by figure-of-eight strokes that churn up the water.

The collected *Daphnia* are best carried home in plastic cans or carboys. Overcrowding should be strictly guarded against or the *Daphnia* will die in transit.

Many attempts have been made to culture *Daphnia*. In artificial concrete ponds this can be done with success. Water and organic material are introduced in the pond to produce a culture of infusoria and algae and the *Daphnia* are then introduced. Dilute suspensions of yeast are also occasionally stirred in to feed the *Daphnia*. As we have seen earlier, the same sort of process can also be carried out with the circulating range system (Chapter IV).

A catch of *Daphnia* usually contains one or more other food organisms such as ghostworms, bloodworms, *Cyclops*, and mosquito larvae. It may also contain some so-called enemies, i.e., creatures that are undesirable or dangerous in the aquarium, like dragonfly larvae, water beetles, water boatmen, leeches, planarians, *Hydra*, fish lice, etc. Most of the trouble-makers can be easily spotted and removed once you learn to identify them (see Chapter XV).

Cyclops

This small crustacean is usually found with *Daphnia*. Indeed, in some catches from the pond there may be more *Cyclops* than *Daphnia*. Being much smaller it is not quite as suitable for larger fishes. It is, however, a valuable food for fishes past the brine shrimp stage, i.e., ¼ inch to ½ inch long. Many breeders believe that *Cyclops* should

F. N. GHADIALLY

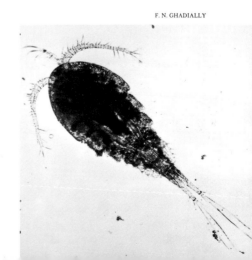

Cyclops (male).

not be allowed to get into tanks containing very small fry. If this happens most of the fry disappear. The mechanism by which this occurs is not clear since *Cyclops* do not appear capable of eating fry. It has been suggested that they bump into, injure, and harass the fry. For whatever reason, my experience bears out the notion that spawnings come to grief if *Cyclops* get into the breeding tank before the fry are large enough to eat them.

Bloodworms

These so-called worms are in fact the larval stage of *Chironomus* midges. They measure approximately ¾ inch in length, are blood red in color, and move through the water tracing figures of eight in a characteristic manner. They occur in modest numbers in *Daphnia* ponds, rain tubs, and other similar small bodies of water. Our interest in these worms lies mainly in the fact that they come in with catches of *Daphnia* and we should be able to identify them as a food organism and not mistake them for one of the enemies.

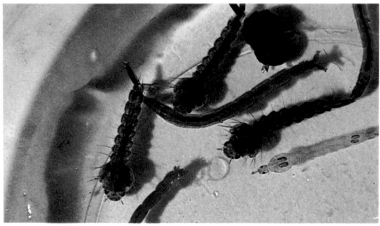

W. TOMEY

Three live foods, all of which are excellent for adult fishes: mosquito larvae (thick bodied), bloodworms (red), and glass larvae (semi-transparent). As all three are immature forms of winged insects, any surplus which is retained should be refrigerated to retard development. Otherwise, their containers should be tightly covered with fine mesh.

Glass- or Ghostworms

These virtually transparent crystal-like creatures measuring approximately ¾″ in length are the larvae of plumed gnats (*Chaoborus*). They are usually found in modest numbers in *Daphnia* ponds, but sometimes very large collections of these larvae can be found in ponds and lakes. They can stand low temperatures very well and aquarists have at times collected them in midwinter after breaking the ice on the surface of *Daphnia* ponds. They are an excellent live food for the larger fishes and are particularly valuable for they are available at a time when other live foods are in scarce supply. Being carnivorous they should be kept out of tanks containing small fishes.

Feeding and Rearing Fry

Although the techniques of spawning fishes vary considerably according to breeding habits of various species, the feeding and rearing of virtually every species of fry follows a stereotyped procedure. Given adequate tank space and correct temperature, the problem resolves itself into one of providing the correct size, quantity, and quality of various food items. It is for this reason that we discuss the problem of rearing fry in this chapter devoted to feeding.

For the first few days after hatching, the fry of egglayers are sustained by nutrient materials lodged in the yolk sac. A functional mouth is not developed and it would be futile to attempt to feed them at this stage. Our work begins once the fry become free-swimming. The first question that the aquarist must ask himself is: What is the largest live food at my disposal that the fry can comfortably swallow? In the case of many bubble-nest builders and Characins that produce very small fry the answer will be infusoria. In the case of large Cichlids and livebearers the choice would fall on newly hatched brine shrimps and microworms.

Many elaborate ways of drip feeding infusoria have been described but I do not consider that they offer any advantage over unceremoniously pouring a cupful or small jarful of mature culture into the tank containing fry. The actual amount added depends on the size of the tank, number of fry, and the quality of the culture.

It is useful to have a small lamp illuminating the fry tank day and night for the first few days, or even weeks. Both infusoria and fry gather under the lamp. The former can easily be spotted as a whirling cloud by the naked eye, or by examining under the microscope a drop of water collected from this site. As the fry eat the infusoria this "cloud" will diminish or disappear and more culture should be added.

Reckless addition of large quantities of culture is harmful for since infusoria use oxygen the fry run the danger of being crowded out. The danger of pollution arises only when a turbid, immature culture teeming with bacteria is employed. The water in the fry tank should at all stages remain clean and wholesome. If some turbidity is noticed, part of the water should be replaced with fresh. This is accomplished by siphoning through an air-stone attached to a length of aeration tubing. The end bearing the air-stone is placed in the tank and the siphon started by sucking. Even when there is no evident pollution it is worthwhile carrying out this procedure once or twice a week.

With good feeding and management the fry will have become large enough to take brine shrimp, usually in just under one week. The change-over to a larger-sized food should always be gradual. Thus for the next few days both infusoria and brine shrimp should be added.

It is important also to time this changeover correctly for if the change from smaller to larger food is unduly delayed the rate of growth of fry is retarded. If the larger food is offered too soon the bigger fry will jump ahead and the smaller ones will lag behind, and probably die or be eaten by their larger brethren. There is no more certain way of accentuating the naturally occurring variation in fry size than by abruptly changing to larger food at the incorrect moment.

Once the fry can take brine shrimp and microworms, growth is usually very rapid. By the end of three weeks or so finely sifted dried food can be added to the menu to ease the strain on the live foods.

From this point, rearing is a simple procedure. All that needs to be done is to provide larger sizes of foods as the fry grow bigger. Thus, Grindal worms, whiteworms, chopped earthworms, and many fresh foods can be added to the menu.

Sifted *Daphnia* must be added only when one is quite certain that the fry are large enough to tackle them. On more than one occasion I have lost spawnings by adding them too soon. If the *Daphnia* are not eaten they will rapidly grow and breed in the infusoria-rich tank and crowd out the fry.

References
Ghadially, F. N. (1957). *Fish Foods and Feeding*. Buckley Press Ltd., Middlesex, England.

IX Plants

Plants are every bit as important as fishes in a decorative aquarium, for their diverse form and color add materially to the aquascape.

Healthy growing plants are an asset for they (1) oxygenate the water (see Chapter II), (2) purify the water by removing inorganic nitrogenous salts (see Chapter IV), (3) provide shade and shelter for fishes, and (4) provide, in the breeding tank, support for eggs and shelter for fry. Dying, unhealthy, or algae-ridden plants are ugly to behold and serve no useful purpose; indeed their dead tissues will add to the pool of organic waste material and encourage pollution and algae growth.

The success of a newly set up tank depends, among other things, on whether the plants start growing quickly. It is for this reason that we advised (Chapter VII) that fishes should not be introduced until a week or so had elapsed after planting. This gives the plants a chance to settle down and start growing. An early introduction of fish might result in the production of nitrogenous salts far in excess of that which the as-yet-unestablished plants can handle. This would give algae the chance to start for there is continuous competition between the major plants and algae for the available metabolites in the tank.

How can good plant growth be encouraged? Although the requirements of different species may vary somewhat, by and large one can lay down certain general principles. The first concerns illumination; this should be of the correct quality, intensity, and duration. Some points regarding this have already been discussed (Chapter V). Here it remains to point out that as a rule green-colored plants need more light than those with brownish, reddish, or purplish tints. Thus most of the *Cryptocorynes* need a smaller intensity of light than, say, *Vallisneria* or *Cabomba*.

Plants, like fishes, can adapt considerably to the prevailing water conditions, but for optimum growth some attention must be paid to the hardness and pH of the water. It is generally held (Sterba, 1967) that *Cryptocoryne*, *Cabomba*, and *Echinodorus* fare best in soft slightly acid water (calcifugous), while such plants as *Elodea*, *Myriophyllum*, *Sagittaria*, and *Vallisneria* (calciphilous) prefer moderately hard, slightly alkaline water. As we mentioned earlier (Chapter III), almost all plants will do fairly well in near neutral to slightly alkaline water with a hardness of about 100-200 ppm.

MICHAEL YOUENS

(1) *Acorus gramineus.* (2) *Anubias congensis.* (3) *Anubias lanceolata.* (4) *Aponogeton ulvaceus.* (5) *Aponogeton undulatus.* (6) *Aponogeton fenestralis.* (7) *Azolla* species. (8) *Bacopa caroliniana.* (9) *Bacopa monnieri.*

(10) *Cabomba caroliniana*. (11) *Cabomba aquatıca*. (12) *Ceratopteris cornuta*. (13) *Ceratopteris thalictroides*. (14) *Cryptocoryne affinis*. (15) *Cryptocoryne nevillii*. (16) *Cryptocoryne beckettii*. (17) *Cryptocoryne willisii*. (18) *Cryptocoryne cordata griffithii*.

(19) *Echinodorus paniculatus* var. *rangeri*. (20) *Echinodorus tenellus*. (21) *Echinodorus cordifolius*. (22) *Eleocharis acicularis*. (23) *Eleocharis vivipara*. (24) *Elodea densa*. (25) *Hygrophila polysperma*. (26) *Lagarosiphon major*. (27) *Lemna minor*. (28) *Limnophila heterophylla*. (29) *Ludwigia natans*. (30) *Marsilea hirsuta*.

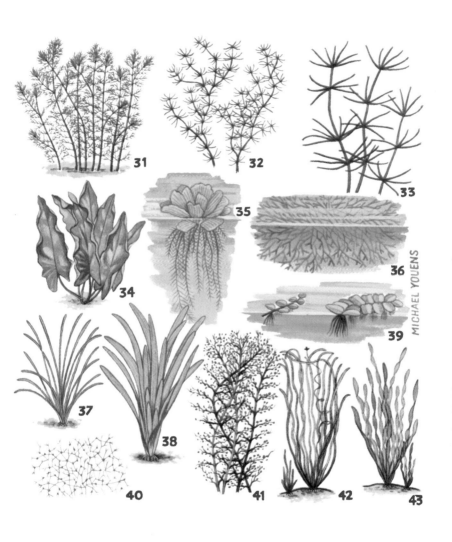

(31)*Myriophyllum elatinoides.* (32) *Nitella flexilis.* (33) *Nitella megacarpa.* (34) *Nuphar sagittifolium.* (35) *Pistia stratiotes.* (36) *Riccia fluitans.* (37) *Sagittaria subulata.* (38) *Sagittaria latifolia.* (39) *Salvinia auriculata.* (40) *Utricularia gibba.* (41) *Utricularia vulgaris.* (42) *Vallisneria spiralis.* (43) *Vallisneria spiralis* var. *tortifolia.*

Fast-growing species making new tissues rapidly use up nitrogenous salts and CO_2. They also produce copious amounts of oxygen in the process of building up starch and cellulose. Thus such plants (*Cabomba, Elodea, Vallisneria*, etc.) are often spoken of as oxygenating plants. One could also aptly call them water-purifying or water-conditioning plants.

Next is the question of "stimulating" plant growth by the use of various materials under the gravel floor of the aquarium or planting special or specimen plants in plastic boxes, clay plant pots, or trays with special media. It should be pointed out at the outset that in tanks well populated with fishes I have observed no benefits to a variety of plants treated in this fashion. Indeed, adverse effects such as rotting roots are more likely to occur.

The media most commonly recommended are peat and well-weathered garden loam, or a mixture of these with a small amount of charcoal. The bottom of a large tank can be covered with about ½ to 1″ of this material and then 3″ or so of gravel placed on top. The plants are carefully rooted without disturbing the subsoil too much. There is some danger of polluting the tank and killing the fishes so one must proceed cautiously. The experiment is much more safely carried out on a small scale in plant trays or pots. It is said that such treatment makes the plants grow and multiply quickly, particularly the so-called gross feeders or fast-growing plants.

It seems to me that in any tank well populated with fish there is more than enough nutriment (often too much) for all, including the gross feeders, and adding more in the form of subsoil is hardly likely to help. In tanks where plants are cultivated commercially, away from the fish, there is little doubt that such methods are useful for many species of plants.

It is interesting to note that a number of plants used in our aquaria can be grown in an emersed state (such as a bog plant, with the lower part of the plant in water), e.g., *Cryptocoryne*; others can be cultivated in trays or pots where the soil is kept soaking wet all the time (e.g., *Ludwigia*). Obviously these plants need a high humidity, to provide which the whole arrangement can be enclosed in clear plastic.

Such methods are commonly employed by commercial firms to produce aquatic plants in quantities. A fancier who has a warm greenhouse could try cultivating aquatic plants in this fashion, for this can be a most interesting pastime.

Now we come to the plants proper. I propose to deal with most of the common and some of the interesting ones, noting as we go along how they may be cultivated, of what use they are to us, and any points of special interest. Plants are listed under genera, which for convenience of reference are arranged in alphabetical order.

The scientific name of a plant, like that of a fish, is made up of two parts. The first indicates the genus, the second the specific name.

Acorus (Japanese Rush or Quillworts)

Three varieties of this popular plant are commonly available, one with bright green spike-leaves growing to a height of about ten inches (*A. gramineus*, Japanese Rush) (see painting 1), another with yellow striped foliage (*A. gramineus* var. *foliis variegatis*, Striped Japanese Rush) and a small variety with two-inch leaves (*A. gramineus* var. *pusillus*, Dwarf Japanese Rush). These are bog plants that grow rather slowly in submerged conditions. They do better at slightly lower temperatures than those encountered in tropical aquaria. When large, these plants can be propagated by splitting up the crowns from which the leaves arise.

Anubias

Recently introduced slow-growing bog plants from Africa. About six species are commonly available. They all have shiny, waxy-looking leaves. These plants grow to a height of six to twelve inches (see paintings 2 and 3).

Aponogeton

Some ten or so species and hybrids are available. There has been much confusion regarding nomenclature and plants are commonly sold under the wrong name. The two most popular species are *A. ulvaceus* (see painting 4) and *A. undulatus* (see painting 5). The former is regarded as one of the most magnificent of aquarium plants. It produces masses of pale green, semitranslucent, spirally twisted leaves. The latter produces long, wavy-edged leaves which can reach a height of some 18 inches. To this genus also belongs the fabulous Lace Plant *A. fenestralis* (see painting 6), a most difficult subject to cultivate.

Aponogetons form tuberous roots and have a resting period in the winter when the leaves die down.

Azolla (Fairy Moss)

To this genus belong two species of small floating plants, which aquarists call Fairy Moss. The tiny leaves have a velvet green to red-brown color, depending upon the season and species. Very prolific in growth so that it can become a nuisance (see painting 7).

Bacopa

Only two species of this genus of bog plants are commonly used by aquarists, *B. caroliniana* (see painting 8) and *B. monnieri* (see painting 9). The former has bright green, oval, slightly pointed fleshy leaves, the latter has smaller, more spatulate leaves. Both grow an erect, usually unbranching stem. They look quite different from most other aquatic plants. Perhaps their rigid appearance, suggesting terrestrial rather than aquatic habit, makes them look a bit out of place in the aquarium. The *Bacopas* are best propagated as bog plants, in trays or pots in a warm greenhouse.

Cabomba

Many species and cultivated varieties of this genus are available, the commoner ones being *C. aquatica* (see painting 11) and *C. caroliniana* var. *paucipartita* (see painting 10). The fan-shaped leaves are produced on ascending stems which can grow many feet in length, winding to and fro over the surface of the tank. The growing ends with a rosette of leaves form a magnificent spectacle in show tanks. These plants grow well over a fairly wide temperature range, 50°F.-80°F. Modest amounts of light, an algae-free tank, and slightly acid water are the main requirements for rapid growth.

Ceratopteris

This genus includes the Floating Fern (*C. cornuta*) (see painting 12) and the Indian Fern (*C. thalictroides*) (see painting 13). Both these quick-growing and easily propagated species are great favorites. The Floating Fern is excellent for discouraging the formation of "green water," for its rapid growth removes nitrogenous salts and its surface-growing habit cuts down the light reaching the water. Both species produce numerous plantlets from the margins of the leaves. The

Indian Fern can grow into magnificent specimens some 18″ in height.

Cryptocoryne

This genus contains many bog and submerged plants, usually of slow-growing habit. Great variation in the color and form of the leaves occurs in various species and under different conditions of growth, even in the same species. The nomenclature of this group was in a confused state but has now been much clarified by Roe (1967). Many species can be identified only when they flower, which further adds to the difficulty. Nevertheless the *Cryptocorynes* are deservedly very popular aquarium plants. They are slow to establish and hence should not be moved about or disturbed. Sometimes almost overnight or within a few days all the leaves on apparently perfectly healthy plants disintegrate into a jellylike mass and disappear. The reason is not clearly understood. Three theories have been proposed to explain this: (1) That it is due to a change in water conditions; (2) That it is some sort of disease, probably caused by a virus; (3) That in some species at least this is probably a reflection of cyclical change similar to that found in the natural state where these plants grow part of the time as bog plants (emersed) and the remainder of the time submerged.

There is little that the aquarist can do when his *Cryptocoryne* disintegrate in this fashion. I have tried various ways of reviving them but without much success; sometimes a few recover but as a rule most of the plants are lost.

These plants thrive best in slightly acid water and a modest amount of light. Only a few of the very large number of species available are mentioned in this book for some of them are rather rare and expensive.

One of the most popular and fastest growing and multiplying of the *Cryptocoryne* is *C. affinis*, also called *C. haerteliana* (see painting 14). It grows to some eight to twelve inches in height and has long bluish-green leaves with a reddish-purple underside. In my experience this species is more prone to sudden collapse as described above than any other.

A very useful small green *Cryptocoryne* that grows to a height of two inches or so used to be called *C. beckettii* but it is now considered that this and another similar but larger-growing variety are both *C. nevillii* (see painting 15). The real *C. beckettii* (see painting 16) is a larger plant with bronze leaves. Another interesting, easily available species is *C. willisii* (see painting 17), which has long, narrow leaves with crinkly edges and a brownish underside; it used to be called *C. undulata*.

A quite distinct and different-looking plant is the magnificent *C. cordata griffithii* (popularly but wrongly called *C. griffithii*, for this is a different species (see painting 18). This bears dark green heart-shaped leaves with a reddish-purple underside on elongated stalks. It grows as high as 16 inches and forms a magnificent centerpiece for modest-sized aquaria.

Echinodorus

This genus contains many attractive and rare species but only two or three are commonly seen. Perhaps the best known is the Amazon Sword Plant (*E. paniculatus*), a magnificent subject which will grow to a height of 18 inches in a large tank. A narrow-leaved variety (*gracilis*) and a broad-leaved variety (*rangeri*) are available (see painting 19). It is a heavy feeder and does best in an established tank housing many fishes. An aerial flower stem is produced which rarely flowers but produces numerous plantlets along its length. This should be laid out on the gravel with small stones placed along its length, between the plantlets, so that the young plants can root and grow. Young plants are best left attached to the parent till they have formed leaves about 6 inches long.

E. tenellus or Pygmy Chain-Sword Plant is another great favorite (see painting 20). This is a very variable species producing thin leaves rather resembling *Sagittaria*; at one time it was called *Sagittaria microfolia*. This plant grows to a height of three feet and in suitable conditions will throw out many runners and soon carpet the floor of the aquarium in a most delightful fashion.

E. cordifolius, once known as *E. radicans*, another beautiful and fairly prolific member of this genus, is strictly for the large aquarium, for it produces large oval leaves some nine inches long and seven inches wide. It also throws up aerial leaves and flower stalks. (See painting 21.)

Eleocharis

Popularly known as Hair Grass, and Needle Spikerush. Three species are available – *E. acicularis*, a dainty plant with a creeping root stock producing three to four inch stems (see painting 22), and *E. obtusa* and *E. vivipara* (see painting 23), which grow to a height of 18 inches and 10 inches respectively. Both develop plantlets from terminal buds on the stems. Once established, these plants grow well if the tank can be kept free of algae.

Elodea

Many species and varieties are available. Most of these are suitable only for the cold-water tank. Perhaps the most attractive and deservedly popular one is *E. densa*, which does well in both tropical and cold aquaria. This is a very rapidly growing and prolific species that can be propagated from small cuttings. The long, sparsely branched stems carry translucent green lanceolate leaves. The stems grow many feet in length. (See painting 24.)

Hygrophila

H. polysperma is a very popular, easily grown plant (see painting 25). The bright green leaves spring from a rather woody central stem. Cuttings root easily and the stems elongate rapidly. A clump of these plants looks most attractive in a decorative tank. Hard pruning can produce a bushy plant. In a poor light the plant tends to become drawn out and leggy. A larger-leaved species popularly called Giant Hygrophila (*H. salicifolia*, or *H. stricta*) is a very useful plant for the large aquarium. It forms woody stems up to ½" thick and bears leaves 5" or so in length. This is a prolific, easily grown species.

Lagarosiphon

L. major (see painting 26) is commonly known as *Elodea crispa*. *Elodeas* carry their leaves in whorls around a central stem, but in this plant the leaves alternate. More suited to cold water.

Lemna

This genus consists of several species of Duckweeds (floating plants), e.g., *L. gibba* and *L. minor* (see painting 27). It is usually introduced with the live food collected from the pond. It soon grows rampantly and becomes quite a nuisance. The excess is best scooped off the surface with a net and fed to such fishes as Goldfish and the larger Barbs.

Limnophila

L. sessiliflora and *L. heterophylla* (see painting 28) are commonly though incorrectly called *Ambulia* by aquarists: light green feathery leaves arising in whorls around a central stem. Easy to grow and propagate if algae-free conditions can be obtained.

Ludwigia

The cultivated form of *L. natans* that is called *L. mullertii* is the best of the Ludwigias (see painting 29). It produces small lanceolate leaves with a pale green upper surface and a reddish or bright red undersurface. This plant has a strong tendency to send shoots out of the water; it can be propagated very well as a bog plant. It grows well at fairly low temperatures (60°F.).

Marsilea

M. hirsuta is the best known member of this genus, which comes from Australia. In appearance it resembles a four-leaved clover. It is suitable for both cold and tropical tanks. Propagation is by runners, which are freely produced in hard alkaline conditions. (See painting 30.)

Myriophyllum

This genus contains many very fine-leaved plants called Water Milfoils. Because of their fine structure they tend to collect floating sediment and algae and are hence not as popular as they used to be. These plants form good spawn receptors but here again they have been replaced by artificial spawning media. Nevertheless, the Water Milfoils are dainty plants worthy of cultivation. They all need fairly strong natural light for their cultivation. Three of the best species for the aquarist are *M. brasiliense*, *M. elatinoides* (see painting 31) and *M. heterophyllum*.

Nitella

This plant is frequently confused with the Lesser Bladderwort (*Utricularia gibba*), but it can be distinguished by the fact that it has no bladder. Two species are available, *N. flexilis* (see painting 32), with translucent green stands from which arise branches forming whorls, and *N. megacarpa* (see painting 33), which looks like a larger version of the former, the branches being about three or four times larger. A somewhat brittle plant, it grows well in hard alkaline water with plenty of light. An ideal plant for spawning egg layers.

Nuphar

To this genus belong plants popularly known as Spatterdocks. Most of them are better suited to cold rather than tropical aquaria. They have a strong tendency to make long stems with floating leaves, a type of growth not suitable for decorative aquaria. The most admired species is the Cape Fear Spatterdock (*N. sagittifolium*) which does well in moderately warm aquaria. It has pale green, narrow, translucent leaves with wavy margins. (See painting 34.)

Pistia stratiotes

A decorative and useful floating plant. Looks like a cabbage lettuce, hence the popular name, Floating Lettuce. It has velvety leaves and long bushy roots, highly suitable for breeding surface spawners. A prolific plant that produces numerous floating runners from which small plants arise. (See painting 35.)

Riccia fluitans

Popularly called Crystalwort. This rootless floating plant with Y-shaped leaves is a prolific grower that forms a dense mat two to three inches thick on the surface of the water. Considered by many to be ideal for spawning and providing refuge for fry. In spite of its prolific growth, many aquarists find it a difficult plant to keep. It gets hopelessly entangled with algae and has a marked tendency to die off in the winter, probably because of lack of adequate illumination. (See painting 36.)

Sagittaria

Over a dozen species occur but only three or four are commonly seen in aquaria. These plants produce long, green, straplike leaves, which vary in length and breadth according to species and cultivation. They also produce aerial leaves, which are often spoon- or arrowhead-shaped. Some species are free-flowering and produce numerous small white flowers. Most of them propagate fairly freely from runners. Perhaps the most commonly available is *S. subulata* (see painting 37). Three different forms of these are known; *f. pusilla* is the smallest, growing to about six inches high, *f. natans* to fifteen inches, and *f. gracillima* to 23 inches.

Another very useful and impressive plant for the really large tank is *S. latifolia* (see painting 38). The submerged leaves, which are about one inch wide under aquarium conditions, usually do not grow beyond 18 inches in length. It produces lanceolate aerial leaves and does well in cold and tropical tanks.

Another popular species is *S. teres*, which grows to six or eight inches and has narrow leaves 3/16 to 3/8 inch wide.

Salvinia

The species commonly seen in tropical aquaria is *S. auriculata*. This is an attractive small floating plant with a branching stem and a row of round or oval leaves on either side. The upper surface of the leaves is hairy. Size of leaves varies from ½ to 1½ inches according to growing conditions. (See painting 39.)

Utricularia

Rootless, free-floating plants with filamentous stems and leaves bearing bladders. The plants belonging to this genus are often referred to as Bladderworts. The bladders are small sacs with hairs on them. When a small animal touches the hairs the bladder opens and the animal is sucked in by the inrush of water. The animal is digested and utilized by this carnivorous plant. The size of animal that the plant will capture depends on the size of the bladder. *U. gibba* with very small bladders (1/32 to 1/16 inch) can catch only infusorians; hence it is safe to use as a spawning medium, for the newly hatched fry are too big for it to capture. Other species with larger bladders are capable of devouring fry. (See paintings 40 and 41.)

Vallisneria

This genus contains two well-known favorites, *V. spiralis* (see painting 42) and *V. spiralis* var. *tortifolia* (43). The former has leaves up to ¾ inch wide, 30 inches long; the latter, which is an all-time favorite, grows up to about 9 or 15 inches and has spirally twisted leaves. Hence it is popularly called Corkscrew Val or Twisted Val. Not every one can grow this plant successfully. Much controversy exists regarding the best way to grow it. Contrary to popular belief it does not need very strong electric light or daylight. Robust plants are often raised under moderately strong artificial illumination. It does not like peat water. Slightly alkaline water of moderate hardness suits it best. If conditions are right, the plant is prolific and soon fills the tank with runners from which numerous plants arise.

References
Roe, C. D. (1967). *A Manual of Aquarium Plants*, pp. 20-55. Birmingham, England.
Sterba, G. (1967). *Aquarium Care*. Studio Vista Ltd. London, p. 28.

X Anatomy and Physiology

External Anatomy

Every aquarist must acquaint himself with the external anatomy of fishes, for the names of various fins and parts of the body continually occur in the description of species. This is best done with the aid of the diagram. Particular attention should be paid to the names and positions of the various fins.

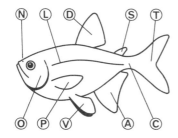

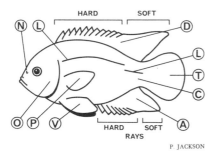

P. JACKSON

External anatomy of two types of fishes; above, a typical Characin — below, a typical Cichlid. (N) nose or nares — (L) lateral line — (D) dorsal fin — (S) adipose fin — (T) tail or caudal fin — (C) caudal peduncle — (A) anal fin — (V) paired ventral or pelvic fins — (P) paired pectoral or breast fins — (O) gill cover or operculum.

Fins

The fins are made of stiff rays covered by fin membrane (skin). Some may be jointed and some divide near the edge of the fin. In certain fishes some of the rays supporting the fin are bony, stiff, and unjointed. They are then referred to as spines. Almost half the fin rays in the dorsal fin of Cichlids are in fact bony spines. Therefore the anterior portion of such a fin is called the spiny dorsal and the posterior part the soft dorsal. In Gobies and some others the spiny dorsal and soft dorsal are totally separated and form two distinct dorsal fins. The number of rays in the fins is of importance in classification (taxonomy). The hard rays are expressed in Roman numerals and the soft rays in Arabic numerals. Thus in the Angel (*Pterophyllum scalare*) there are eleven or twelve hard rays and 24 or 25 soft rays in the dorsal fin. This is written briefly like this: D XI-XII/24-25. The ray counts in other fins are expressed in a similar fashion.

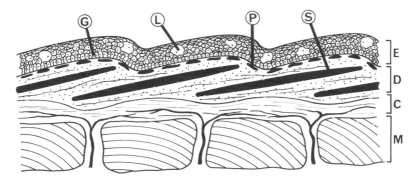

P. JACKSON

Diagramatic cross-section of the skin of a fish: (E) epidermis or outer layer, resting on (D) dermis. The subcutaneous connective tissue is shown as (C) and the muscles as (M). Basal or germinal cells (G) from which the epidermis regenerates and the slime or mucoid cells (L) are clearly defined. The pigment cells (P) lie at the dermo-epidermal junction. The scales (S) are embedded in the dermis.

Skin

As in the case of other vertebrates the skin of fishes is divided into two layers (see illustration): the superficially placed epidermis is supported underneath by the dermis. The epidermis is made of epithelial cells, arranged in layers one above the other (hence called stratified epithelium). These cells are shed continually at the surface and replaced by the proliferation of cells in the deepest layer of the epidermis, called the basal cell layer or germinal layer (*stratum germinativum*). Interspersed between the epithelial cells are mucous or slime cells which produce slimy or mucoid secretions that form a protective covering on the fish.

Scales

The deeper-placed dermis is made up of connective tissue (fibroblasts and collagen fibers) and blood vessels. The scales (mainly bony) lie in pockets in the dermis and in fact arise from this connective tissue. It will be noted that the scales do not stick out of the skin like hairs; each scale is covered by the epidermis. The scales overlap and thus form a protective flexible armor capable of withstanding blows and buffeting.

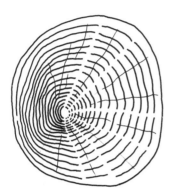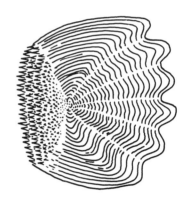

P. JACKSON

Two common types of scales – (Left) Cycloid, (Right) Ctenoid.

The morphology of scales is complex and many varieties occur, but only two main types concern us here (see illustration). Both are round or oval flat plates, but in one variety (ctenoid scales) one edge is serrated while in the other (cycloid scales) there is no serration on any edge. In some families scales are entirely lacking, as in some Catfishes described in this book as naked Catfishes. In others they are so small that they cannot be seen with the naked eye. In armored Catfishes and some others the scales are replaced by bony plates. The head is usually free of scales.

Scales are arranged in rows and scale counts play an important part in distinguishing closely related species. Two counts are usually made, a longitudinal and a transverse. The former is carried out along the length of the body, usually along the lateral line, and the latter at the greatest body height.

Surface views of scales seen under the microscope reveal rings similar to those found in tree trunks and indicate periods of active growth and relative quiescence. As such they can give a rough idea of the age of the fish.

Pigment Cells

The many beautiful colors and color patterns seen in fishes are produced by pigment cells lying in the dermis.

These cells are named according to the pigment they contain. Thus *melanophores* contain brownish-black pigment called melanin, *erythrophores* contain red pigment (pterins), *xanthophores* contain yellow pigment (pterins also), and *guanophores* or *iridophores* contain crystals of guanin which reflect and/or refract the light. Thus the metallic look of Goldfish, the mirrorlike silvery surface of many fishes, and the grey, green and blue iridescences in Fighters are largely due to these cells, assisted in some instances by the overlying colored pigment cells.

Fishes can change color from one moment to the next. We have all seen Angels at one moment displaying beautiful dark bands, which disappear in a few moments if the fish is frightened. This kind of rapid change is achieved by the movement of melanin granules within the cells (see illustration). When the granules are dispersed they provide a large surface for light absorption, hence the area containing these cells with dispersed or expanded pigment looks black. When the pigment comes together to form a small clump around the nucleus (contracted stage) the fish goes pale.

P. JACKSON

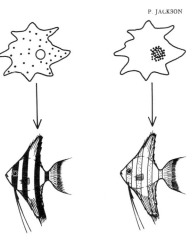

This diagram illustrates the manner in which the black bands of an angelfish seem to disappear when the fish is frightened. In the fish at the left, the melanin granules are dispersed, providing a broader dark area. In the fish at the right, the granules have contracted to form a small clump around the nucleus, making the fish appear light.

Skeleton and Muscles

This subject is of considerable interest to taxonomists but of little interest to aquarists. The bony skeleton supports the fish and provides attachments for the powerful muscles. These are arranged in segments or myotomes, a fact easily verified when you are eating cooked fish. The musculature is transparent in some species, as the aquarist knows: e.g., Glass Catfish, X-Ray Fish, etc. In others, such as the Mormyridae and Electrophoridae, some of the muscle segments are modified into electric organs.

Respiratory System

Aquatic respiration is carried out by means of gills lodged under the gill covers. The wall of the pharynx is perforated by five slitlike apertures. The tissue between the slits is referred to as a gill arch; thus on each side of the fish there are five gill slits and four gill arches. On the gill arches are mounted the gills, a delicate system of blood vessels covered by very thin epithelium through which gaseous exchanges can occur (see Chapter II).

The actual respiratory cycle can be easily observed in the aquarium, where one can see the fish alternately shutting and opening its mouth

When respiring, a fish opens its mouth to suck in water which is then forced through the gills and out from behind the gill covers.

and gill covers. What happens during such a cycle is as follows: the fish opens its mouth and water is sucked in. Next the mouth shuts and muscles in the mouth begin to contract. This closes the oral valves (see illustration) so that water is forced through the gill slits, over the gills and under the gill covers, which are now moving outward. Two skin folds at the posterior edge of the gill covers and the gill covers themselves act as valves hindering the passage of water in the reverse direction when the fish opens its mouth. Nevertheless, fishes can reverse the flow and expel water from the mouth to assist in clearing the gills of debris.

Other Forms of Respiration

Gaseous exchanges probably occur over the skin of fishes. While in young fry before gills have developed this is vital and in small fishes it may be important, its occurrence in large adult fishes is doubtful. Some fishes have developed accessory organs to utilize atmospheric oxygen. One such, the labyrinth organ, is described elsewhere (Chapter XIII), as is intestinal respiration (see below, Swim Bladder) by which oxygen is removed from a quantity of air swallowed by the fish.

Alimentary System

This is best regarded as a long tubelike structure extending from mouth to anus. The alimentary canal can be divided into three parts: (1) The fore-gut, made up of mouth, pharynx, and esophagus; (2) The mid-gut, made up of stomach, duodenum, and ilium, and (3) The hind-gut, a short segment where feces accumulate before excretion.

Carnivores have a shorter midgut than herbivores. Into the midgut are poured secretions from the liver and the pancreas (absent in some fishes). The liver is a large reddish-brown organ that can be easily recognized; it is sometimes fatty, in which event it is yellow in color. The function of the midgut is to digest the food and absorb the simpler substances derived by this process.

Circulatory System

The main function of this system is to transport essential metabolites and oxygen to the tissues. This is achieved by pumping blood along a system of vessels. The motive force for the circulation is provided by the heart. Venous blood is first collected into the sinus venosus; from here it goes to the auricle, and thence to a strong muscular ventricle which pumps out the blood into the main artery, called the ventral aorta. From here the blood proceeds to the gills (via branches of the ventral aorta known as the afferent branchial arteries). These arteries break up into capillaries; passing through the gills the blood gives up carbon dioxide and picks up oxygen. The oxygenated blood now flows from the afferent branchial arteries, into two large vessels on the left and right respectively. Cerebral arteries carry blood forward, and the two vessels unite behind to form the dorsal aorta, which distributes blood to other parts of the body. The impure blood is collected by a system of veins and brought back to the sinus venosus, thus completing the circulation.

Kidneys

Excretion of nitrogenous waste products from the blood is carried out by kidneys, which lie just under the vertebral column. Many and varied morphological differences are seen in the kidneys, too numerous to detail here. The kidneys terminate in ureters which lead the urine to one or two openings just behind the genital opening.

Brain and Spinal Cord

The forebrain in man is large and highly developed; in fishes it is small and serves the sense of smell. The spinal cord and other parts of the brain, like the cerebellum and midbrain which serve the locomotor system, are well developed.

Special Senses

Man has five senses: vision, hearing, smell, taste and touch. Fishes have all these and at least one more, a sort of sixth sense which allows them to detect low frequency vibrations. Humans have always been keenly interested in knowing what and how their pets sense and feel. Aquarists are no exception; they frequently ask whether their fish can see and recognize them, whether they feel pain, whether they can hear music, whether they can smell, and if so how can one smell under water? To these and hundreds of similar questions one cannot give quick easy answers. A great deal of work has been done that throws light on these problems. The special senses of fishes will be covered in rather more detail than is customary.

The Lateral Line

The lateral line consists of a series of scales, each modified by a tube or pore, which connects with a system of canals housing sensory cells (called neuromasts) and nerve fibers. It runs in a continuous or interrupted line from the gills up to the tail fin of the fish and may easily be seen with the naked eye in many of our aquarium fishes. Similar canals also ramify over the head and face.

It is now clear that this organ is concerned with the detection of water currents. In practical terms, such a system allows the fish to detect vibrations in the water produced by prey or predator at a distance. It is also thought that the waves set up by the movement of the fish itself are reflected back by the surrounding objects and picked up by the sensory organs of the lateral canal. A computation of the direction and time of arrival of such waves could give the fish an accurate three-dimensional topography of its environment. The resemblance between this and our echo location systems will be readily appreciated. Obviously, such a system is particularly useful in the absence of visual orientation in darkness or in turbid waters.

Olfactory Sense

In most fishes the sense of smell is very highly developed and is probably of greater use to them in seeking out food than the sense of vision.

In the Teleostei the olfactory pits are responsible for the sense of smell. Two of these are found in each fish, situated on either side on the snout, and communicate to the exterior usually by two openings, an anterior inlet and a posterior outlet. In certain fishes such as the Cichlids the pits communicate to the exterior by only a single opening. It will be noted that the fish's nose does not communicate with the respiratory system as in man.

The olfactory pouch is lined by a membrane (thrown into folds to increase its surface area) containing smell receptors (olfactory cells) and numerous nerve fibers which convey impulses to the brain, there producing the sensation of smell.

Odor perception in all animals is a chemically induced phenomenon.

Thus the odor-producing substance has to dissolve in the layer of mucus in the human nose before it can exite our olfactory cells. In the case of fishes the substance is already dissolved in the surrounding water. Thus in the final analysis there is no fundamental difference between the way we smell things and the way the fishes do, for all olfaction is aquatic.

Vision

Vision under water poses many special problems. Perhaps the most significant is the small amount of light available in any but the superficial layers of water. This is because light from the sun, as it hits the water, is largely lost by reflection at the surface, absorption in the water, and diffusion by myriads of particles present even in clean-looking waters.

Since vision under water is limited to a few yards, even in fairly clean waters, and not to miles as on land, it is not surprising to find that the fish eye is designed to see objects in the near distance and not at infinity. Focusing is carried out by moving the lens backward or forward as in a camera and not as in the human eye, where the curvature (and hence the focal length) of the lens surface is altered by muscular action.

The lens of the fish eye must have a greater curvature than the lens of terrestrial animals for the refractive index of water is much higher than that of air. The fish lens is in fact a sphere, i.e., it has maximum possible curvature; but even so, many consider that it may be inadequate to produce a sharply focused picture on the retina.

Two main types of cells are seen in the retina of vertebrates, rods and cones. The rods can be stimulated by low thresholds of light and are useful when the light is poor, but fine details and colors cannot be discerned by these cells. The cones operate when light is plentiful; the quality of the image is much better and colors can be appreciated.

The cartilaginous fishes, sharks and their relatives, have only rods in their retinas and are obviously color-blind. Much controversy has raged in the past as to whether even the bony fishes, which have both rods and cones, experience any true color sensation. Today, however, it is generally accepted that most of these have at least a limited power to recognize color as color and not merely as different shades of gray. Some of the Cichlids seem to have a strong color-differentiation.

Fishermen know that different colored bait attracts different fishes.

Since the eyes of fishes are placed one on each side of the head the vision is largely monocular. Such an arrangement gives fishes a very wide field of vision but is of little use in judging distances. There are, however, grounds for believing that in many species there is an overlapping of the visual fields in the front of the fish and a limited zone of binocular or stereoscopic vision is in fact experienced.

Hearing

A massive body of scientific evidence now exists which shows that fishes are capable of hearing, that is to say, responding to a range of vibrations, which we call sound waves. Although we are uncertain about the precise mechanisms involved, we do know a good deal about the threshold, range, and pitch discrimination in various species (Lowenstein, 1957).

This subject should be of special interest to aquarists for many aquarium fishes have been investigated in this fashion. Thus various Anabantidae, such as *Betta splendens, Colisa lalia, Macropodus opercularis, Trichogaster leeri, Trichogaster trichopterus*, can hear notes with an upper limit of between 2637 and 4699 cycles per second (CPS). The Guppy will respond to sounds between 44 and 2068 CPS. The Gobies fare rather poorly for their top limit is only 800 CPS.

So far we have considered fishes that do not belong to the order Ostariophysi.

In these the swim bladder is connected to the inner ear or labyrinth (organs of balance and hearing in fishes must not be confused with the respiratory labyrinth of the Anabantidae) by a chain of small bones called Weberian ossicles. The swim bladder in these fishes could act as an efficient sound resonator and we would expect them to hear better, and this seems to be the case for at least some of the Ostariophysi. Thus Characins such as *Hemigrammus caudovittatus* and *Hyphessobrycon flammeus*, which belong to this order, can hear notes up to 6960 CPS while the Cyprinid *Phoxinus phoxinus* can hear 7000 CPS (this is a little better than the range of frequencies found on old 78 rpm phonograph records). They can distinguish between semitones in the range 987.7 to 1046.5 CPS and quarter tones in the 400 to 800 CPS range.

The threshold of audibility (i.e., the softest sound one can hear) has been measured in only a few species but it appears that it is of the same magnitude as in man.

Gustatory Sense (Taste)

The situation here is strikingly different from that in terrestrial vertebrates. In fishes, taste buds are found not only in the mouth but also in the skin covering the head, body, fins, barbels, and lips. Many Catfishes have taste buds on their flanks. This would suggest that fishes can taste food before it even enters the mouth. Such a notion derived from anatomical considerations is also supported by some ingenious experiments.

Other Senses

The abundance of touch receptors and nerves in the fish skin clearly shows that they have a sense of touch. Such receptors are often carried on barbels or the whiskers of Catfishes. An important question that aquarists frequently ask is: Can fishes feel pain? To this we can give no clear answer. On anatomical grounds it can be argued that it is in the cortex of the human brain that pain is perceived and since fishes have no truly comparable structure they cannot perceive pain, at least in the sense we use the word. Pain in man has a physical and a psychological component. As far as fishes are concerned, the latter could be ruled out at once. Regarding the former we can only observe that fishes can detect harmful or noxious stimuli and attempt to withdraw from them, but whether they feel pain from such noxious stimulation is highly debatable.

Swim Bladder

Lying just under the spine of many teleostean fishes (usually between the kidneys and the gut) is found a hollow membranous sac called the gas bladder or swim bladder. Embryologically, the swim bladder develops as a pouchlike extension (diverticulum) from the gut. In the adult of some species (physoclistous teleosts) the connection between the gas bladder and the gut (called the pneumatic duct) is lost, but it is retained in a few (physostomous teleosts).

Thus in physoclistous teleosts the swim bladder is a closed sac containing gas which arrives and leaves via the blood and the activity of gas-secreting and gas-absorbing glands in the walls of this organ. Analysis of the gas shows that it is composed of a mixture of oxygen, carbon dioxide, and nitrogen. The proportions vary in different species but the figures clearly indicate that the gas could not have got there by simple diffusion from the blood stream.

The main function of the swim bladder appears to be as a hydrostatic organ. The amount of gas is regulated to give the fish the correct buoyancy at the depth it lives. Fishes without swim bladders (e.g., sharks and rays) would sink to the bottom if they kept still. They have to swim constantly and use muscular energy to maintain any position off the bottom of the water.

Fast free-swimming midwater teleostean fishes have a well-developed swim bladder; those living on the bottom have a very small or no swim bladder. As every swimmer knows, the density of sea water is greater than fresh water and hence is more buoyant. It is therefore

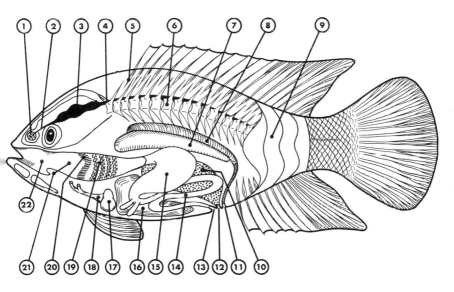

The internal anatomy of the fish.
(1) olfactory bulb. (2) olfactory nerve. (3) brain. (4) spinal cord. (5) fin ray supports. (6) vertebral column. (7) swim bladder. (8) kidneys leading to ureter. (9) myotomes (muscle segments). (10) gonads. (11) and (12) urogenital opening (openings of oviduct and ureter). (13) anus. (14) intestine. (15) stomach. (16) liver. (17) heart. (18) ventral aorta. (19) gill slits. (20) gill rakers. (21) pharynx and tongue. (22) buccal or oral cavity.

not surprising to find that in marine fishes the swim bladder occupies only about 5 per cent of the fish's total volume but in corresponding fresh water fishes the volume is 7 to 10 per cent.

Gas bladders, however, limit a fish's range of diving and rising, for gaseous exchange between the blood and the bladder is a slow process. If a deep-sea fish is hooked and suddenly brought to the surface the bladder will expand and push the stomach out of the mouth of the fish.

Besides the hydrostatic function mentioned the swim bladder has, or may have in certain species, additional functions. It can serve as an accessory breathing organ, but the amount of oxygen available in this way is rather small. It can, as we have already seen (see above, Hearing), serve as a receptor for sound stimuli in fishes (Ostariophysi) where the swim bladder is connected to the inner ear by the Weberian ossicles. In some fishes it acts as a sound producer; this is achieved by vibration of the walls by attached muscles or by expulsion of gas through the pneumatic duct. It can also act as a sound resonator in fishes which produce sounds by the grating of pharyngeal teeth.

Genital System and Reproduction

Both the male and female gonads, that is, the testes and ovaries, are essentially paired hollow organs, but in some species the members of the pair are fused. The cavity in the gonads is continued posteriorly to form the oviduct in the female and the spermatic duct in the male. These open just behind the anus on a small papilla.

Except for one or two rare exceptions reproduction in fishes is sexual, that is to say it involves the fusion of a male sex cell called the spermatozoon with a female sex cell called the ovum to produce a fertilized egg or zygote, which then proceeds to divide and differentiate to form a new individual. In most species the males and females are separate individuals but in some families (*Sparidae* and *Serranidae*) true functional hermaphrodites occur, that is to say, ovarian and testicular tissue occur in the same individual and they are capable of self-fertilization.

In the Amazon Mollie we have another peculiarity of reproduction (Atz, 1961). Here the females mate with males of other *Mollienesia* (Poecilia) species, but the sperms do not fuse with the ova. The unfertilized egg then proceeds to divide and produces broods of female Mollies. Such a phenomenon is called gynogenesis or pseudogamy.

The occurence of parthenogenesis, by which the ovum in the female proceeds to divide and form a young individual without any help from the male, is also claimed to occur at times in *Gambusia affinis*.

The teleostean fishes show a wide and varied spectrum of reproductive devices and behavior. Much of this has been dealt with in other parts of the book, particularly under individual species. However, a brief account of the main features is necessary.

In many of our aquarium fishes fertilization of the eggs occurs outside the body. The male and female come close together and ova and sperms are liberated and unite in the water. (The sperms cannot survive in the water for more than a few seconds to a few minutes.) This form of reproduction is spoken of as oviparous, i.e., the eggs are fertilized and develop outside the mother, deriving sustenance from the yolk stored in them.

Two other forms of reproduction are encountered, ovoviviparous and viviparous, but much confusion exists regarding the precise meanings of these terms.

Kallman (1967) aptly describes this state as follows: "Ovoviviparity implies that the zygote is retained and develops inside the female parent but that no food materials are transferred from the mother to the embryo." In short, the fertilized eggs derive shelter but not sustenance from the mother. Ovoviviparity is seen in certain Characins such as *Corynopoma riisei* and others where the male attaches himself for a brief moment to the female and expels a packet of sperms into her oviduct. The female then proceeds to lay fertilized eggs for many months. In some species the eggs may be fertilized immediately before laying, in others the fertilized egg (zygote) is retained for variable periods and fertilized eggs or embryos at various stages of development are liberated. An intermediate state between true viviparity and ovoviviparity is seen in *Xiphophorus*, *Gambusia*, and *Poecilia*, where the embryo derives nutrition partly from the egg yolk and partly from the maternal blood stream.

In some other species, however, a situation similar to that seen in mammals develops, where a structure analogous to the placenta is developed and the fertilized egg is nourished virtually entirely by the mother (viviparous). In the family Embiotocidae, the young are nourished by the mother, grow to 1¾ inches, and the males are sexually mature when born. Another interesting variation is seen in the small livebearer *Heterandria formosa* (Mosquito Fish). Here at any given moment the ovarian cavity contains a number of embryos in different stages of development. As the eggs mature in the ovaries they are released into the ovarian cavity and fertilized by the stored sperms. This state of affairs is called superfoetation. The fish delivers two or three young daily over a period of a week or two.

Some peculiarities of gonopodial development and sex reversal in livebearers have been dealt with in Chapter XIII.

References

Atz, J. W. (1961). "Fish Without Fathers," *Aquarist, 26, 176-179.*

Kallman, K. (1967). *Enjoy your Platies and Swordtails.* Edited by E. Schneider, Pet Library, New York.

Lowenstein, O. (1957). "The Acoustico-lateralis System," *The Physiology of Fishes,* vol. 2, 178-182. Edited by M. E. Brown. Academic Press, New York.

XI Genetics

Genetics is the study of heredity. That offspring resemble their par
ents is common knowledge, but how the various physical and other
characteristics making up an individual are handed down from generation to generation can only be comprehended by a study of genetics. Obviously, the characteristics themselves are not handed down;
for the fertilized egg bears little resemblance to the parents, but the
potentiality for their inheritance is. In order to understand this it is
first essential to grasp certain simple biological facts.

Chromosomes

Chromosomes are threadlike structures found in the nucleus of all
cells, but they can be seen only, or best, when the cell is dividing.
They contain deoxyribonucleic acid (DNA) and some protein. In
somatic cells (cells of the body as contrasted with those in gonads) we
find several different pairs of chromosomes in the nucleus. The actual
number is usually constant for a species. Thus in man we have 23
pairs or 46 chromosomes.

This is called the diploid state or condition. When somatic cells
divide (mitosis) the DNA is duplicated and each chromosome divides
along its long axis so that at the end of division each daughter cell
has 46 chromosomes.

In the gonads we have primitive sex cells, which are also in the
diploid state, that is to say they have 46 chromosomes (23 pairs). During division to form the mature sex cells (gametes) they undergo what
is known as reduction division (meiosis) so that the spermatozoon and
ovum end up with only half the number of chromosomes, 23 chromosomes, i.e., only one member of each original pair. This is called the
haploid state and how this occurs in the male and female is shown in
the diagram. In the case of the male all the products of division are
utilized to form sperms; in the female only one part survives to form
a large ovum. The rest, called polar bodies, are discarded.

When the sperm and ovum unite the normal diploid number for the
species is restored (23 + 23 = 46). You will see that one member of
each pair comes from the male and the other from the female, and
also that by this method the number of chromosomes for the species
remains unaltered.

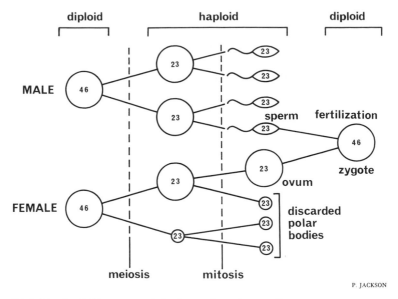

Diploid – haploid states and the formation of sex cells.

Sex Chromosomes

In human males we have 22 pairs of chromosomes where the partners resemble each other and one pair in which they do not. The former are referred to as autosomal chromosomes and the latter as sex chromosomes. In the unequal sex chromosomes the larger member of the pair is called the X chromosome, the small one Y chromosome. In females we have a pair of X chromosomes (XX), in males an X and a Y chromosome (XY). This is also true of many fish species (e.g., *Xiphophorus variatus*, and *Poecilia reticulata*), but in domesticated *Xiphophorus maculatus* the situation is reversed, for the male carries the similar pair and the female the dissimilar pair of chromosomes.

Genes

The gene is defined as the material of inheritance or the unit of inheritance. At one time it was thought that genes were small particles carried on chromosomes; current opinion, however, regards the gene as a small segment of a chromosome influencing a particular character in a certain definite way. The material of which it is made is called deoxyribonucleic acid (DNA). (An exception to this is seen in some viruses where the material is RNA, ribonucleic acid.) One of the greatest discoveries of our time is that we now know that DNA is a chain molecule, the links of which consist of four chemical compounds called nucleotides. The complexity and sequence in which they occur constitutes the genetic code, i.e., the information, message, or blueprint for building a new individual. If this seems far-fetched we should perhaps recall that complex human thoughts can be transmitted by the Morse code, which consists of nothing more than a sequence of dots, dashes, and spaces.

Individuals may be looked upon as the sum total of a very large number of characteristics. Each characteristic is controlled by a single pair or multiple pairs of genes. However, the members of the pair may be similar or dissimilar. When they are similar we speak of them as being in the homozygous state, when dissimilar, the heterozygous state. Because of reduction division when sex cells are formed, only one member of a pair of genes is carried in any given sperm or ovum. It will be seen that on fertilization we once more have a pair of genes but one has come from the father, the other from the mother. Thus the offspring inherits a double set of information on any particular point. This may, of course, be similar (homozygous) or dissimilar (heterozygous). If it is dissimilar then one set of information takes precedence over the other. To put it in another way, one gene will be dominant, the other recessive. How this operates in practice can be best appreciated by the experiment of Gregor Mendel, the father of genetics.

Dominant and Recessive Genes

Mendel had a race of tall peas which always bred true and produced tall plants. He also had another race of peas which always produced short plants. If we now use the symbol T for tallness and t for not tall, or short, we can see what is happening. The somatic cells of tall peas will have two genes TT, they will form male and female gametes, sex cells, each containing only one T. When they unite we once more have the situation TT or a tall plant. We can show this diagrammatically thus:

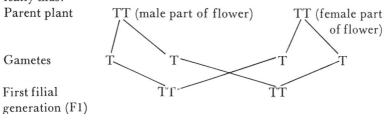

Parent plant   TT (male part of flower)   TT (female part of flower)

Gametes   T   T   T   T

First filial generation (F1)   TT   TT

Thus we see that inbreeding a pure-line homozygous strain of tall peas, all the offspring will be tall like the parents.

In the same way homozygous short peas will also breed true. Let us now see what happens when the tall peas ((TT) are crossed with the short ones. This is best seen in the following diagram.

Parent plants

Gametes

F1 generation

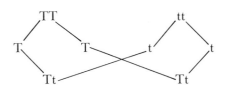

It will be observed from the above that all the offspring will be heterozygous and will have the genetic constitution (genotype) Tt. Mendel observed that in fact all the plants were tall like one of the parents – *they were not of an intermediate height.* We can therefore say that tallness is dominant over shortness. Whether the genotype is TT (homozygous) or Tt (heterozygous) makes no difference to the appearance (phenotype) of the plant in regard to its height.

Let us now see what happens when we mate these heterozygous plants of the first filial generation (F1) among themselves. Obviously many male gametes carrying either T or t will be formed as will many female gametes carrying either T or t. Three types of plants are now possible, TT, Tt, or tt. The frequency with which they occur will be dependent on chance and the probability can be worked out by a simple block diagram, thus:

<table>
<tr><td colspan="3" align="center">Male</td></tr>
</table>

	T	t
T	TT	Tt
t	Tt	tt

Female (for the left of the table)

We see now that the offspring will be in the ratio of one TT, two Tt, one tt; one TT and two Tt will be all tall plants but one tt will be a short plant. Thus there will be a 3 : 1 ratio of tall to short plants. This is spoken of as the usual Mendelian ratio, and it indicates that we are dealing with inheritance based on a single pair of a dominant and a recessive gene.

Examples of Dominant and Recessive Inheritance in Fishes

Once the above principles of Mendelian inheritance are understood they can be applied to a variety of cases in other animals. It is convenient to remember that most of the characters we consider desirable in our fishes are usually recessive. Thus wild-type coloration (gray) is dominant over gold or blond coloration. If a gray Platy or Guppy is mated to a gold Platy or Guppy the offspring will all be gray, for gray is dominant over gold. If brother-sister matings are carried out between members of the first filial generation we will have the usual Mendelian ratio of three gray to one gold. The blond, being recessive and homozygous, will breed true and produce nothing but gold Guppies; they will in no way be tainted or "spoiled" by having gray ancestors. The moon (complete moon) marking on the Platy is dominant over no marking.

Recessive Inheritance of the Albino

Albinism is a condition (can also be looked upon as a disease) in which melanocytes and melanophores (melanin-producing cells) fail to produce the brownish-black pigment melanin. An enzyme called tyrosinase is essential for the conversion of tyrosin (an amino acid) into the pigment melanin. This enzyme is present in the pigment-producing cells of the normal individual but is absent in the albino. A single gene controls the production of the enzyme in the normal state but the altered or mutated gene of the albino animal lacks the genetic code needed to direct the synthesis of this enzyme. This mutated albino gene is recessive to the normal.

It will be appreciated from previous examples that being recessive, albinos breed true and produce only other albino animals. If crossed to a normal pigmented (homozygous) individual the offspring will all be pigmented.

The Intermediate Phenotype

In the examples we have studied so far we have seen that an individual with heterozygous genotype is indistinguishable from the dominant homozygous genotype by external examination alone. That is to say they have the same phenotype.

Thus, by just looking at a tall pea we cannot say whether its genotype is TT or Tt. There are, however, examples in piscine genetics where you can do just that, for the heterozygous animal is either intermediate in appearance between the two parents or shows a different color. This is spoken of as the intermediate phenotype or by the not as accurate term incomplete dominance. This is a situation of some practical interest and importance to aquarists. For generations now aquarists have tried to produce a pure strain of Blue Fighters or a pure strain of nacreous Goldfish, and have failed to do so. The reason for this is that the Blue Fighter and the nacreous Goldfish are heterozygous animals and thus cannot possibly breed true. Let us examine these fascinating examples in a little more detail.

In the Fighting Fish the colors gray, blue, and green are produced by the amount and manner in which guanine crystals are arranged in certain cells in the skin, called iridophores. These crystals reflect and refract the light, producing the above-mentioned colors, and also give the metallic sheen to the Fighter. The colors gray, green, and blue are controlled by the gene *viridis* (green). When the gene is in the homozygous dominant phase (VV) it produces a gray fish (sometimes called steel blue), when in the homozygous recessive phase (vv) a green fish. The heterozygous state (Vv) produces the much-admired Cornflower Blue Fighter.

We can now see why a pure line of Blue Fighters is impossible to produce. If we interbreed Blue Fighters of genetic constitution Vv we get offspring of the genetic constitution 1VV, 2 Vv, 1vv. That is to say, 25 per cent of the fish will be gray, 25 per cent green, and 50 per cent blue. We can carry this on forever without getting any closer to producing a pure line of Blue Fighters. In fact, the only way to get 100 per cent Blue fish would be to mate gray (VV) fish with green (vv) each time.

Let us now see the situation in the Goldfish (whether they are Fantails, Veiltails, or Lionheads is of no concern in this example). Basically, one can define three forms as far as the reflectile guanine crystals in iridophores in the skin is concerned: Transparent (also called matt) (TT), nacreous (Tt), and metallic (tt). The gene T causes the scales to be transparent, the gene t causes them to be reflectile or metallic. The heterozygous state Tt gives the much-desired nacreous fish with its pearly luster.

The nacreous Goldfish is a heterozygous animal and cannot possibly breed true; it will perennially throw 25 per cent ordinary metallic goldfish, 25 per cent transparents, and 50 per cent nacreous.

Genetic Determination of Sex and Sex-linked Inheritance

We can find many examples of color or color patterns present in only one sex and not in the other. This is in some instances explained by the fact that genes responsible for this are contained in the sex chromosomes. Before we examine this let us see how sex is genetically determined. We have already seen earlier that the sex chromosome pair can be represented in the male as XY and in the female as XX in man and many species of fish. When gametes (mature sex cells) are formed it is easily seen that all the ova will carry an X chromosome but there will be two types of sperms; one half will carry Y chromosomes the others X chromosomes. An egg fertilized by the former will produce a female, that fertilized by the latter, a male. This is shown in the diagram below:

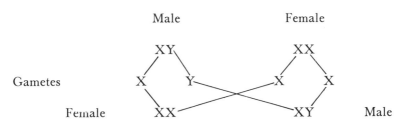

Not only do the genes responsible for determining sex reside in these chromosomes but so do many other factors. The Y chromosome in most groups of animals rarely carries dominant genes but in fishes many dominant genes are known to occur in the Y chromosome.

Thus the dominant gene responsible for black spotting on the flanks of male *Xiphophorus variatus* is carried by the Y chromosome and hence this spotting develops only on the male.

Linkage

Since the number of genes is infinitely greater than the number of chromosomes, it follows that, when chromosomes divide, blocks of genes will be transferred. Such genes which go together are spoken of as linked genes and the characters determined by them will appear in the same individual. Conversely, when we see two or more characters always appearing together we suspect that the genes responsible for them reside in the same chromosome.

Gene Exchange

Reduction division or meiosis is a very complicated biological process, which we could not examine in detail in this small chapter on genetics. At one stage the chromosome pairs come very close together and even wrap around each other. At this stage pieces can break off. On reassembly a bit belonging to one member of the pair can become exchanged for a similar piece from the other. The genes in the two chromosomes are thus exchanged. Gene exchanges between X and Y chromosomes are most interesting, for colors and color patterns restricted, say, to the male may now begin to appear in the female.

Mutation

We commenced our discussion on genetics by stating that offspring resemble their parents. If this were always strictly true, no new characters could develop and evolution would hardly be possible. It is believed that mutations are the raw material of evolution. What happens is that there is a sudden change in the chromosomal DNA. If such a change occurs in a gamete (sex cell) it will be replicated and transmitted to the offspring (genetic mutation). The function of the gene will be altered and new characters may appear. Classic examples of these are the many characters seen in fancy Goldfish, e.g., veiltails, telescope eyes, Lionhead, etc. Mutations of somatic cells (cells of the body) are held to be responsible for the production of tumors. These neoplastic mutations can be produced by chemicals, ionizing radiations, or viruses. Such agents can also increase the rate of genetic mutation. Most mutations are unfavorable; gross mutations can so upset biological mechanisms that they are usually lethal. But every now and again a mutation arises that allows better adaptation to the environment; such a mutation operated on by the forces of natural and/or sexual selection gives rise in time to new species.

Practical Aspects of Genetics in Fish Breeding

It is well known that many beautiful strains of domestic animals (including fishes) have been developed by persons with little or no knowledge of genetics. This does not detract from the obvious advantage of possessing such knowledge, a fact which I trust has been amply demonstrated in the previous pages.

Common sense and a knowledge of genetics both indicate that if we wish to produce bigger and better-colored fish we should breed from the biggest and best colored specimens at our disposal. This is the concept of selective breeding. The parents may or may not be related. If such selection is repeated over many generations, the chances are that we will ultimately produce a group of fishes noticeably larger and better colored than those with which we started.

Another device commonly employed is inbreeding, that is to say, mating closely related individuals: i.e., brother to sister, father to daughter, or son to mother. This is done in an attempt to fix a new desirable character that may have appeared in the family. Such desirable characters are more often than not recessive, so if we can find a brother and sister showing the particular trait we wish to fix, these two should be paired together. However, susceptibility to various diseases is also frequently transmitted as a Mendelian recessive, so this too may become unmasked and fixed. It is for this reason that breeders have sometimes found that strains which have been carried on by inbreeding begin to show such undesirable traits as wasting, sterility, proneness to shimmers, swim bladder trouble, and the like.

At the first sign of weakening of the strain, or even earlier, many breeders bring in "fresh blood," that is to say, acquire fishes from other sources to mate with their own. This often works, but with the return of health there is also likely to be deterioration of the desired characters for which one is breeding. However, should inbreeding appear too discouraging, let us not forget that but for inbreeding the numerous varieties of domestic and farm animals would never have been evolved or fixed.

XII   Classification and Nomenclature

The aim of any classification is to arrange a collection of diverse things into groups and subgroups of similar or related individuals. Thus the individuals in a given group resemble one another more closely than they resemble members of other groups. Such a system not only brings order out of chaos but is also an indispensable aid to clear thinking. The details and intricacies of classification are truly for the taxonomist but what the aquarist needs to know is quite easy to understand.

All the fishes described in this book and virtually all the fishes that aquarists keep belong to the great group of bony fishes called Teleostei. The Teleostei are subdivided into various orders. The orders are subdivided into families, the families into genera, and the genera into species. Our interest as aquarists lies mainly with the last subdivisions, namely, families, genera, and species, but let us for the sake of clarity look first at a couple of the many orders into which Teleostei are divided to see how the system works. The number of these orders is too great to be dealt with here.

The first order of interest to aquarists is the order Isospondyli, which contains the primitive herringlike fishes. Of the many families in this order there are only two of interest to us, the Pantodontidae and the Mormyridae. The former contains only one fish, the Butterfly Fish *Pantodon buchholzi*; the latter contains our so-called Elephant Fishes, e.g., *Gnathonemus petersi*.

The order Ostariophysi is of the utmost interest to us as aquarists, for some three quarters of the commonly kept aquarium fishes belong to this order. It is divided into a number of families, too many to list here, so a few examples should suffice. Thus in this order we have the family Characidae to which our popular Characins or Tetras belong. Also included are the families Gasteropelecidae (Hatchet Fishes), Siluridae (Catfishes), Cyprinodontidae (egg-laying and livebearing Tooth Carps), and a host of others.

We have seen that the Teleostei are divided into orders and families. It now remains to point out that these families are divided into genera and species. The scientific name of a fish is in fact composed on this basis: the first word in the name of the fish tells us the genus to which it belongs, the second indicates the species. Thus the popular Tiger or Sumatra Barb has the scientific name *Barbus tetrazona*.

There are many other Barbs, such as *Barbus nigrofasciatus* (Black Ruby). Each of these may have more than one common name, depending on local preferences, but only one scientific name which will be accepted world wide and in all languages. Thus each fish has a definite name by which all of us throughout the world know it. This is the great virtue of scientific nomenclature in contrast to the popular names we give our fishes. These frequently apply to more than one species. Thus the term Pencil Fish has been employed to describe a number of different fishes belonging to the genus *Nannostomus*, and the terms Glass Fish, Glass Tetra, and X-Ray Fish have been applied in a confusing fashion to many widely different species, apparently the only requirement being that the fish should be translucent or semitranslucent.

Nevertheless there is no harm in using such names among a circle of friends, for each knows what is meant and any ambiguity can be quickly cleared up by asking questions. It would be inadvisable to use such names alone when writing about fishes, or lecturing to strange audiences. In this book I have tried as far as possible to give the scientific as well as the most widely known popular names of fishes.

We have now examined the main points regarding classification and nomenclature (both scientific and popular). There are, however, a few points which I omitted in the interest of continuity so let us deal with them now.

Sometimes in a given species we find many color varieties as well as different degrees of fin development. Thus we have many color varieties of Platies, all of which bear the scientific name *Xiphophorus maculatus*. To indicate that we are referring to, say, the red variety we would write *Xiphophorus maculatus* var. *rubra*.

Sometimes it may happen that we know the genus to which the fish belongs but we do not know the species. For instance, there are believed to be three species of Angelfish – *Pterophyllum altum*, *P. eimekei*, *P. scalare*. If, like most of us, you do not know which particular species of Angel you have, then you could refer to it as *Pterophyllum* sp. If, like some, you believe that the aquarium-bred Angel is a hybrid derived from the species, you could call it *Pterophyllum hybrida*.

You will have noticed that the first letter of the name of the genus is a capital and of the species a small letter, and also that when the genus is repeatedly mentioned it can be abbreviated as shown above.

So far, the virtues of scientific classification and nomenclature have been stressed; it is only fair to point out that they can be the source of much annoyance and headache to both aquarists and scientists alike.

As ichthyological research continues, fishes have to be reclassified, and old favorites appear under new and unfamiliar names. This is because the nature and relationships have been discovered; we can do nothing about it but learn the new name.

The fishes in this book are arranged in families and the families are arranged in taxonomic order. Thus we begin with the early-evolved Pantodontidae and end with the highly evolved Cichlidae and Anabantidae.

The aquarist may well wonder what criteria are used to arrive at this hierarchy. Broadly speaking, this is decided on anatomical grounds. Externally, this increasing complexity of structure and evolution is demonstrated chiefly by a greater number of spines in the dorsal and anal fins and a more forward position of the ventral fins. Other major anatomical differences are internal and as such beyond the scope of most aquarists. A simple example, however, is the labyrinth organ of the Anabantidae. This allows the fish to utilize atmospheric oxygen, in contrast to many other fishes which rely solely on oxygen dissolved in the water. Obviously, here we have a fish that has a great advantage and one that has traveled high up the evolutionary ladder.

Pantodon buchholzi – Butterfly Fish.

XIII   The Fishes

There is only one species in this family.

Pantodon buchholzi   Peters 1876

Popular name   Butterfly Fish, Fresh Water Flying Fish.
Origin   West Africa.
Size   4 inches.
Appearance   Boat-shaped body with upward-facing mouth. Large winglike pectorals. Greenish gray to brown body with many dark spots and streaks.
Behavior   Reasonably peaceful. Can be kept with fishes its own size.
Feeding   Will not feed off the bottom. Live insects and small fishes are readily accepted. Can be trained to take worms and other meaty foods from the end of a stick.

Water conditions   Prefers moderately soft water at a temperature of 80°F. Butterfly Fish are best kept in a well-covered aquarium half filled with water, planted with a few thickets of plants that send some shoots above the water surface.

Sexing   Posterior end of anal fin shows a notch in the male; same zone straight in the female. When ripe, females show the usual fuller appearance.

Breeding   Difficult to breed. At mating the fish wrap themselves around each other and release eggs which float to the surface. Young hatch after three days and need minute insects (e.g., plant aphids) for their diet.

MORMYRIDAE

These fishes occur commonly in many stagnant pools in Central and South Africa. The ratio of brain weight to body weight compares favorably with that in man. They have a remarkable ability for learning and an inquisitive, playful nature. Some of them have weak electric organs. It is important to ascertain that the fish is feeding properly before purchase. Often starved, wasted specimens have been offered. These usually refuse to eat and perish.

Gnathonemus petersi   Günther 1862

Popular name   Elephant Nosed Fish.
Origin   Congo and Cameroons.
Size   Up to 9 inches. In aquaria 4 inches.
Appearance   Elongated, laterally compressed body with dorsal and anal fins set well back on the body. Mental (chin) projection surmounted by a small mouth. Over-all coloration dark brown to black with two white bands on posterior part of the body.
Behavior   A shy, peaceful fish. Can be kept in a community tank with even small fishes. Other fishes seem to leave it alone. Feeds at dusk, hides most of the day.
Feeding   *Tubifex* and freshly dead *Daphnia* are favorite foods. Will seek all sorts of foods, including dried foods, at the bottom.
Water conditions   Fairly soft neutral water at 80°F. Well-planted tank with shady spots and hiding places. Does not like strong light.
Sexing, Breeding   Little is known about this. Not bred in captivity.

Gnathonemus petersi
Elephant Nosed Fish (p. 140).

Gnathonemus schilthuisi
Elephant Trunk Fish (p. 143).

errasalmus rhombeus - White Piranha,
or Spotted Piranha (p. 146).

Metynnis roosevelti - Silver Dollar
(p. 147).

Metynnis schreitmuelleri
Schreitmueller's Metynnis (p. 147).

Hyphessobrycon pulchripinnis
Lemon Tetra (p. 153).

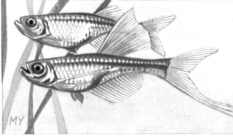

Hyphessobrycon innesi - Neon Tetra
(p. 152).

Corynopoma riisei - Swordtail Characin
(p. 155).

Gnathonemus schilthuisi Boulenger 1899

Popular name Elephant Trunk Fish.
Origin Middle Congo.
Size 4 inches.
Appearance Similar in appearance to G. *petersi* except that it has a much lighter silvery-brown body with one dark band and a blunt tubercule instead of the elongated chin process. Scales rather prominent.
Behavior, Feeding, Water conditions, Sexing, Breeding Similar to G. *petersi*.

CHARACIDAE

Many Characins are distinguished by the possession of a small adipose fin. Also, Characins usually have teeth in the jaws. Like Carps and some Catfishes, they belong to the order Ostariophysi; hence they have Weberian ossicles linking the swim bladder with the inner ear (Chapter X). Most of them come from Central and South America, a few from Central Africa. Some of these fishes are carnivores, others are omnivorous, and some predominantly herbivorous. The last will nibble or totally destroy aquarium plants. Most of the aquarium Characins are small species which inflict little damage with their teeth, beyond occasionally nipping the fins of such slower-moving fishes as Angels or Fighters. However, to this family also belong the Piranhas which, with their powerful teeth, can strip the flesh off even large terrestrial animals in a very short time.

The majority of Characins prefer soft peaty water and breed best under such conditions. They lay adhesive or semiadhesive eggs, which they are likely to devour, given the chance.

Some aquarium Characins are easy to breed, most require some skill and knowledge on the part of the aquarist, while a few demand expert treatment. When you have bred these you have really reached the pinnacle of achievement in the aquarist fraternity. It is advisable to separate and condition the fish prior to spawning.

Choosing and Conditioning the Fish

Much of the success in breeding Characins depends on the treatment the fish have received months before actual spawning. In order to breed a given species it is best to obtain half a dozen or more young-sters from a reliable source and then rear them to maturity. When the females begin to fill up with eggs the sexes are separated for a week or two and given the best in the way of aquarium management and feeding. This process is called conditioning.

The Planted Tank Method

This is perhaps the oldest method of breeding Characins. A small or medium-sized tank of about five or ten gallons is furnished with fine-leaved plants, coarse gravel (⅛" diameter) or pebbles (½" diameter) and water suitable for breeding the species concerned. Care is taken to see that no snails, planarians, or other egg- or fry-destroying crea-tures are introduced.

When all is ready the conditioned pair are transferred to the breed-ing tank. This is usually done late in the evening. By next morning, if all goes well, the fish will have settled and commence spawning. In most species fertilization of the eggs occurs in the water. These then adhere to plants; a few fall to the bottom. The end of the spawn-ing session is heralded by the pair losing interest in each other and starting to browse around in the plant thickets or on the aquarium floor, seeking eggs to devour. At this stage the parents are removed.

The eggs hatch in a few days and the fry can be seen hanging on the plants and the glass wall of the tank. A few days later they become free-swimming and can be reared in the way described in another part of this book (Chapter VIII). Characin fry are very small and need infusoria as first food.

Method of Breeding Characins on Artificial Spawning Media

In Chapter VII we have already pointed out the many advantages of using artificial spawning media such as willow root and nylon mops over fine-leaved green plants. Briefly, the main advantage is that with this system one can have a clean, easily reproducible setup free from snails and planarians, for breeding fishes.

In this technique for breeding Characins a 5- or 10-gallon tank is first thoroughly cleaned out. Soap, detergents, or chemicals may be used if thoroughly rinsed out as routine; simple scrubbing and rinsing is usually quite adequate. However, there are times when something stronger may be necessary. In such instances I like to use ammonia (specific gravity 0.8), rather than any other chemical. About 50 to 100 ml. of this are added to the tank full of water and allowed to stand a few hours. The ammonia-containing water is now removed and the tank filled and emptied with fresh water five times. This rinses out the ammonia and leaves the tank clean and free from pests and their eggs, all of which are killed by this process.

In the bottom of the tank is now placed an inch layer of boiled pebbles. (Some aquarists like to use glass marbles instead of pebbles, but I do not recommend them as many fish are frightened and refuse to spawn or burrow under them. I have found fish trapped and dead next morning when using glass marbles in breeding tanks.)

The tank is now filled with tap water, tap water plus distilled water (or rainwater), or peat water as needed for the species. A handful of cleaned and boiled willow root (see Chapter VII) or some nylon mops are introduced. The tank is now ready to receive the conditioned fishes. The procedure from here on is the same as described earlier in breeding Characins in planted tanks.

The Acriflavine Adsorption Method for Breeding Characins

Acriflavine and various other dyes are commonly employed when breeding Cichlids to prevent eggs from becoming covered with fungus. There is another distinct and different way in which this dye can be employed to assist in breeding the problem fishes. The method I am about to describe was first evolved by Jacobs. Later, unaware of this work, I also evolved a similar method (Ghadially, 1957). I have used this method extensively to produce large numbers of Glowlights while Jacobs has used it for both Glowlights and Neon Tetras.

For this method a tank is cleaned and filled with suitable water (not treated with peat). Now enough of a solution of acriflavine is added to produce a final concentration of about 1 milligram/gallon in the tank. (The amount is not very critical.) Let this stand for a day or two and then add boiled willow root. The dye will be adsorbed by the root and the water will become crystal clear in a few hours. The breeding pair is now introduced. After spawning is completed the pair is removed and the tank covered so as to exclude most of the light. It is thought that strong light will ruin the eggs of some of the more difficult-to-breed Characins. The fry hatch out after a few days and are fed in the usual way. It is interesting to note that with this method both Jacobs and I have been able to breed Glowlights not only in soft acid waters but also in alkaline waters of moderate hardness.

If willow root is not available for adsorption and spawning, a charcoal filter could be used to remove the dye from the water. It is important to remove the dye prior to spawning. If fishes are allowed to spawn in water containing acriflavine the eggs will be infertile, for acriflavine will kill the sperms before they can fertilize the eggs.

Peat Water for Breeding Characins

German aquarists were the first to report that certain difficult-to-breed Characins (problem fishes), such as the Neon Tetra, could be bred successfully in water that had been allowed to stand in contact with peat, oak bark, or oak leaves.

Peat water is prepared by adding handfuls of scalded peat to a quantity of rainwater (see Chapter III). In time the peat sinks and the water becomes amber colored; pH and hardness readings are taken and more peat added if necessary. Over a period of some months pH and hardness value decline.

According to McInnery (1966) the final water must have a hardness not exeeding 10 ppm and should ideally be as low as 2 ppm for successful breeding of neons. The pH can be anywhere between 5 and 6.8.

A small, clean tank (preferably but not necessarily all glass) is filled to a depth of 4″ or so with this water. No gravel or pebbles are used. Nylon mops serve as spawn receptors. A conditioned pair of Neons is introduced. These should spawn within 24 hours.

Peat water not quite as soft as that used for Neons has been employed for breeding not only difficult-to-breed Characins but also a variety of fishes belonging to other families.

Although many aquarists are convinced of the benefits of peat water or soft acid water in breeding a variety of fishes, there are those who point out that virtually every fish, including Neons, on more than one occasion has also been bred in moderately hard alkaline water. Further, the fact that peat water is soft does not permit us to conclude that this is the factor responsible for success, even though it may serve as a good index for judging the suitability of the water for breeding fishes. This and related points are discussed more fully in Chapter III.

Serrasalmus rhombeus Linnaeus 1766

Popular name White Piranha, or Spotted Piranha.
Origin South America, Amazon Basin.
Size Up to 10 inches. Aquarium specimens 6 inches.
Appearance A deep-bodied, strongly compressed, olive-green to silvery fish, with many strong teeth set in a large mouth with protruding lower jaw giving a bulldoglike appearance.
Behavior Piranhas are aggressive to any fishes, smaller or larger than themselves. Even during transport they will attack other fishes. Best kept as single specimens. Care required when netting. One's hand should not be placed in the tank. This fish, like other Piranhas, must be kept out of reach of children. A good showpiece because of its savage reputation.
Feeding Carnivorous. Other fishes, pieces of lean meat.
Water conditions Not critical.
Sexing, Breeding Not bred in captivity. When a pair are brought together one will probably eat the other!

Rooseveltiella (Serrasalmo) nattereri – Red-breasted Piranha, or Natterer's Piranha.

Rooseveltiella nattereri Kner 1859

Popular name   Red-breasted Piranha, or Natterer's Piranha.
Origin   Amazon and Orinoco systems.
Size   Up to 12 inches. In aquarium 4 inches-6 inches.
Appearance   Perhaps the handsomest and most macabre Piranha.
Deeply compressed body, blue-gray with red underside. Numerous
metallic spots.
Behavior, Feeding, Water conditions, Sexing, Breeding   Same as for
Serrasalmus rhombeus.

Metynnis rooselvelti Eigenmann 1915

Popular name   Silver Dollar.
Origin   Amazon Basin.
Size   5 inches.
Appearance   One of the most popular *Metynnis* species available.
Strongly compressed oval body with length slightly greater than
depth.
Behavior   A shy, peaceful, schooling fish best kept in the company
of its own kind in a large tank. A predominantly herbivorous fish,
which destroys aquarium plants rapidly. A single specimen will mow
down a tank full of *Vallisneria* within a few days.
Feeding   Vegetable food, such as lettuce, spinach, and sprouts should
be provided. Must also be given some standard meaty fresh foods.
Water conditions   Slightly acid, moderately soft water.
Sexing, Breeding   Bred on only a few occasions. The anterior portion
of the anal fin is markedly convex in the male but angular in the
female. At spawning time the caudal and anal fins show a bright red
border surrounded in the case of the caudal by a black margin. Approximately 200 eggs are laid. These hatch in a few days. Fry become
free-swimming four to five days later and are easily reared on the
usual foods plus vegetable material.

Metynnis schreitmuelleri E. Ahl 1922

Popular name   Schreitmueller's Metynnis.
Origin   Amazon Basin.
Size   6 inches.
Appearance   Strongly compressed oval body, with length slightly

greater than depth.

Behavior, Feeding, and Water conditions   Same as *M. roosevelti.*

Sexing, Breeding   Similar to *M. roosevelti* except that some 2000 nonadhesive eggs are laid. These fall to the bottom of the tank. Young hatch in 70 hours at 82°F. Young only half the size of *M. roosevelti.*

GENE WOLFSHEIMER

Gymnocorymbus ternetzi – Black Tetra, Blackamoor, or Petticoat Fish. (Female above – male below.)

Gymnocorymbus ternetzi   Boulenger 1895

Popular names   Black Tetra, Blackamoor, or Petticoat Fish.
Origin   Brazil, Argentina, and Bolivia.
Size   2 inches.
Appearance   A pert fish with large black dorsal and anal fins giving it a fanlike appearance. In well-marked specimens the posterior half of the fish, excluding the caudal fin, is jet black. Two vertical black bars adorn the silvery flank. A truly unique, deservedly popular aquarium fish. Unfortunately becomes a bit drab when over 1¼ inch long.

Behavior   Inclined to some fin-nipping. Nevertheless a good community fish.

Feeding   All foods, including dried foods.

Water conditions   Not critical. Does better at 68°F. to 70°F. rather than at the usual 80°F. Black pigmentation best developed when kept at cooler temperature.

Sexing, Breeding   Males slightly longer, females slightly deeper. In mature specimens the fuller shape of the female is unmistakable. Can be bred in near neutral water of moderate hardness; 100 to 200 adhesive eggs are laid, which hatch in 24 hours. Fry free-swimming in about three days. They need infusoria as first food.

GENE WOLFSHEIMER

Pristella riddlei – X-Ray Fish (albino variety). (Female above – male below.)

Pristella riddlei   Meek 1907

Popular name   X-ray Fish, or Water Goldfinch.

Origin   Northern South America.

Size   1½ inches.

Appearance   Translucent body of the fish gives it its popular name. This is not a very colorful fish; nevertheless, it is interestingly marked and is a great old-time favorite.

Behavior   Very peaceful. Ideal for community tank.

Feeding   Eats all foods.

Water conditions   Temperature 72°F. to 78°F. pH and hardness not critical.

Sexing   The fuller form of the female and the flat, at times concave contour of the male makes sexing easy. Black spot on anal completely crosses the fin in the female but only partially in the male.

Breeding   One of the easiest Characins to breed, once a good pair has been found. Lays 400 to 500 eggs which hatch within 24 hours. Fry very hardy and easy to rear.

A. VAN DEN NIEUWENHUIZEN

Hemigrammus erythrozonus – Glowlight Tetra. (Male above – female below.)

Hemigrammus erythrozonus   Durbin 1909

Popular name   Glowlight Tetra. Before 1955 this fish was mistaken for *Hyphessobrycon gracilis*. It has also been called *Hemigrammus gracilis*.

Origin   British Guiana.

Size   1¾ inches.

Appearance   The most attractive feature is the glowing ruby-red line which runs along the length of this fish. In certain strains and in fish kept under unfavorable conditions this line is pale amber.

Behavior   Peaceful community fish.

Feeding   Eats all foods.

Water conditions   Peat water heightens coloration. Temperature 78°F.-80°F. Seen at best when a group is kept on its own in a thickly planted tank with a dark background.

Sexing Females are larger and more robust looking. Belly contour convex. Males are slenderer and the belly is flat or even concave.

Breeding Considered to be only a little less difficult to breed than the Neon Tetra. Either the acriflavine adsorption method or the peat water method should be tried (see above, Characins). If they spawn they lay 200 to 400 eggs. The young hatch in 24 hours. If conditions are suitable one can expect to rear most of them. However, to rear anything over 50 from a spawning is considered pretty good going.

A. VAN DEN NIEUWENHUIZEN

Hemigrammus rhodostomus – Red or Rummy Nosed Tetra. (Two males.)

Hemigrammus rhodostomus Ahl 1924

Popular name Red or Rummy Nosed Tetra.
Origin Amazon.
Size 2 inches.
Appearance A beautifully marked fish with a bright red snout.
Behavior Very hardy and peaceful.
Feeding Eats all foods.
Water conditions Moderately soft slightly acid water. 78°F.
Sexing Males smaller and slenderer than females. Nose a little more red.
Breeding One of the more difficult-to-breed Characins. Methods similar to those recommended for Glowlight have proved moderately successful.

Hyphessobrycon flammeus – Tetra von Rio, or Flame Tetra. (Female above – male below.)

Hyphessobrycon flammeus Myers 1924

Popular name   Tetra von Rio, or Flame Tetra.
Origin   Neighborhood of Rio de Janeiro.
Size   1½ inches.
Appearance   A short fish. Posterior half of the body and fins gleaming red.
Behavior   A hardy old favorite. Good community fish.
Feeding   Accepts all foods including dried foods.
Water conditions   Not critical.
Sexing   Males smaller, slimmer, and more colorful. Anal fin of male shows a black edge.
Breeding   Easy to breed, and will breed freely in most waters; 100 to 200 eggs laid, which hatch in 24 hours.

Hyphessobrycon innesi Myers 1936

Popular name   Neon Tetra.
Origin   Peru, Brazil.
Size   1¼ inches.
Appearance   Widely accepted as one of the most beautiful of aquarium fishes. The iridescent greenish-blue strip and the deep red band have an intensity rarely matched in other species.
Behavior   This is a rather hardy fish, well able to look after itself

even in company of fishes twice its size. An ideal community fish which usually swims in the lower half of the tank.

Feeding Takes all foods.

Sexing The females are unmistakably larger and fatter than the male, the belly of which is flat or slightly sunken.

Breeding This is considered to be a difficult feat. Suitable methods have already been described earlier (see above).

Hyphessobrycon pulchripinnis – Lemon Tetra. (All three fish appear to be males.)

Hyphessobrycon pulchripinnis E. Ahl 1937

Popular name Lemon Tetra. At one time called *Hemigrammus erythrophthalmus.*

Origin Amazon.

Size 1¾ inches.

Appearance This fish is outstanding because of the pale lemon-tinted body and the bright red color in the upper part of the eye.

Behavior A peaceful community fish.

Feeding Accepts all foods.

Water conditions Moderately soft, slightly acid water. Temperature 80°F.

Sexing   Male slightly slimmer and more colorful.
Breeding   Not very easy. Peat water method should be employed.

Anoptichthys jordani   Hubbs and Innes 1938

Popular name   Blind Cave Tetra.
Origin   Subterranean streams and pools in Mexico.
Size   2¾ inches.
Appearance   A silvery rose-tinted fish. Vestigial eyes and orbits overgrown with skin. These fish are derived from *Astyanax fasciatus mexicanus* which have normal eyes. It is believed that a long time ago these fish were carried by currents into subterranean streams and the eyes atrophied and became useless.
Behavior   Blindness does not present a serious handicap to this fish. It can be kept in a community tank with other fishes. A heightened sense of smell and vibration enables the fish to find its food and avoid bumping into other fishes.
Water conditions   Can be kept and bred in moderately soft or moderately hard, nearly neutral waters. Temperature 78°F.

Anoptichthys jordani – Blind Cave Tetra. (Female above – male below.)

Sexing Shape is the only guide. Males are distinctly slimmer than females.

Breeding This is easy with large mature specimens; 400 to 800 semi-adhesive eggs are laid, which hatch in 36 hours. Fry have small eyes, which are probably functional. They can be reared in the usual manner, commencing with infusoria as first food.

Corynopoma riisei Gill 1858

Popular name Swordtail Characin.
Origin Trinidad, Colombia, Venezuela.
Size 2½ inches.
Appearance A cream-colored fish with rather long translucent fins.
Behaviour, Feeding An undemanding peaceful species of interesting breeding behavior. Will take dried foods but needs a reasonable amount of live or fresh foods.
Sexing The male has a peculiar, long, oarlike or spoonlike extrusion from the gill cover which extends halfway down the body. Its fins are longer and the lower lobe of the caudal is elongated. Hence the popular name Swordtail Characin.
Breeding This is fairly easy but what happens during the mating act is as yet uncertain. The male approaches the female and extends his gill appendages so that they stand off at right angles to the body. The female sometimes turns around to snap at one of them. It is believed that at this stage the male somehow transfers a package of sperms (spermatophores) into the oviduct of the female. Once the female is fertilized in this fashion she will go on delivering fertile eggs for many months or even the rest of her life without further assistance from the male. This is a fairly easy fish to breed and is not critical of water requirements. About 100 eggs are laid and the female looks after them and transfers them from leaf to leaf. The male should be removed after spawning; the female when the fry become free-swimming.

Cheirodon axelrodi Schultz 1956
At one stage called *Hyphessobrycon cardinalis.*

Popular name Cardinal Tetra.
Origin Upper Rio Negro.
Size 1¾ inches.

Cheirodon axelrodi – Cardinal Tetra (upper fish female – two lower fish males) (p. 155).

Appearance   This fish resembles the Neon Tetra (*Hyphessobrycon innesi*). It differs from it by being somewhat larger and more colorful, for whereas the red band in the Neon extends from the tail to the middle of the body, in the Cardinal it carries on to the gill covers.
Behavior, Feeding, Water conditions, Sexing, Breeding   Same as for Neon Tetra.

Copeina arnoldi   Regan 1912

Popular name   Spraying Characin.
Origin   Venezuela, Brazil, Guiana.
Size   3 inches.
Appearance   An elegantly shaped slender fish with elongated fins.
Feeding   Accepts all foods.
Water conditions   Moderately soft neutral water.
Sexing   The male has longer fins and there is a white spot at the root of its dorsal fin.
Breeding   This fish is kept mainly because of its unusual breeding habit. It spawns outside water, e.g., on the surface of an overhanging leaf or on the undersurface of the aquarium cover glass. The conditioned pair are introduced in a 10- to 15-gallon, sparsely planted tank with the water level lying about 1″ to 1½″ below the cover glass. The pair swim side by side and together jump out of the water to the

undersurface of the cover glass, where they adhere for a moment, deposit 10 to 15 eggs, and fall back into the tank. This act is repeated until some 100 eggs are laid. When spawning is completed the female should be removed. The male looks after the eggs and prevents them from drying by splashing them with water. This process sometimes dislodges the eggs or newly hatched fry which, when they fall into the water, are devoured by the male. If this is seen to happen, the male should be removed and an aerator stone fixed in the tank so that the spray from the bursting bubbles keeps the eggs damp. By about the fourth day the fry drop into the water and swim about freely. Just before this happens it is best to remove the male and rear the fry in the usual way.

Copeina guttata Steindachner 1875

Popular name   Redspotted Copeina.
Origin   Central Amazon.
Size   4 inches. Aquarium specimens up to 5 inches.
Appearance   Not as elegant or streamlined as *C. arnoldi*. It has a bluish silvery body and yellowish fins with orange-red margins.
Behavior   Reasonably peaceful, but it is rather large for the average community collection.
Feeding, Water conditions   Same as *C. arnoldi*.
Sexing   The male is more colorful than the female. It also shows rows of tiny red dots on the flank. Few or no such dots occur on the female.
Breeding   This is another Characin with an unusual breeding habit. It lays its eggs in depressions in the gravel or on a flat stone. The male fans the eggs and looks after them. The breeding procedure is reminiscent of Cichlids and Sunfishes rather than Characins. About 200 to 300 eggs are laid, which hatch in 2 days. The female should be removed after spawning and the male soon after the fry become free-swimming.

ANOSTOMIDAE

These Central and South American fishes are often very beautifully marked but unfortunately most of them are a bit too large for the usual community aquarium. Many of them have a habit of drifting about with the head down and aquarists therefore call them Headstanders.

Copeina guttata - Redspotted Copeina (p. 157).

Copeina arnoldi - Spraying Characin (p. 156).

Chilodus punctatus - Pearl Headstander (p. 159).

Anostomus anostomus
Striped Anostomus (p. 159).

Nannostomus eques
Tube Mouthed Pencilfish (p. 161).

Nannostomus anomalus
Anomalous Pencilfish (p. 160).

Nannostomus trifasciatus
Three Banded Pencilfish (p. 162).

Nannostomus ocellatus
Tail-eye Pencilfish (p. 162).

Anostomus anostomus   Linnaeus 1758

Popular name   Striped Anostomus.
Origin   South America.
Size   6 inches.
Appearance   A rather startling fish with a long cylindrical body and pointed snout. The body is traversed by longitudinal strips of black and gold; a red spot on the root of the caudal fin which leaves the lobes colorless completes the bizarre color combination.
Behavior   Swims in a head-down fashion but straightens up when it darts forward. Can be kept in company with other large fishes.
Feeding   Mainly live and frozen foods supplemented with green foods such as lettuce.
Water conditions   Not critical. Temperature 78°F.
Sexing, Breeding   Not known.

Chilodus punctatus   Müller and Troschel 1845

Popular name   Pearl Headstander.
Origin   Northern South America.
Size   3½ inches.
Appearance   The elongated grayish-green body is covered by rows of brown spots. The fish swims head down at an angle of 45° from the horizontal.
Behavior   Very peaceful; can be kept in community aquaria.
Feeding   Eats all foods but must be provided with fresh green foods such as lettuce and spinach.
Water conditions   Moderately soft, slightly acid water. Temperature 80°F.
Sexing   Females plumper than males.
Breeding   Has been seldom bred. Method same as that described for other Characins. About 150 to 200 brownish eggs are laid. Fry difficult to rear.

HEMIODONTIDAE

The Hemiodontidae resemble the Characins in many respects but differ from them in that in most of them the lower jaw is toothless. Some of the smallest and prettiest aquarium fishes belong to this family. They come from South America. Most of them have a thin elongated body and are popularly called Pencilfishes. The scientific nomenclature of the fishes in this family is truly chaotic.

The genus *Nannostomus* was described by Günther in 1872. In 1909 Eigenmann removed one of the fishes from this genus and established a new genus called *Poecilobrycon* for it. This was done on the basis of differences in the adipose fin. Some subsequent workers have accepted this and placed other fishes in the genus *Poecilobrycon*; others, however, have refused to accept the genus *Poecilobrycon* on the ground that these differences are neither constant nor clear-cut. To add to the difficulty, fishes of the genus *Nannostomus* show remarkable changes of color pattern during their life and even during a single day.

Nannostomus anomalus   Steindachner 1876
(also called *Nannostomus beckfordi anomalus*).

Popular name   Anomalous Pencilfish, or Golden Pencilfish
Origin   Amazon Basin. British Guiana.
Size   1¾ inches.
Appearance   The elongated body has a golden-brown tint and is traversed by a longitudinal black band edged with gold and sometimes with red. At night the horizontal band fades and dark bands or blotches appear on the sides.
Behavior   A peaceful fish suitable for the community tank; hardy in spite of its delicate appearance.
Water conditions   Moderately soft to moderately hard, near neutral to slightly acidic water. Temperature 80°F.
Sexing   The plump shape of the female is the main guide. The male is slightly more colorful. Red coloration in fins and on the body is almost exclusive to the male.
Breeding   This is one of the easiest aquarium fishes to breed. It does not destroy its eggs or young. It can be bred in the usual Characin fashion but the number of young produced is likely to be small. A simpler method is to place three or four females with two males in a well-planted tank or a tank containing a fair amount of some artifical spawning medium, and feed them well. The tank will soon be seen to contain many (50 to 100) young fry in various stages of development. Either the adults can now be moved to a fresh tank or the fry ladled out and reared elsewhere.

Nannostomus eques   Steindachner 1876
(also called *Poecilobrycon* or *Nannobrycon eques*).

Popular name   Tube Mouthed Pencilfish.
Origin   Amazon.
Size   2 inches.
Appearance   Another Pencilfish which swims at an angle. It has an elongated snout.
Behavior   A peaceful fish.
Feeding, Water conditions   Same as other *Nannostomus* species.
Sexing   Males slimmer than females.
Breeding   Usual Characin method but seem to prefer spawning on broad-leaved plants such as *Hygrophila* and *Ludwigia*.

Nannostomus marginatus   Eigenmann 1909

Popular name   Dwarf Pencilfish.
Origin   West Guiana.
Size   1¼ inches.

Nannostomus marginatus – Dwarf Pencilfish. (Two males.)

Appearance This is the smallest *Nannostomus*. It is rather more stocky than others. A pretty black-banded fish with splashes of red in the fins.

Behavior Very peaceful, rather shy. Best kept with other small fishes.

Feeding, Water conditions Same as for *N. anomalus*.

Sexing The males are brighter in color than females.

Breeding Eats its own eggs so cannot be bred like *N. anomalus*, but can be bred like other Characins; 25 to 75 eggs laid at a spawning which hatch in 2 days. However, the same pair can spawn again in three or four days.

Nannostomus ocellatus Eigenmann 1909

Popular name Tail-eyed Pencilfish.

Origin Guiana, Amazon.

Size 2 inches.

Appearance One of the handsomest Pencilfishes. It swims head up at an angle of 30° to the horizontal. The lower lobe of the caudal fin is enlarged and carries a large, colorful spot.

Behavior A peaceful fish suitable for the community tank.

Feeding, Water conditions Similar to other *Nannostomus* species.

Sexing, Breeding Males slimmer than females. Have been bred occasionally but reports are scanty and inconclusive.

Nannostomus trifasciatus Steindachner 1876

Popular name Three Banded Pencilfish.

Origin West Guiana, Amazon.

Size 1½ inches.

Appearance Universally accepted as the prettiest *Nannostomus*, but unfortunately rather rare. As its name implies, it has three black lines running along a gold-colored body. Numerous vivid red marks on the body and fins.

Behavior Peaceful community fish.

Feeding, Water conditions Same as other *Nannostomus* species.

Sexing Difficult. Female slightly paler and plumper.

Breeding Difficult to breed. It is said that they can be induced to spawn in plant thickets in peaty water of pH 6.5 and hardness 60 ppm. Only 30 to 70 eggs are laid. Fry difficult to rear.

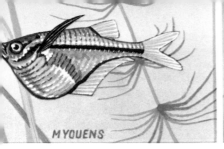

Carnegiella marthae
Blackwinged Hatchetfish (p. 164).

Brachydanio albolineatus
Pearl Danio, or Gold Danio (p. 165).

Tanichthys albonubes
White Cloud Mountain Minnow (p. 169).

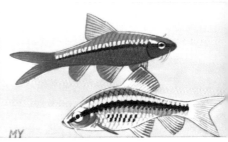

Danio malabaricus - Giant Danio (p. 168).

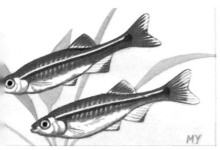

Acanthophthalmus semicinctus
Half Banded Coolie Loach (p. 175).

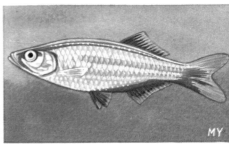

Barbus titteya - Cherry Barb (p. 173).

Malapterurus electricus
Electric Catfish (p. 178).

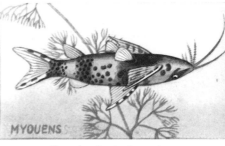

Synodontis nigriventris
Upside-down Catfish (p. 178).

GASTEROPELECIDAE (Hatchetfishes)

These markedly compressed, extremely deep-bodied fishes come mainly from northern South America. Some species are capable of rapidly flapping their pectoral fins and are probably the only true "flying fishes." They can jump out of the water and "fly" or glide some 10 to 15 feet.

Carnegiella marthae   Myers 1927

Popular name   Blackwinged Hatchetfish.
Origin   Venezuela, Peru, Amazon, Rio Negro, Orinoco.
Size   1¼ inches.
Appearance   A small and delicate species. The middle portions of the pectorals are black; so is the keel.
Behavior   A small, peaceful fish, best kept with others of its own kind.
Feeding   Accepts all foods.
Water conditions   Very soft, slightly acid water.
Sexing, Breeding   Not much is known about this; they have been bred occasionally. Method recommended is similar to that employed for *Hyphessobrycon* species.

Gasteropelecus levis   Eigenmann 1909

Popular name   Silver Hatchetfish (Giant).
Origin   Lower Amazon.
Size   2½ inches.
Appearance   This is a silvery fish with a single slim blue-black horizontal band.
Behavior   Perhaps the most robust of all the Hatchetfishes available to the aquarist; does fairly well in a community tank, if given good conditions.
Feeding, Water conditions   Same as for other Hatchetfishes.
Sexing, Breeding   Not known. Has not been bred in captivity.

FAMILY CYPRINIDAE (Carps and Carplike Fishes)

This, the largest family of bony fishes, is widely distributed: in Asia, Africa, Europe, and North America. Carps do not occur naturally

Gasteropelecus levis – Silver Hatchetfish (Giant).

in Northern Canada, South America, Australia, New Zealand, or Madagascar.

Most of them have the classical fish shape: not too compressed body, with a convex dorsal and ventral profile. Carps do not have teeth in the mouth but they have pharyngeal bones surmounted by grinding teeth. No Carp has an adipose fin. Some of them have one or two pairs of barbels. The largest Carp grows to about 8 ft. in length (*Barbus tor*, one of the Indian Mahseers) but there are many that are small and suitable for the aquarium. Of the aquarium Carps, a number (like the Goldfish) are cold water fishes and do not concern us here.

Brachydanio albolineatus   Blyth 1860

Popular name   Pearl Danio, or Gold Danio.
Origin   India and Sumatra.
Size   2 inches.
Appearance   Slim, moderately compressed, iridescent body. Mother-of-pearl appearance when viewed by reflected light. Different strains have been developed, some showing predominantly red and yellow iridescence, others green and blue iridescence.

Behavior   A peaceful schooling fish which makes a good community inhabitant. For a spectacular display a number of these should be housed in a well-planted tank with dark gravel at the bottom. Light should be arranged so that it strikes the fish from the front.

Feeding, Water conditions   As for *Brachydanio rerio.*

Sexing   Males more colorful and slimmer than females.

Breeding   Same as for *B. rerio.*

A. VAN DEN NIEUWENHUIZEN

Brachydanio nigrofasciatus – Spotted Danio. (Female above – male below.)

Brachydanio nigrofasciatus   Day 1869

Popular name   Spotted Danio.

Origin   Burma, India.

Size   1½ inches.

Appearance   Similar in shape and appearance to *B. rerio* except that it has fewer stripes and some spots on its sides.

Behavior, Feeding, Water conditions, Sexing, Breeding   Same as for *B. rerio* except that it is a bit more difficult to induce spawning.

Brachydanio rerio   Hamilton-Buchanan 1822

Popular name   Zebra Danio.

Origin   Eastern part of India.

Size   1¾ inches.

Appearance   Slim, almost cylindrical body with attractive bluish black and silvery or golden stripes.

Behavior   A peaceful schooling fish which contributes much to the community tank by its constant, but not restless, movement.

Feeding   Accepts all food.

Water conditions   Not critical.

Sexing   Females obviously plumper. Mature males have a yellowish cast, the bands appearing golden rather than silver.

Breeding   Considered to be one of the easiest fishes to breed. Lays nonadhesive eggs, which fall to the bottom of the tank; avid spawn eaters, hence the eggs must be protected. One of the simplest ways of breeding this fish is to cover the bottom of the tank with a 1 inch layer of pebbles (½ inch diam.). A few fine-leaved plants or nylon mops may or may not be introduced. Water depth not more than 3 inches for the fish eat many eggs as they fall slowly through the water. It is generally recommended that a long tank should be used so as to allow these fish chasing room during spawning. It is not absolutely necessary, for personal experience has shown that they will spawn equally readily in a goldfish globe with nothing more than a few pebbles at the bottom. For large-scale breeding, trays with a plastic mesh bottom can be employed. The mesh size should be such that the eggs but not the fish can pass through. Half a dozen or more fish can be placed in the

Brachydanio rerio – Zebra Danio. (Male left – female right.)

trays at a time. When spawning is complete, the fish are removed. Eggs usually hatch in 2 or 3 days but at times this may be delayed to as long as 5 or 6 days, even when the temperature is held at 80°F. The fry need infusoria as first food. They are easily reared, for they can be given substantial quantities of dried foods from an early age.

Danio malabaricus   Jerdon 1849

Popular name   Giant Danio.
Origin   Ceylon, West coast of India (Malabar).
Size   Up to 4 inches.
Appearance   A silvery fish with blue and yellow longitudinal stripes. When in breeding condition most of the fins show a reddish hue.
Behavior   Peaceful – can be kept in company of larger fishes. A restless swimmer difficult to net.
Feeding   Huge appetite. Eats all foods.
Water conditions   Not critical. A species that does reasonably well in moderate to fairly hard neutral or alkaline water; lives best in a large long tank with plenty of swimming space. Temperature 80°F.
Sexing   Specimens over 2½ inch in length can be sexed by the fuller shape of the female. The blue and yellow bands are more interrupted in the male. Reddish hue in the fins is more marked in male.
Breeding   A fairly large tank (10 to 15 gallons) with a 1 inch layer of pebbles on the bottom and some nylon mops or fine-leaved plants should be prepared and the conditioned pair introduced; 200 to 300 semiadhesive eggs are laid. Fry hatch in 3 days and become free-swimming on the 6th day.

Labeo bicolor   Smith 1931

Popular name   Redtailed Black Shark.
Origin   Thailand.
Size   4½ inches.
Appearance   As its popular name implies, this fish has the torpedo-shaped body and flaglike dorsal of a shark. The body is velvety black and the tail crimson red in the good specimens. Yellow or orange caudal fin indicates unsuitable aquarium conditions or a poor strain of fish.
Behavior   An excellent fish for the community tank. Its large sucker-like mouth helps to keep plants and front glass clean. Of peaceful

Labeo bicolor – Redtailed Black Shark.

temperament, but bullies smaller members of its own kind.
Feeding   A scavenger. Eats all foods, including algae.
Water conditions   Not critical. Some authorities advocate hard alkaline water, others soft acid water.
Sexing, Breeding   Has been bred but no details available.

Tanichthys albonubes   Lin 1932

Popular name   White Cloud Mountain Minnow.
Origin   China, Canton, from the rivers of the White Cloud Mountains.
Size   1¼ inches.
Appearance   An olive-brown fish with a bright golden longitudinal band extending from snout to root of caudal peduncle. Yellow and red markings in dorsal and caudal fins.
Behavior   Peaceful community fish.
Feeding   Eats all foods.
Water conditions   Near neutral water of moderate hardness. Temperature 50°F.‒75°F. Thrives at about 70°F.
Sexing   Males noticeably slimmer than females.

Breeding This fish breeds like the *Brachydanios*, laying nonadhesive eggs. If fed well, most pairs do not molest eggs or fry. If a few fish are kept in a planted tank, numerous babies will be soon found swimming among the adults. They can also be spawned in pairs in breeding traps or over pebbles and fine plants or nylon mops. A drop in temperature of about 5°F. often starts them spawning.

GENUS BARBUS

This genus (Family *Cyprinidae*) provides an unusually large number of very popular aquarium fishes. Most Barbs are gay, colorful, active fishes, easy to feed, not choosy about water conditions, and breed readily. It is useful to divide aquarium Barbs into two groups, small Barbs which grow to 2 or 3 inches in size and large Barbs that grow to larger sizes.

The small Barbs are ideal community fishes; the larger ones can be a nuisance for they are likely to stir up the mulm, uproot plants, and generally behave like a bull in a china shop. However, the larger Barbs, too, are attractive fishes. As a rule the smaller fry of the small Barbs need infusoria as first food. The fry of larger Barbs can usually manage brine shrimps.

Barbs thrive in mature well-oxygenated water with plenty of swimming space. In an overcrowded tank they are usually the first to show distress.

Recently some of the smaller Barbs have been moved to a new genus called *Puntius*. The limits and characteristics of this genus are not clear so we retain here the old nomenclature, but indicate those considered by some to be *Puntius*.

Most Barbs lay adhesive or semiadhesive eggs; hence they can be spawned by the methods described under Characins. Briefly, this consists of providing a fairly well-planted tank with pebbles on the bottom. They can also be spawned on nylon or willow root. Barbs are avid spawn eaters and should be removed immediately spawning is completed.

Barbus conchonius Hamilton-Buchanan 1822

Popular name Rosy Barb, or Red Barb.
Origin India.
Size 2½ inches.

A Rosy Barb/Ruby Barb hybrid male with Rosy Barb Female (lower fish).

Appearance One of the prettiest Barbs when in good condition. Basically, this is a silvery fish which becomes suffused with a deep rosy red or pale green tint when conditions suit it. The fins show a variable amount of black pigmentation.

Behavior Peaceful but rather boisterous. Should not be kept with very small fishes.

Feeding Hearty appetite. Eats all foods.

Water condition Near neutral to slightly alkaline, moderately hard to hard water. Temperature 78°F.

Sexing When in color the rosy hue of the male contrasts with the predominantly yellowish-green of the female. Tip of dorsal fin in male is black. In female this area shows a dark tint; all her other fins are clear.

Breeding One of the easiest egg layers to breed. Beginners could start with this one. The eggs are adhesive; 200 to 300 are produced at a spawning. Method of breeding as described earlier. (See above under Charicidae.)

Barbus nigrofasciatus Günther 1868

Popular name Black Ruby, or Purple-headed Barb.
Origin Ceylon.
Size 2½ inches.

171

Barbus nigrofasciatus – Black Ruby or Purple-headed Barb. (Female above – male below.)

Appearance   The female is a yellowish-gray fish with three to four dark vertical bands or blotches. The male is brownish black to black and the anterior part of the fish is vermilion-red.

Behavior   An attractive and popular community fish.

Feeding   Accepts all foods.

Water conditions   Not critical, but shows off best in near neutral water of moderate hardness.

Sexing   As described above.

Breeding   Another easily bred Barb; it lays 200 to 300 eggs. Method same as for other Barbs (see above, Genus *Barbus*).

Barbus tetrazona   Bleeker 1855

Popular name   Tiger Barb, or Sumatra Barb.

Origin   Sumatra, Borneo.

Size   2 inches.

Appearance   Reddish-yellow fish with four broad black evenly spaced bands.

Behavior   Variable. Some aquarists find this a peaceful community fish. Others complain that it is a bully and fin nipper. Nevertheless it is widely held to be one of the prettiest community fishes.

Feeding, Water conditions   Same as other Barbs.

Sexing   The slimmer, more colorful males are easily picked out from the plainer, plumper females. There is more red in all the fins of the male. The author has noticed that very young fish can be sexed by studying the distribution of red pigment in the ventral fins. In the female the red pigment is concentrated at the root of the fin while the free edge is transparent and colorless. In the male the entire fin is red and the pigment is more concentrated in the free edge.

Breeding   Same as other Barbs. Fry susceptible to fin rot and swim bladder trouble. Telescope-eyed mutants (similar to those in Goldfish) are sometimes encountered. Extremely clean conditions must be maintained when rearing the young.

Barbus tetrazona – Sumatra Barb, or Tiger Barb. (Female left – male right.)

Barbus titteya   Deraniyagala 1929

Popular name   Cherry Barb.
Origin   Ceylon.
Size   2 inches.
Appearance   Yellowish-brown or reddish-brown fish with dark

longitudinal black band.

Behavior An ideal community fish.

Feeding, Water conditions Same as other Barbs.

Sexing The male is darker. At breeding time it turns cherry red and the black band disappears almost completely. The female is noticeably plumper and lighter colored.

Breeding Same as other Barbs; it lays 100 to 200 eggs. Some pairs are avid egg eaters. Others leave both eggs and fry alone.

Rasbora heteromorpha – (Red) Rasbora, or Harlequin Fish. The pair is shown spawning upside down on the underside of a broad-leafed plant. The female is in the foreground.

Rasbora heteromorpha Duncker 1904

Popular name (Red) Rasbora, or Harlequin Fish.

Origin Malaya, Sumatra, Thailand.

Size 1¾ inches.

Appearance This is an old favorite. The large wedge-shaped blue-black area is set on a violet- and rose-pink-shaded body.

Behavior A schooling fish of great beauty, which deserves to be given a tank to itself. It is also suitable as a community fish.

Feeding   Accepts all foods.

Water conditions   Soft, slightly acid, peaty water. Temperature 80°F.

Sexing   Mature males are slimmer and have more red in dorsal and caudal fin. Sexing by extent of wedge-shaped blotch is unreliable.

Breeding   This is a difficult fish to breed. A well-conditioned pair should be placed in a tank containing peaty water (pH 6.2, hardness under 40 ppm) and some *Cryptocoryne*. The pair usually spawn upside-down on the under surface of the leaf. It is said that not every male will breed with every female so if no spawning is obtained one of the partners should be substituted. Usually less than 100 eggs are laid, which hatch in 24 hours.

COBITIDAE

This family, which includes Loaches and *Botias*, provides some quaint but useful scavengers and algae eaters.

The Cobitidae come from the old world, and like the Carps they have no teeth in their jaws. They have three or more pairs of barbels. Some members of the family, the spiny Loaches, have a simple or bifid spine just under each eye. Normally this lies folded flat, but if threatened it is erected with the result that any predator attempting to swallow it receives an unpleasant surprise.

These fishes are scavengers that live at the bottom of the pond in muddy, poorly oxygenated water. To compensate for this some species come to the surface and swallow air. They carry on a form of intestinal respiration, extracting oxygen via the mucosa of the hind gut. The spent air is expelled through the vent. Some Loaches are believed to be sensitive to changes in atmospheric pressure (Weather Fish).

Acanthophthalmus semicinctus   Fraser-Brunner 1940

Popular name   Half Banded Coolie Loach.

Origin   East Indies.

Size   3½ inches.

Appearance   Many fishes with a tubular snakelike body covered by black and yellow markings are offered to the aquarist. Some are distinct species, others are subspecies of *A. kuhlii*. The fish we are considering has a salmon-pink belly and the black and yellow markings extend only halfway round the fish.

Behavior   A peaceful fish that is often kept in community tanks. Since it is of nocturnal habit and hides at the bottom, it is rarely seen by its owner. The best way is to keep a collection of these Loaches in a small, sparsely planted tank with some peat on the bottom and many hiding places; then one can study their interesting behavior.

Feeding   All food, particularly algae and *Tubifex*.

Water conditions   Not critical; near neutral, moderately hard water at 78°F.

Sexing   The females become noticeably plumper at spawning time.

Breeding   Not much is known about this. When these fishes are kept on their own as described above, small Loaches appear. If this is seen adults should be removed to another tank and the young reared in the usual way.

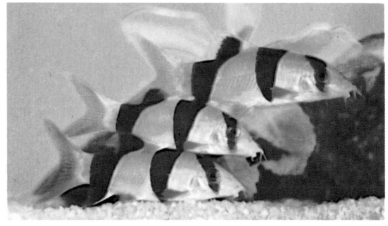

Botia macracantha – Clown Loach, or Tiger Botia.

Botia macracantha   Bleeker 1852

Popular name   Clown Loach, or Tiger Botia.

Origin   Sumatra, Borneo.

Size   4½ inches.

Appearance   The color pattern of this *Botia* bears an amazing resemblance to a Tiger Barb (*Barbus tetrazona*). The body is golden-yellow with three dark blue-black bands.

Behavior   A peaceful community fish. A fairly good scavenger. Does not like strong light. Should have hiding places.

Water conditions Most *Botias* prefer alkaline, moderately hard to hard water. This one is fairly tolerant regarding water requirements but the other extreme of soft acid water must be avoided. Temperature 70°F.-75°F.

Sexing, Breeding Not bred in captivity.

SILURIDAE

This family contains Asiatic and European Catfishes with a naked skin. Eyes are usually covered by a transparent layer of skin. Adipose fin absent. Only a few species are of interest to aquarists.

Kryptopterus bicirrhis Cuvier and Valenciennes 1839

Popular name Glass Catfish.
Origin India, Greater Sunda Islands.
Size 3½ inches.
Appearance Strongly compressed transparent glasslike body with a long-based anal fin, which is continually undulated by the fish. A pair of long maxillary barbels (whiskers).
Behavior Can be kept in a community tank but it is inclined to lurk at the back of the tank, standing in one spot undulating its anal fin. An interesting fish best kept with its own kind.
Feeding Mainly live foods; will not pick up food from bottom but will take dried food as it descends in the tank.
Water condition Not critical.
Sexing, Breeding Not bred in captivity.

Kryptopterus bicirrhis – Glass Catfish.

A. VAN DEN NIEUWENHUIZEN

This family contains naked Catfishes from Africa. Adipose fin present.

Synodontis nigriventris   David 1936

Popular name   Upside-down Catfish.
Origin   Belgian Congo.
Size   2 inches.
Appearance   Body shape similar to *Corydoras*. Ventral surface dark. This represents a reversal of normal obliterative coloring of fishes that have a dark dorsal surface and a light ventral surface.
Behavior   Kept mainly for its interesting habit of swimming upside down. Peaceful community fish.
Feeding   Live foods and algae, which it obtains from undersurface of leaves.
Water conditions   Not critical.
Sexing, Breeding   Not known. Has spawned inside a flowerpot.

MALAPTERURIDAE

There is only one species in this family.

Malapterurus electricus   Gmelin 1789

Popular name   Electric Catfish.
Origin   In some lakes and rivers of central and west Africa.
Size   2 feet, aquarium specimens 10 inches.
Appearance   Long, almost cylindrical body. It has a large adipose fin but the dorsal fin is absent. Small phosphorescent eyes. The main interest lies in the electric organs.
Behavior   Has to be kept in solitary confinement. Can give a considerable shock if disturbed or touched. The discharge is weaker than that produced by the electric eel (*Electrophorus electricus*) but stronger than that produced by the Mormyridae. It is not clear whether the electric organ is used to stun and catch smaller fishes or whether it serves as a kind of sonar.
Feeding   A voracious nocturnal feeder. Eats earthworms, meat, and smaller fishes.

Water conditions   Not critical.
Sexing, Breeding   Not accomplished in captivity.

CALLICHTHYIDAE (Armored Catfishes, Mailed Catfishes)

This family contains the mailed or armored Catfishes of South America and Trinidad. The flanks are covered by a double series of overlapping bony plates; the head and back are also similarly covered in some species. The adipose fin is supported by a mobile spine, and a large spine also occurs in the dorsal fin. With such protection it is not surprising that even large fishes leave them strictly alone. The mouth is small and toothless and is surmounted by one or two pairs of barbels. The eyes have a limited movement in their sockets, a fact which adds considerably to their droll appearance. Like the Cobitidae, these fishes are adapted for intestinal respiration. The swim bladder occurs in two parts and is surrounded by a bony capsule.

GENUS CORYDORAS

The family Callichthyidae contains the genus *Corydoras*, a most charming and popular group of small Catfishes suitable for the aquarium. Not only are they hardy, inquisitive, droll creatures interesting in their own right but they also perform a useful sanitary function by going over the aquarium floor and disposing of food left by other fishes, which might otherwise cause pollution.

Although a number of them have been bred occasionally, they are somewhat difficult to induce to spawn. This is perhaps because most aquarists keep them as scavengers and not as interesting fish in their own right, whose dietetic and other needs are studied and provided for. For breeding *Corydoras* it is best to give a group of these fishes a tank to themselves, and feed them well. A large part of the diet should be comprised of various worms and a fair amount of other usual fresh foods. The sexes are not hard to distinguish in many *Corydoras*, for when viewed from above the female will be seen to be much broader and fuller than the male. Often the fins of the male tend to be longer and somewhat more pointed than those of the female.

The tank should be provided with a fairly dark-colored fine gravel bottom. It should be lightly planted with *Cryptocoryne* and provided with hiding places, such as broken flowerpots or stones arranged to

Corydoras paleatus
Peppered Corydoras (p. 183).

Corydoras julii - Leopard Corydoras
(p. 182).

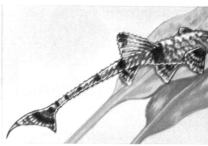

Otocinclus affinis
Midget Sucker Catfish (p. 185).

Loricaria parva - Alligator Catfish
(p. 184).

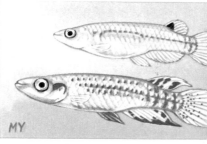

Oryzias latipes - Geisha Girl Medaka,
Japanese Medaka, or Ricefish (p. 188).

Aplocheilus blocki
Dwarf or Green Panchax (p. 188).

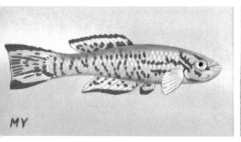
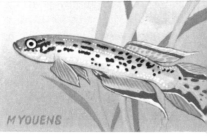

Aphyosemion gardneri
Steel Blue Aphyosemion (p. 193).

Aphyosemion australe australe
Lyretail Panchax, or Cape Lopez (p. 192).

form arches and tunnels. Temperature should not be too high for most species like cooler conditions (around 72°F.) than other tropicals, and strong light should be avoided. It is generally accepted that most *Corydoras* do best in neutral to slightly alkaline water of moderate hardness. As the fishes mature and the sexes become distinguishable, another tank should be set up similar to the one already described so that the sexes can be segregated and conditioned.

As mating time approaches there is a heightening of their colors. Some species take on a pale rosy hue. It is now time to set up a spawning tank of about 10- to 15-gallon capacity, in the same way as the main tanks. The chosen pair is now introduced and should spawn in a day or two. If they fail to do so try dropping the temperature to 62°F. by adding fresh cold water. This sometimes brings on the spawning urge. If the pair have not spawned within a week try another pair, or try one female with two or three males.

The premating behavior of the *Corydoras* is worth watching. The male continually nudges the excited female, who swims restlessly all over the tank; often the male swims over the female's back. The male then lies on his back or side or rises slightly so as to present his ventral surface to the female. What happens now is not at all clear. Some maintain that the female collects the sperm in her mouth by sucking it out of the male's genital papilla; others believe that at this point she extrudes some eggs, which stick to her ventral fin, and that these are fertilized by the sperm liberated by the male and brought to her ventral fin by the movement of her fins and gill cover. When the embrace is over the female swims away, cleans a spot on the glass wall of the tank or a leaf, and deposits her eggs. Those who maintain that the female carries the sperm in her mouth believe that the cleaning act prior to deposition of the eggs is in fact concerned with spitting out the collected sperm prior to deposition of the eggs.

After numerous embraces some 200-400 eggs are laid. These are very large (2 mm.) and clear at first but become amber-colored later. Many eggs are usually infertile or do not hatch for other reasons; they go chalky white. The fish, once they have spawned, should be removed; even though they are not avid spawn eaters they have no further duties to perform and are best out of the way. In order to prevent too much fungus growth and bacterial activity from the rotten eggs it is best to tint the water a light blue with some methylene blue. It takes about six days for the eggs to hatch. The young are large and easily reared on brine shrimps, with microworms as first food.

Corydoras aeneus –
Bronze Corydoras. (Male)

Corydoras aeneus   Gill 1858

Popular name   Bronze Corydoras.
Origin   Trinidad, Venezuela.
Size   2½ inches.
Appearance   One of the hardiest and most popular of aquarium
Catfishes. It has a greenish flank and a pinkish body.
Behavior   A perfect community fish. Very peaceful – will not molest
even very tiny fishes.
Feeding   Eats dried food that falls to the bottom. Loves whiteworms
and *Tubifex*.
Water conditions   Neutral to alkaline, moderately hard water. In-
tolerant of salt (NaCl) in water.
Sexing, Breeding   As described earlier for *Corydoras*.

Corydoras julii   Steindachner *1906*.
(*Corydoras leopardus*   Myers 1933 is either the same fish or a subspecies.)

Popular name   Leopard Corydoras.
Origin   Tributaries of the Lower Amazon.
Size   2½ inches.
Appearance   Probably the most attractively marked *Corydoras*. The
silver-gray body is traversed by a longitudinal stripe and numerous
dark spots.
Behavior   Typical peaceful *Corydoras*.
Feeding, Water conditions, Sexing, Breeding   As for other *Cory-
doras*.

182

Corydoras melanistius – Blackspotted Corydoras. (Sex indeterminate.)

Corydoras melanistius   Regan 1912

Popular name   Black-spotted Corydoras.
Origin   Guiana, Venezuela.
Size   2½ inches.
Appearance   Silver-gray body covered with evenly placed small black dots. Wedge-shaped blotch on nape of neck extending to dorsal fin. Black band across eye and head.
Behavior, Water conditions, Feeding, Sexing, Breeding   As described earlier for other *Corydoras*.

Corydoras paleatus   Jenyns 1842

Popular name   Peppered Corydoras.
Origin   Brazil and La Plata Basin.
Size   2¾ inches.
Appearance   Body of an olive-brown color, with dark almost black blotches. As popular and common as *C. aeneus*. An albino strain has been developed.
Behavior   A peaceful community fish which loves to disport at the front part of the aquarium floor, keeping area under feeding ring tidy. Amuses onlookers by frequent movement of eye.

Feeding Dried food. *Tubifex* and white worms.
Water conditions, Sexing, Breeding As described earlier for *Corydoras*.

The Loricariidae, like the Callichthyidae, are armored Catfishes from Northern and Central America. They have three or four series of bony plates on their sides, in contrast to the Callichthyidae which have only two. The head and the dorsal (back) and ventral (under) surfaces (except the abdomen) are also protected by bony plates in most species. The first ray of all fins except the caudal is stiffened to form a spine.

The mouth is placed on the ventral (under) surface of the flattened head. These fishes are popularly known as sucking Catfishes because the mouth is surrounded by broad-lobed lips, which form a sucking disc by which they anchor themselves to objects in the aquarium. These fishes are also sometimes referred to as algae-eating Catfishes because with their rough rasp-like lips they can scrape off algae from rockwork, plants, and glass walls of the tank. The importance of this to aquarists can hardly be overstated and many consider that no decorative community tank should be without one or more fishes belonging to this family.

While no Catfish can completely eliminate the need for cleaning the front glass of the tank, members of this family do cut down the frequency with which this not too pleasant task has to be performed by the aquarist. Further, the removal of algae and debris from the leaves of aquatic plants not only enhances their appearance but also promotes healthy condition and better growth.

Loricaria parva Boulenger 1895

Popular name Alligator Catfish, Whiptail Catfish.
Origin Paraguay.
Size 4½ inches.
Appearance The main interest here is in the long tapering body and the upper lobe of the caudal fin, which terminates in a long whiplike filament. It is a brownish fish with mottled black markings, which blend with the aquarium gravel.
Behavior A peaceful community fish, which would no doubt be more

popular if it were freely available.

Feeding Must have plenty of algae supplemented with other green foods such as lettuce leaves. Also accepts various fresh protein foods such as shrimps or fish roe. Will also eat a little dried food.

Water conditions It comes from fast-moving water so a well-oxygenated tank is needed. Slightly acid soft to medium hard water. Happier at lower temperatures around 70°F.

Sexing, Breeding Has been accomplished on a few occasions only. The females are slightly plumper than the males. They spawn on flat stones, under arches, or in tubes about 2 inches in diameter. The male guards eggs until they hatch in just over a week. Fry reared on mashed worms, dried food, and algae.

Otocinclus affinis Steindachner 1876

Popular name Midget Sucker Catfish.

Origin Southeast Brazil.

Size 2 inches.

Appearance A gray-green to brown fish of not very attractive appearance.

Behavior This is the supreme algae eater for the usual community tank, which will not damage even the finest-leaved plant. One or more should be used, depending on the size of the tank. A long-lived hardy species if right conditions are provided.

Feeding Unless algae are available this fish will not survive long. Also accepts the other usual foods including dried foods.

Water conditions Not critical. Wide temperature range, does well at 78°F. and also at 65°F. for considerable periods. I have kept them in tanks housing fancy Goldfish.

Sexing Adult female markedly fatter than male.

Breeding This is similar to the *Corydoras*. Eggs are laid on the glass and on plant leaves. Young hatch in 2 or 3 days and cling to glass or plants for a similar period before they drop to the bottom searching for food. Fry reared on mashed worms, algae, and dried foods.

CYPRINODONTIDAE (Tooth-carps)

This large family of fishes is widely distributed in the tropical and subtropical region of every continent except Australia. The distinction between these fishes and the true Carps is clearly indicated by both the scientific and the popular name of this family. Carps have pharyngeal teeth but a toothless mouth. The Cyprinodontidae have both oral and pharyngeal teeth.

These fishes usually have a flattened head with an upturned mouth. No barbels or adipose fins occur.

Some of the Cyprinodontidae are egglayers, others livebearers. In the latter the anal fin is modified to form an intromittent organ called the gonopodium. So varied are the aquatic needs and methods of reproduction in this family that broad generalizations are inadequate. It is essential to consider each genus, and at times each species, separately. It should be noted that the distinction between the egg-laying and livebearing species is one of convenience. Taxonomically some of the livebearers are more closely allied to some egglaying forms than to other livebearers.

GENERA APLOCHEILUS AND ORYZIAS
(Asiatic Tooth-carps)

The Asiatic Tooth-carps are mainly surface-living fishes that are found in fast-moving streams, ponds, and small drainage ditches. Little wonder then that they are not very demanding in their water conditions or temperature requirements. They do well in a temperature range between 70°F. and 80°F., in all except very hard alkaline water. In their native habitat they live on mosquito larvae and other insect life. In the aquarium too it is advisable to give them a fair amount of live and fresh meaty food, and only occasionally dried foods.

Most of the species are easily bred in small or medium-sized tanks (2 to 10 gallons) containing neutral or slightly acid peat-filtered water of moderate hardness. The tank should be furnished with lime-free gravel, fine-leaved plants, and floating plants. Next the conditioned pair is introduced in the tank. They lay a few eggs each day for a period of one to three weeks, which hatch in about ten to fifteen days. In many species the eggs are at first attached to the ventral fins or ventral surface of the female and later brushed off on the floating plants. Most parents do not molest the eggs, but may devour the fry when they hatch out. To prevent this three courses of action are open to the aquarist: (1) He can keep the fish in the spawning tank for a week or ten days and then move them to a fresh tank before the eggs

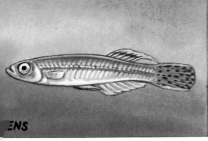

Micropanchax macrophthalmus
Lampeyed Panchax (p. 194).

Aphyosemion gulare coeruleum
Blue Gularis (p. 193).

Epiplatys sexfasciatus
Six Barred Epiplatys (p. 196).

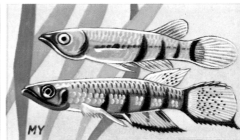

Epiplatys chaperi - Firemouth Epiplatys
(p. 195).

Pachypanchax playfairi
Playfair's Panchax (p. 197).

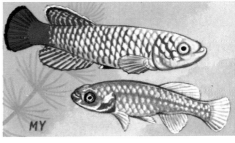

Nothobranchius guentheri
Guenther's Nothobranchius (p. 197).

Cynolebias nigripinnis
Blackfinned Pearlfish (p. 199).

Cynolebias belotti - Argentine Pearlfish
(p. 198).

hatch out. (2) He can remove egg-laden plants to a separate hatching tank and supply fresh plants for the fish to spawn on, or (3) He can knock off the eggs from the floating plants into the hatching tank and return the plants to the spawning tank. I prefer the first method, which is the least time-consuming.

If one is not concerned with the loss of a few fry one can leave the pair permanently in the spawning tank and ladle out the young as they hatch out each day.

Since the "old" eggs hatch before the newly laid ones, there will be a considerable disparity of size among youngsters in a spawning. In order to prevent cannibalism it is advisable to sort out the youngsters by size occasionally.

Most of these fishes can also be spawned on nylon mops. These are best suspended in the water to imitate rootlets of floating plants. When the mop is laden with eggs either the mops or eggs are removed in the same manner as that described earlier with floating plants.

Aplocheilus blocki   Arnold 1911

Popular name   Dwarf or Green Panchax (also called Panchax Parvus).
Origin   India and Ceylon.
Size   1¾ inches.
Appearance   This is the smallest Panchax known to aquarists. It has a metallic greenish-yellow body with rows of red and yellow dots.
Behavior   Reasonably peaceful. Can be kept with others in a community tank.
Feeding   Mainly live foods. Takes dried foods.
Water conditions   As described earlier.
Sexing   Female less colorful than the male and also slightly smaller. The fins of the female are shorter and rounded and there is a black mark at the base of the dorsal.
Breeding   As described above, genera *Aplocheilus* and *Oryzias*. Can be spawned either in pairs or in groups, e.g., two males with four or five females. Eggs hatch in 12-14 days at 78°F.

Oryzias latipes   Schlegel 1850

Popular name   Geisha Girl Medaka, Japanese Medaka, or Ricefish.
Origin   Japan.
Size   1½ inches.

Appearance A rather prosaic grayish-green fish kept mainly for its interesting breeding habit. Strains with a golden and reddish body color have also been developed.

Behavior A delicate fish unlikely to fare well in a community tank with more boisterous companions. Best kept with its own kind.

Feeding Accepts all foods.

Water conditions Moderately soft, slightly acid water to which approximately 1 level teaspoonful of salt per 3 gallons of water is added. Temperature range 75°F.-80°F. Does best at 78°F.

Sexing Females are plumper and have shorter, rounder fins.

Breeding Set up as described above, genera *Aplocheilus* and *Oryzias*. Can be spawned in pairs or in small groups. Since parents molest neither eggs nor fry, breeding is a simple matter of feeding parents adequately and collecting fry as they hatch out for rearing in separate tanks. Breeding behavior particularly interesting.

After the male and female have come together the fertilized eggs are carried on the ventral surface of the female, attached by a fine mucoid thread for many hours before they are brushed off on plants. Eggs hatch in 10-14 days.

GENUS APHYOSEMION
(African Tooth-Carps)

This genus contains many brilliantly colored fishes, which unfortunately fare rather poorly in community tanks. Under such circumstances they go about with folded fins, hide in corners, and rarely last very long. To appreciate the breath-taking beauty of these fishes it is best to give each species a separate tank. Further, in many of the larger species the males are so aggressive toward each other that it is best to keep only one male with three or four females. The tank should be placed in a shaded position and surface-floating plants provided. The bottom is best covered with well-washed scalded peat prepared as described in Chapter III.

All species thrive in slightly acid soft to moderately hard water, although some of them have occasionally been bred in somewhat hard alkaline waters (see Chapter III). Most authors recommend the addition of 1 teaspoonful of salt per gallon of water.

In nature these fishes often occur in small pools or drainage ditches, which in some instances dry up during the summer. Survival of the species in such instances is assured by eggs lying dormant in the

An annual fish, the Blue Gularis spawning. (1) The parent fish spawn, laying their eggs beneath the mud. (2) As the dry season arrives the eggs remain safely buried. (3) With the advent of the rainy season, the pool is again flooded and the fry hatch. (4) The pool fills with water, aquatic organisms and insects nourish the fry which start to grow, ultimately to repeat the cycle all over again.

damp mud at the bottom of the pond, Although adults die, when the rains come the young hatch out and carry on the species,

As far as their breeding habits in the aquarium are concerned it is customary to divide these fishes into two or three groups: (1) Surface spawners, which lay adhesive eggs on floating plants; (2) Mid-level spawners, which lay eggs on fine-leaved plants in the tank; (3) Bottom spawners, which lay eggs on the bottom of the tank in the peat or other medium provided.

Convenient though such a division is for descriptive purposes, it must be clearly recognized that this is an arbitrary division and that in different circumstances not only the same species (e.g., *A. australe*) but even the same pair will at one time spawn at the surface and at another time on the bottom of the tank. Therefore two divisions: (1) The surface spawners and (2) The bottom spawners, are adequate for our purpose and we shall now proceed to study them in detail.

Breeding the Surface Spawners

For most species rather small all-glass tanks or even large battery jars are adequate. Larger species are better bred in larger conventional aquaria. A layer of scalded peat at the bottom and some floating plants or suspended nylon mops complete the breeding setup. A conditioned pair or a group comprising one male and two or three plump females is now introduced. Often spawning commences in a few hours or within a few minutes and continues for many days. The procedure from here on is the same as that described above for the genus *Aplocheilus* in that the parents are moved on to another tank or the eggs removed from the parents at intervals.

Surface-spawning *Aphyosemion* eggs usually hatch out in about 12 to 18 days at 76°F. However, when stored in damp peat at lower temperatures (65°F.) the hatching is considerably delayed, so that these eggs can be sent by post to fellow aquarists in other countries. At no stage should the peat dry out completely or the eggs will perish. Slightly damp but not too wet peat is best for this purpose.

To hatch the eggs the peat is shaken in a quantity of soft water (or rainwater) and placed in a hatching tank, and the temperature raised to 75°F. Some recommend adding acriflavine, others a quantity of infusoria culture to insure or hasten the hatching process. The rational behind the latter suggestion is that in nature the dried-up pools containing eggs are covered with fallen leaves; when the rains come, a culture of bacteria and infusoria develops which in some way helps the disintegration of the rather tough egg shells.

Breeding the Bottom Spawners

The breeding habits of this group resemble that of the South American *Cynolebias* and *Pterolebias*. These fishes spawn after lying side by side on the surface of the peat at the bottom of the tank. The eggs are buried by lashing movements of body and fins, which stir up the peat. They as a rule do not burrow or sink into the bottom as do their South American counterparts.

The breeding set up for these fishes is very simple indeed. All that is needed is a small tank with some scalded peat at the bottom. Plants, floating or otherwise, may be added to make the fishes comfortable but this is not absolutely essential. The fishes, either a pair or a group, are next introduced and allowed to spawn for a week or so and then they are removed. The water from the tank is now carefully siphoned out with a fine tube, leaving the peat and eggs undisturbed. The peat is now allowed to dry out a bit (but not completely) by laying the covered tank aside (temperature 70°F.) approximately for 2 to 3 weeks. The lumpy peat may now be removed from the bottom of the tank and the lumps broken up by hand and the peat and eggs can be stored for many months at about 65°F. in a jam jar or other container. An occasional drop to 60°F. does no harm, so transporting these eggs presents little difficulty. At the end of a further month or two (or even longer) the eggs can be hatched out by shaking the peat in water as described immediately above, Breeding the Surface Spawners.

Not all species need long resting periods or drying out. The important point to note is that at no stage must the peat become completely dry or the temperature fall too low.

Aphyosemion australe australe   Rachow 1921

Popular name   Lyretail Panchax, or Cape Lopez.
Origin   Cape Lopez, Gabon delta.
Size   2¼ inches.
Appearance   This is undoubtedly one of the most beautiful of aquarium fishes. Body color reddish-brown peppered with red spots. The caudal fin of the male is lyre-shaped and brilliantly decorated with many colors.
Behavior   Can be kept in community tank with smaller species, but does best in a special tank with its own kind. Temperature 75°F.
Feeding   A favorite item of diet is whiteworms. Accepts dried foods.
Water conditions   Slightly acid, moderately soft water with or without salt as recommended for the genus (see above, *Aphyosemion*).
Sexing   Easily told at a glance for only the male has the lyretail.
Breeding   Easily accomplished even with young fishes 2 to 3 months

old. This is a predominantly surface spawner and should be bred as described above, Genera *Aplocheilus* and *Oryzias*. Eggs hatch in 12 to 15 days at 75°F.

Aphyosemion gardneri   Boulenger 1911

Popular name   Steel Blue Aphyosemion.
Origin   W. Africa.
Size   2¼ inches.
Appearance   The gorgeously colored male has a pale green body with red underside. Head and sides covered with many red streaks and spots. The female is olive brown in color and has smaller fins.
Behavior   Reasonably peaceful in a community tank, but do not show off well. Males aggressive to each other.
Feeding   Small live foods. Accepts dried foods.
Water conditions   Moderately soft, slightly acid water with salt added as described above, under genus *Aphyosemion*.
Sex   The more colorful males are easily picked out.
Breeding   Spawns on either surface plants or on peat bottom. Long resting period with drying out not absolutely essential. Eggs hatch in two to four weeks

Aphyosemion gulare coeruleum   Boulenger 1915

Popular name   Blue Gularis.
Origin   Cameroons, Niger delta.
Size   4½ inches.
Appearance   Another outstandingly beautiful *Aphyosemion* of very variable coloration. Usually the male has a predominantly blue or bluish green body with red or red-brown dorsum. Brilliant red and blue dots and streaks cover the fish. The brownish-green female is less colorful and has smaller rounded fins.
Behavior   A hardy, pugnacious species but can be kept in the usual community tank when young, or in company with larger fishes when older. Temperature 72°F.-75°F.
Feeding   This is a large carnivorous fish best fed in cichlid fashion with earthworms, Guppies, and other meaty foods. It will, however, accept some dried food.
Water conditions   As described for the genus.
Sexing   Already indicated under Appearance.

Breeding   As described for the genus. A bottom spawner. Eggs hatch after one or two months at 75°F.

GENUS MICROPANCHAX
(African Tooth-Carps)

These fishes come from the Nile and tropical Africa. Most but not all of them are rather prosaic silvery or brownish fishes whose main attraction is that they have an iridescent area surmounting a rather large eye. Their breeding behavior and water requirement are similar to the *Oryzias* in that the fertilized eggs hang on the female for a while before they are brushed off onto plants. The parents do not molest the eggs and rarely eat the young. The breeding set up for *Oryzias latipes* will be found adequate in most instances (see above, *Oryzias latipes*). Many of them are annual fishes that live under one year.

Micropanchax macrophthalmus   Meinken 1932
(also called *Aplocheilichthys macrophthalmus*)

Popular name   Lampeyed Panchax.
Origin   Lagos.
Size   1¼ inches.
Appearance   Translucent silvery body. Large eye surmounted by iridescent bluish-green spot. A faintly iridescent longitudinal band runs across the fish.
Behavior   A small peaceful species best kept as a school in a tank with dark bottom, fine-leaved vegetation, and a dim top light. Given such a setting, the iridescent spot glows like a lamp and the effect can be impressive.
Feeding   Accepts all foods.
Water conditions   Peat-filtered water that is neutral or slightly acid and moderately soft. 76°F.-78°F.
Sexing   Males have more pointed fins, females slightly plumper.
Breeding   Can be bred in pairs or in groups. The breeding setup is similar to that needed for *Oryzias* (see above, *Oryzias latipes*). They spawn over a period of several days and only a few young are produced. Eggs take about 10 days to hatch at 76°F. Fry grow very slowly.

These West African Cyprinodontidae are rather sluggish fishes, which bask at the surface of the water. They can, however, dart with lightning rapidity to seize their prey. They inhabit stagnant waters and are hence not comfortable if the water surface is continually disturbed by strong aeration or filtration. They do not need water as soft as do some of the other Cyprinodonts; near neutral water of moderate hardness to which 1 teaspoonful of salt is added per three gallons of water is quite adequate. They do, however, prefer a somewhat warmer environment, between 78°F. and 82°F.

Their large mouth and Pike-like appearance clearly indicate their predatory nature, and their unsuitability for community life with fishes less than a third their size.

Most of these fishes are easily bred. They lay hard-shelled adhesive eggs in surface vegetation, so the methods described for breeding surface spawners should be employed (see above, Genera *Aplocheilus* and *Oryzias*). Either a conditioned pair or one male and three or four females are used for spawning.

Most of these fishes leave the eggs alone but anything that moves is considered as food so the fry are in danger soon after they become free-swimming. For the same reason there should not be too great a disparity of size between the fry, or else the larger ones will devour their smaller brethren.

Epiplatys chaperi   Sauvage 1882

Popular name   Firemouth Epiplatys.
Origin   West Africa.
Size   2 inches.
Appearance   An attractive old favorite. This is an olive-green fish with a bluish sheen in places. The body bears approximately six black transverse bars. The main attraction here is the ruby-red throat of the male.
Behavior   This fish can be kept in a community tank for it is of medium size and well behaved. The males are not quarrelsome so more than one can be kept in the tank.
Feeding   Accepts all foods.
Water conditions   Not critical. No salt needed. Breeds over a wide range of pH and hardness.

Sexing   Female has rounded fins. Red throat coloration occurs only in males.

Breeding   Two males and three or four females should be brought together in a 10 to 15-gallon tank furnished as described immediately above, under Genus *Epiplatys*. Prolific breeders, as many as 100-200 eggs may be laid by a female in one week. Eggs hatch in 9-11 days at 80°F.

Epiplatys sexfasciatus   Gill 1862

Popular name   Six-barred Epiplatys.
Origin   Tropical West Africa.
Size   4 inches.
Appearance   A greenish-yellow banded fish of Pike-like appearance.
Behavior   Can be kept in community with fishes of similar size.
Feeding   Mainly live meaty foods. Reluctant to accept fresh or dried foods.
Water conditions   Neutral water of moderate hardness.
Sexing   Females paler with rounded fins.
Breeding   Use one male to three females. Procedure as described for genus. A surface spawner that lays 100-200 eggs, which hatch in 10-14 days at 80°F.

GENUS NOTHOBRANCHIUS

This genus contains short-lived fishes, commonly referred to as annual fishes, for their usual life span is under one year.

In their native habitat (East and Central Africa) the pools and ditches they inhabit dry up during the hot season and the adult fishes die; the species survives, for eggs are laid in the mud at the bottom of the pool. This does not dry out completely even though the surface becomes dry and fissured. When the rainy season comes and the pools fill up with water, the fishes hatch out in a few minutes. They grow and mature at an amazing pace and start breeding in preparation for the next drought.

In the aquarium also, even though the water does not dry up, the fishes still rarely live over a year (usually more like six to eight months). Hence they must be bred each year to replace the parents. Sometimes this is difficult, for the youngsters fail to attain a size suitable for breeding.

At the moment our knowledge of the biology and breeding of Nothobranchius is rather scanty, but rapid strides have been made in recent years by aquarists who have specialized in looking after these fishes. There is little doubt that some of the most outstandingly colorful fishes belong to this genus and every effort should be made to learn more about them.

Nothobranchius guentheri   Pfeffer 1893

Popular name   Günther's Nothobranchius.
Origin   East Africa.
Size   2 inches.
Appearance   Predominant body color of the male is green with shades of brown, yellow, and blue. Scales edged with red. Tail vermilion red. Females yellowish brown with almost colorless fins.
Behavior   Pugnacious. Best kept with own kind in pairs or in groups of one male to two or three females.
Feeding   Live and fresh foods only.
Water conditions   In natural state known to survive considerable changes in water chemistry and temperature. Usually kept in moderately soft, slightly acid peat water, with scalded peat at bottom of tank.
Sexing   As described above.
Breeding   A bottom spawner which breeds as described immediately above, under Genus *Nothobranchius*. Allow pair or trio to bury eggs in peat for seven to ten days. Dry off peat and store for three to four months at 70°F.-75°F. Hatch by adding rainwater.

Pachypanchax playfairi   Günther 1866

Popular name   Playfair's Panchax.
Origin   East Africa, Seychelles, Madagascar.
Size   3 inches.
Appearance   This is a yellowish-orange fish speckled with tiny red dots. An interesting, perhaps unique feature is that the scales (especially along the back) in this species (particularly in the males) do not lie down flat as in other species. They stand slightly on end as if the fish were suffering from dropsy.
Behavior   An aggressive fish unsuited for the community tank.
Feeding   Mainly live foods. Will take dried foods.

Water conditions   Moderately soft, slightly acid water. Temperature 76°F.-80°F.

Sexing   Male more colorful, with larger fins.

Breeding   A surface spawner that can be easily bred as described above, Genera *Aplocheilus* and *Oryzias*.

GENUS CYNOLEBIAS

(Central and South American Cyprinodontidae)

Members of this genus are annual fishes, very similar in breeding behavior to members of the genus *Nothobranchius* and some of the bottom-spawning *Aphyosemions*. The breeding setup required is similar to that needed for other bottom-spawning Cyprinodontidae and has already been dealt with (see above, Genus *Aphyosemion*). It only remains to point out some of the relevant details.

It is generally believed that soft acid water suits most *Cynolebias*; on the other hand it would be equally true to say that some of them at any rate are not too critical about water conditions. They can also tolerate a fairly wide temperature range but appear to do best at around 75°F. Most of them are gluttonous and need plenty of live food. They spawn readily when a suitable pair is brought together, the individuals diving deep into the peat at the bottom of the tank. Often they disappear from sight during this process. It follows, therefore, that a fairly deep layer of peat, 1½" or more, should be provided.

For good results it is essential to dry out the peat partially – not entirely – over a period of two weeks and allow the temperature to fall to about 72°F. The slightly damp peat can now be stored in plastic bags or jam jars for another 3 weeks or more. Hatching of eggs is accomplished by shaking peat in water, when fry appear in 1 to 2 hours.

Cynolebias belotti   Steindachner 1881

Popular name   Argentine Pearlfish.

Origin   La Plata region.

Size   2 inches.

Appearance   Deeply compressed body showing a predominantly dark blue coloration in the male. Numerous pearly-white spots on body and fins. Female less colorful, of a green-yellow hue.

Behavior   A small but rather aggressive fish. Best kept in pairs, because of hostility among rival males.

Feeding   Large amounts of live and fresh foods. May accept dried foods occasionally.

Sexing   As described above.

Water conditions, Breeding   As for genus (see immediately above, Genus *Cynolebias*).

Cynolebias nigripinnis   Regan 1912

Popular name   Blackfinned Pearlfish.

Origin   Paraná River in Argentina.

Size   1¾ inch.

Appearance   Male has a velvety black body and fins covered with numerous light green or blue spots. Female is ochre-colored with irregular markings.

Behavior   A delicate, fairly peaceful species.

Feeding   Live and fresh foods.

Water conditions   Moderately soft, slightly acid water.

Sexing   As above.

Breeding   As for genus (see Genus *Cynolebias*). Difficult to breed and rear young.

GENUS FUNDULUS

(North and Middle American Cyprinodontidae)

This widely distributed genus contains many species. They have an elongated, almost cylindrical body and a flattened head. They are popularly referred to as Killifishes or Top Minnows. The temperature and water requirements of different species, living as they do in such widely distributed habitats, is bound to show many differences. Some live in brackish or even sea water, others in fresh waters of varying composition. A few are happy at 78°F.-80°F. but most others are comfortable at fairly low temperatures (70°F.) and do not tolerate our usual tropical tank temperatures for long. Hardiness and breeding urge are often enhanced by a drop in temperature for a few weeks.

Many species of *Fundulus* live at the surface; a few spend their time at the bottom or even in the mud. The surface-living varieties are distinguished by a conspicuous golden spot on the top of the head. They spawn among floating plants. Most of them will eat their own eggs and fry. Since only a few eggs are laid daily over a period of time, breeding them can be a tedious affair. The procedures for breeding surface spawners on plants or nylon mops described above under Genera *Aplocheilus* and *Oryzias* are also suitable for this genus.

Fundulus chrysotus   Holbrook 1866

Popular name   Golden Ear.
Origin   Eastern coast of U.S.A. from South Carolina to Florida.
Size   3 inches.
Appearance   An olive-green fish with numerous green and red spots on flanks and fins.
Behavior   Can be kept in community tank with fish its own size.
Feeding   Accepts all foods.
Water conditions   Slightly brackish to fresh water (1 teaspoonful of salt to 3 gallons of water). Not critical regarding pH and hardness. Temperature 73°F.-78°F.
Sexing   Females are paler and less colorful.
Breeding   Lays a few eggs each day in thick bushy plants, which must be removed to separate tank for hatching. Eggs hatch in 8 to 12 days. See also breeding surface spawners above, under Genus *Aphyosemion*.

Fundulus heteroclitus   Linnaeus 1766

Popular name   Local or Bait Killie.
Origin   Atlantic Coast from Canada to Mexico.
Size   To 4½ inches.
Appearance   Very variable. The male is often greenish-brown with transverse iridescent blue bands on flank. The female is ochre and only very faintly banded. Different varieties have yellowish or reddish fins.
Behavior   Rather peaceful for such a large fish.
Feeding   Accepts all foods.
Water conditions   Hard alkaline water with salt added at the rate of one or two teaspoonfuls per gallon. Temperature dependent on origin, usually between 65°F.-72°F.
Sexing   As above.
Breeding   See breeding surface spawners above, under Genera *Aplocheilus* and *Oryzias*. Spawns over one or two weeks. Eggs hatch in 12 to 14 days.

These Cyprinodontidae come from Southern U.S.A., Middle and South America. They have long cylindrical bodies and rounded fins. The females of many species show what is popularly known as the "rivulus spot." This is a dark spot surrounded by a lighter area on the upper edge of the caudal fin, which is also referred to as an eye spot or ocellus. The males are more brilliantly colored than females although it must be noted that many species are of a rather prosaic appearance.

Regarding temperature, most species do well between the usual 75°F. and 78°F. but they are tolerant to drops in temperatures to 60°F.

These fishes like a sunny, well-planted tank. Most of them are not at all critical regarding water conditions. In their native habitat *Rivulus* are known to jump out of the water and rest on floating plants. In the aquarium too they sometimes jump and adhere to the cover glass and stay there for many minutes before dropping back into the water. They spawn in surface vegetation and hence can be bred by methods described above, under Genera *Aplocheilus* and *Oryzias* and under Genus *Aphyosemion*.

If well fed they rarely molest the eggs, so breeding them is a fairly simple matter.

Rivulus cylindraceus   Poey 1861

Popular name   Green, Brown, or Cuban Rivulus.
Origin   Cuba, Florida.
Size   Male 1¾ inches; Female 2 inches.
Appearance   A greenish-brown fish, with yellow to orange belly. The body is sprinkled with green and red spots.
Behavior   Fairly peaceful, suitable for community tank.
Feeding   Accepts all foods.
Water conditions   Not critical. Usually bred in neutral to slightly acid, moderately soft water.
Sexing   Ocellus on caudal peduncle of female.
Breeding   A surface spawner (see above, under Genus *Aphyosemion*.) Best to breed with one male and two or three females; 100-150 eggs laid by female in about 8 days. Eggs hatch in 10-15 days at 78°F.

Rivulus urophthalmus   Günther 1866

Popular name   Golden or Green Rivulus.
Origin   From Guianas to lower Amazon region.
Size   2¼ inches.
Appearance   At least two distinct color varieties exist. In one we have a brownish fish with rows of red spots on the side, and the female shows the rivulus spot. The other is a xanthic mutant. This is a golden-yellow fish in which the red spots are much better discerned. The female lacks the eye spot. There is less melanin in this fish; hence it can also be regarded as a partial albino. The eyes are, however, black.
Behavior   All varieties fairly hardy and can be kept in a community tank.
Feeding   Mainly live food but will accept some dried food.
Water conditions   Neutral to slightly acid water of moderate hardness.
Sexing   In the brown variety the ocellus of the female is distinctive. In the golden variety the female carries very few small or no red spots on the body.
Breeding   Similar to *Rivulus cylindraceus*.

GENERA POECILIA AND XIPHOPHORUS
(Livebearing Tooth-Carps)

These genera contain some of our most popular aquarium fishes: the Guppies, Mollies, Platies, and Swordtails. The former two have now been placed under the genus *Poecilia* and the latter two belong to the genus *Xiphophorus* (Rosen and Bailey 1963). Many other livebearing genera are known but are seldom seen in aquaria today. Wild specimens of *Poecilia* and *Xiphophorus* are also rarely obtainable for they have been superseded by many attractive aquariumbred varieties and hybrids.

These fishes are not critical of water conditions, However, they do not like peaty water. Most do well in slightly alkaline, moderately hard to hard water at a temperature between 72° and 80°F.

The males and females are easily distinguished by the difference in the anal fin. In the male this fin is modified to form a rodshaped copulatory organ called the gonopodium. This change may occur either early or late in life. At birth and for some time afterward the anal fin of both sexes is similar.

ındulus chrysotus - Golden Ear (p. 200).

Rivulus cylindraceus
Green, Brown or Cuban Rivulus (p. 201).

Fundulus heteroclitus
Local or Bait Killie (p. 200).

Rivulus urophthalmus
Golden or Green Rivulus (p. 202).

oecilia sphenops - Liberty Molly (Male)
(p. 211).

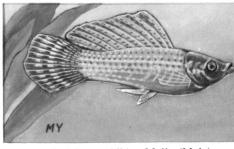

Poecilia latipinna - Albino Molly (Male)
(p. 206).

Poecilia latipinna
Permablack Molly (Male) (p. 206).

Poecilia latipinna
Permablack Molly (Female) (p. 206).

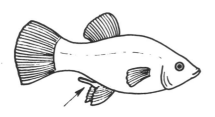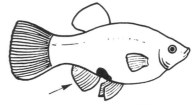

Sexing livebearers. The male is on the left, the female on the right. The arrows point to the anal fins, which are the distinguishing characteristic.

Differences in the structure of the gonopodium in different species have assisted classification. This organ is very mobile and can be moved forward, backward, and sideways in most species. In two genera, however (*Jenynsia* and *Anableps*), the gonopodium can be moved to one side only, i.e., either right or left. Since the genital opening of the females is also not centrally placed we find that males with right-moving gonopodia can mate only with females with left-sided genital opening and vice versa.

Once a female has been mated with a male, she can store the sperms and deliver a number of successive broods without any further contact with a male. The many peculiarities of development have already been discussed in detail in Chapter X.

The gravid female is easily recognized by the distended abdomen and a large, usually black, crescentic or triangular area in front of the anal fin. This is known as the gravid spot. This is due to the black pigment on the peritoneum (a thin membrane which lines the abdominal wall and various internal organs) showing through the distended (hence thinned and rendered translucent) abdominal wall of the pregnant female.

In the Black Molly, of course, the intense black color of the abdominal wall, even when thinned as a result of advanced pregnancy, prevents a view of the peritoneum and hence no gravid spot is seen. In the albinos such as the albino Swordtails, red-eyed Red Swordtails, etc., the "gravid spot" of course lacks the black pigment for no black pigment is developed anywhere in the fish. The crescentic area here presents a pinkish appearance; just as the pink in the eye of the albino, this is due to the color of the blood seen in the vessels in this region. On closer examination (preferably with a light situated behind the fish), spherical translucent structures (eggs or developing embryos) can be seen in this area. In the Wagtail Platy again this area shows practically no black pigment; it presents a translucent golden-yellow appearance and fine black dots may be seen in this area when it is examined by transmitted light. These are the eyes of the developing embryos. The gravid spot is not an absolutely certain indication that a fish has been fertilized and is carrying young, for even virgin females at times show it. Finally, one may say that it is no proof of sex either, for the male *Xiphophorus variatus* shows a very well-marked dark spot but this to my knowledge is the only exception.

The period of gestation, that is to say the time interval elapsing between the fertilization of the egg and the delivery of the young, is very variable, in sharp contrast to the more definite gestation period of the higher vertebrates. One of the main factors influencing the period of gestation in these fishes appears to be temperature. The time taken also varies, of course, with species and with other factors but as a broad generalization one could say that the gestation period is usually 4 to 6 weeks, at a temperature of 78°F. to 80°F., but is extended to as long as 8 to 10 weeks or more at a temperature of about 70°F. The number of young produced is also very variable. This depends on the species and the size and age of the female. Most livebearers bear broods throughout the year but the tempo is slower in the winter. Mollies frequently pause delivering during this period.

Livebearers with similarly shaped gonopodia can be hybridized. Thus Platies will cross easily with Swordtails, and Guppies have been crossed with Mollies.

Besides the late maturation of some males, there is another situation that the aquarist sometimes encounters. A true female, i.e., one which has delivered numerous healthy youngsters, gradually develops a gonopodium and other external characteristics of a male (e.g., sword development in Swordtails) but these fishes, though they look like males, cannot function as such and do not father any progeny. It has been claimed that on occasions a fertile male may be produced by sex reversal from a true female but this is doubtful. The reverse change from male to female is also unknown.

Breeding Methods

The fact that one fertilization can suffice for the production of numerous successive broods must be borne in mind by the breeder. A female that is to be kept for mating later must be isolated from all other males; if this is not done – and even if the desired male is later introduced – one cannot be certain of the male parentage of the future progeny. Thus when line breeding the first step is to pick out those fishes whose anal fin begins to show signs of elongating into a gonopodium and separate them from the rest without any delay. Then when the separated males and females are mature the best male is mated to two or three of the best females by bringing them together in a well-planted tank with surface vegetation. If fed well, nothing more need be done for under such circumstances the parents will eat few if any young when they are delivered. All that needs doing now is to catch the youngsters and rear them in another tank. For serious breeding, however, the female should be isolated in a well-planted tank or a breeding trap to provide maximum security for the fry. Of these two the planted-tank method is the better, for while Guppies and Platies do not suffer much from a short stay in a breeding trap, Swordtails resent this treatment. Mollies should never be treated in this manner; the female may die or deliver young prematurely.

As a general rule the gravid female should be moved to the breeding trap or planted tank a week before delivery. Netting her too late may injure her or lead to premature delivery with resultant loss of young.

Poecilia latipinna   Le Sueur 1821
(until recently *Mollienesia latipinna*)

Popular name   Green Sailfin Molly.
Origin   Southern and Gulf States of U.S.A., ranging into Mexico.
Size   5 inches, in the aquarium just under 4 inches.
Appearance   This is the Molly usually available to aquarists, *P. velifera* being much more difficult to come by. Both Mollies have large sail-like dorsals, that in *P. latipinna* being smaller and much less handsome (see *P. velifera* below). The dorsal in *P. latipinna* is very variable. In only a few specimens is it fully developed. The body of the fish is olive brown with a pearly or bluish sheen in places.
Behavior   Good community fish.
Feeding, Water conditions, and Sexing   As for *P. velifera*.
Breeding   (See details of breeding livebearers above, under Genera *Poecilia* and *Xiphophorus*.) Large females may produce just over

Poecilia latipinna – Green Sailfin Molly. The fish in the foreground is a male.

100 young, each measuring approximately 1/3 inch in length. Fry must have plenty of swimming room. Large dorsals develop in large outdoor pools, not in tanks. Tank-bred males usually remain rather small. Dorsal fin development occurs in the second year.

Poecilia reticulata
Wild Type Guppy (Male) (p. 210).

Poecilia reticulata
Wild Type Guppy (Female) (p. 210).

Poecilia reticulata - Pintail Guppy (Male)
(p. 211).

Poecilia reticulata
King Cobra Guppy (Male) (p. 210).

Poecilia reticulata
Flame Gold Guppy (Male) (p. 210).

Poecilia reticulata - Red Veiltail
Half Black Guppy (Male) (p. 210).

Poecilia reticulata
Bottom Swordtail Guppy (Male) (p. 210).

Poecilia reticulata
Double Swordtail Guppy (Male) (p. 21)

MABEL ERVIN

Black Lyretail Molly. Originally bred as a strain of the *Poecilia latipinna* with an infusion of *P. sphenops,* the Black Molly is one of our most popular aquarium fishes. In recent years a so-called "lyretail" strain has been developed, which is distinguished by the presence of extremely elongated rays on the upper and lower portion of the tail, as well as elongated ventral fins which form tassels. This is a male (p. 212).

A good way of breeding these Mollies is to set up a very large tank with half a dozen or so large females and two or three males. If the parents are well fed, few if any babies are eaten. In this method all that needs doing is to remove the babies as and when they appear.

The Black Molly is a melanistic phase of the *latipinna* which breeds true. There has been some hybridizing with *P. sphenops*. These crosses may be distinguished by the location of the dorsal; the leading edge in *sphenops* begins after the anal fin, in *latipinna* the dorsal begins before the anal fin.

PHOTOGRAPHED AT MAC GUPPY HATCHERY

Albino Veiltail King Cobra Guppies. Not all albinos are colorless. It is the absence of black pigment in the body and the eyes that distinguishes the albino.

Poecilia reticulata   Peters 1859
(until recently *Lebistes reticulatus*)

Popular name   Guppy, or Millions Fish.
Origin   Venezuela. Barbados, Trinidad, Brazil, Guiana.
Size   Males 1½ inches, Females 2 inches.
Appearance   This fish shows a number of forms and color variations, even in the wild state. As a result of selective breeding and crossing established strains, a host of new strains have been developed. These are largely classified according to the color and finnage of the male. The size and shape of the caudal fin is of prime importance in this respect. The terms used are self-explanatory, e.g., Cofertail, Pintail, Speartail, Robson (round tail), Top Sword, Bottom Sword, Double Sword, Lyretail, Deltatail, Flagtail, Scarftail, and Veiltail.

The varieties are also classified by color and color patterns. Thus we have Red, Green, Gold, Chain, Chinese, Lace, Bird's Eye, and many others. It will be readily appreciated that permutations and combinations of colors, color patterns, and fin forms can, theoretically at least, yield endless varieties or strains of Guppies. An amazing degree of success has already been achieved, for not only have large colorful males with flowing fins been developed but the size of the female has also been increased and in recent years females with enlarged colored caudal fins have been produced.

Behavior The popularity of the Guppy stems not only from its beauty but also from its almost unique hardiness, and its impeccable behavior in the community tank. This is a peaceful, lively fish impossible to fault on any point. As is only to be expected, some of the highly inbred strains are not very hardy. Such strains should be kept on their own.

Feeding Here again Guppies are most accommodating. They will accept all foods at all levels of the tank. To rear firstclass specimens, however, they should be fed at least twice a day; preferably more often. The diet should also contain a fair amount of live and fresh foods.

Water conditions This fish is uncritical of water conditions or overcrowding. However, to produce fine specimens, well-planted tanks with ample swimming room should be provided. Temperature 74°F.-78°F. Tolerates temperatures down to 60°F.

Sexing As described earlier for *Poecilia*.

Breeding Techniques described above, under Genera *Poecilia* and *Xiphophorus*, for livebearers are adequate. Female Guppies tolerate life in plastic breeding traps better than other live bearers. To create new strains or improve existing ones, some knowledge of genetics is helpful. This is dealt with in Chapter XI of this book.

Poecilia sphenops   Cuvier and Valenciennes 1846
(until recently *Mollienesia sphenops*)

Popular names   Molly, or Sphenops Molly.
Origin   Mexico to Colombia.
Size   3½ inches.
Appearance   The dorsal fin of this species is smaller (fin ray count 8-10) and set further back than in Sailfin Mollies.

Many color varieties of *P. sphenops* occur. The common brownish-olive *sphenops* with a pale orange caudal fin is rarely seen. Very popular is an all-black variety called Perma-black, which breeds true in that it produces all black young or only occasionally produces a few speckled young. Black speckled Mollies are attractive fishes but are not prized as they are looked upon as poor blacks. Yet another recently produced variety is an all-black Molly in which the dorsal is enlarged and the caudal lyre-shaped. This is the Lyretail Molly.

Another attractive but hard-to-come-by variety of *sphenops* is the Liberty Molly, which comes from Yucatan. It has a silvery-blue body. The dorsal and caudal fins are red and orange, streaked with black.

Behavior   A good community fish. An ardent algae eater, which helps to keep plants clean.

Feeding   All foods. Must have vegetable foods such as algae, lettuce, and spinach.

Water conditions   Moderately hard to hard alkaline water. It is doubtful whether it is advantageous to add salt to the water for this species. Temperature 80°F.

Sexing   Presence of gonopodium easily identifies the male.

Breeding   See Breeding above, under Genera *Poecilia* and *Xiphophorus*. *P. sphenops* is easier to breed and rear than Sailfin Mollies. It is not as demanding in its water conditions or space requirements. A large female produces between 30 and 70 young. The Lyretail variety is probably even hardier than the Perma-black.

Poecilia velifera   Regan 1914
(until recently *Mollienesia velifera*)

Popular name   Sailfin Molly.
Origin   Coastal districts of Yucatan.
Size   5 foot in the wild, under 4½ inches in aquaria.
Appearance   Chief interest lies in its saillike dorsal fin, which is larger than that borne by any other Molly. It has a fin ray count of approximately 18 while *P. latipinna* with the next largest dorsal fin has a count of approximately 13. The body of the fish is olive green with a bluish sheen. The body and fins are decorated with dark reticulations and spots.

Behavior   Can be kept in a community tank, but best kept with its own kind in a large, well-planted, sunny tank.

Feeding   Besides usual foods must have vegetable matter such as algae, spinach, or lettuce.

Xiphophorus helleri
Red Wagtail Swordtail (Male) (p. 214).

Xiphophorus helleri
Green Swordtail (Male) (p. 214).

Xiphophorus helleri
Red Swordtail (Male) (p. 214).

Xiphophorus helleri
Red Swordtail (Female) (p. 215).

Xiphophorus helleri
Black Swordtail (Female) (p. 214).

Xiphophorus helleri
Albino Swordtail (Male) (p. 214).

Xiphophorus helleri - Simpson Hi-Fin
Swordtail (Male) (p. 214).

Xiphophorus helleri - Simpson Hi-Fin
Swordtail (Female) (p. 214).

Water conditions   Alkaline, moderately hard water to which salt has been added at the rate of 1 teaspoonful per 3 gallons. Temperature 80°F.

Sexing   Females too have a large dorsal fin but this is very modest compared to the male. Best guide is the gonopodium of the male.

Breeding   See above, under Genera *Poecilia* and *Xiphophorus*.

Xiphophorus helleri – Simpson Hi-Fin Swordtail. (Male left – female right.)

Xiphophorus helleri   Heckel 1848

Popular name   Swordtail.

Origin   Mexico, Guatemala.

Size   3½ inches (excluding sword).

Appearance   The wild variety (Green Swordtail) is now rarely seen in aquaria; it has been replaced by many very attractive color variations and hybrids with *X. maculatus*. The best known are (1) The Red Swordtail, whose origin is a mystery, but it probably arose as a cross between a Green Swordtail (*X. helleri*) and a Red Platy (*X. maculatus* var. *rubra*). (2) Red-eyed Red Swordtail. Perhaps the most attractive Swordtail. This is an albinistic mutation. (Note: An albino is an animal lacking the brownish-black pigment melanin. It need not necessarily be colorless.) (3) Albino Swordtail. A pink or creamy fish with pink eyes. (Again the black pigment is gone but some yellow pigments remains.) (4) Gold Swordtail. The body color is yellow. Almost complete loss of black pigment in the body. Eye black. (5) Black Swordtail (red and green varieties). Produced by crossing Red or Green Swordtail with Black Platy (*X. maculatus* var. *nigra*). This strain is highly susceptible to melanoma production (see Chapter XIV). (6) Berlin Swordtail. The posterior half of this fish is black, the anterior red or green. Produced by selective breeding from progeny of black-sided or spotted Platy with Red or Green Swordtail. Very prone to melanoma production. Wagtail Swordtail, red, yellow, or green. From appropriate colored Swordtail mated with similar colored Wagtail Platy. (7) Simpson Hi-Fin Swordtail. A mutant with an enlarged dorsal fin.

Behavior   Swordtails and their hybrids are boisterous fish inclined to chase and bully other fishes. They should be kept with fairly large fishes only. All albino mutants are distinctly less hardy and less aggressive. (Terrestrial albino animals, e.g., albino rats or mice, are usually more jumpy and more likely to bite than pigmented strains. This is probably due to their poor eyesight.)

Feeding   Accepts all food. Also browses on algae.

Water conditions   Slightly alkaline, moderately hard water. Soft acid water definitely inimical to growth and well-being.

Sexing   Presence of a gonopodium and the "swordtail" permit easy identification of males. For sex reversal and other points of interest see above, Genera *Poecilia* and *Xiphophorus*.

Breeding   For methods see above, Genera *Poecilia* and *Xiphophorus*. The gravid female is best delivered in a planted tank or a very large breeding trap. Estimates as to number of babies per brood vary. The maximum I have personally noted is 180. Reports claim that this can be as high as 250. The usual number is more likely to be between 50 and 100.

Xiphophorus maculatus   Günther 1866

Popular name   Platy.
Origin   Mexico and Guatemala.
Size   2 inches.
Appearance   This species is shorter and chunkier than *X. helleri*, and does not bear a sword. Numerous varieties and hybrids with

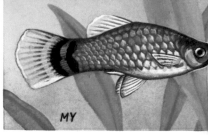

Xiphophorus maculatus
Red Platy (Male) (p. 217).

Xiphophorus maculatus
Blue Platy (Male) (p. 215).

Xiphophorus maculatus
Red Tuxedo Platy (Female) (p. 217).

Xiphophorus maculatus
Red Wagtail Platy (Male) (p. 217).

Xiphophorus maculatus
Gold Wagtail Platy (Male) (p. 217).

Xiphophorus maculatus
Gold Wagtail Platy (Female) (p. 217).

Xiphophorus variatus
Sunset Platy (Male) (p. 218).

Xiphophorus variatus
Sunset Platy (Female) (p. 218).

Xiphophorus variatus – Sunset Platy or Platy Variatus.

X. helleri and *X. variatus* have been developed. Some of the most popular are Red, Gold, Blue, Black, Tuxedo, Moon, Comet, Red-wag, Yellow-wag, and Bleeding Heart. Like the *X. variatus*, the *maculatus* Platies have been bred in all color varieties with elongated fins. These are called "Topsails." Varieties with black fins are called "Wags."

Behavior Its size, attractive colors, peaceful disposition, and algae-nibbling habit make it an ideal community fish.

Feeding, Water conditions, Sexing, Breeding Same as for other livebearers. A good-sized female produces 25 to 80 young.

Xiphophorus maculatus – Gold Wag Topsail Platy (Male) (p. 215).

Xiphophorus variatus Meek 1904

Popular name Platy, or Variegated Platy.
Origin Southern Mexico.
Size 2 inches.
Appearance The males of the species have brilliant canary-yellow sides and red tails. The females are nondescript olive-green fish. The males commence to develop the colors rather late (4 to 6 months). Many strains have now been developed; the best known is called Sunset. As mentioned *variatus* with oversized fins have been developed and are called Topsails.
Behavior, Feeding, Water conditions. Sexing, Breeding Same as for *X. maculatus.*

Redtail Black Topsail Variatus Platy. (Male.)

CENTROPOMIDAE (Glassfishes)

This family was at one time called Ambassidae. It contains some very transparent-bodied fishes popularly called Glassfishes, most of which come from the sea or brackish water. Only one or two small fresh- or brackish-water Glassfishes are usually offered to the aquarist. One of the distinguishing characteristics of this species, which is sometimes mistaken by the novice for a Characin, is that the dorsal fin is in two parts separated by a deep notch.

Chanda ranga – Indian Glassfish. (Male.)

Toxotes jaculator - Archerfish (p. 222).

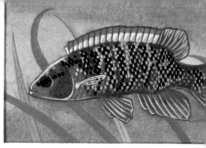
Badis badis - Badis (p. 223).

Colisa lalia - Dwarf Gourami (p. 248).

Monocirrhus polyacanthus - Leaf Fish (p. 223).

Betta splendens
Cambodia Fighter (Male) (p. 247).

Betta splendens
Red and Blue Fighter (Female) (p. 2-

Betta splendens
Red Fighter (Male) (p. 247).

Betta splendens
Blue Fighter (Male) (p. 247).

Chanda ranga Hamilton-Buchanan 1822

Popular name Indian Glassfish.
Origin India and Burma.
Size 2½ inches. Aquarium specimen 1¾ inches.
Appearance By transmitted light the body is transparent; by reflected light it shows many prismatic hues: yellow, gold, and blue.
Behavior Difficult to keep in a community tank as it needs special water conditions and cannot compete well for food with other fishes.
Feeding Almost entirely small live foods.
Water conditions Hard (300 ppm) alkaline water (pH 8.2) to which is added 1 teaspoonful of salt per gallon. Temperature 80°F.
Sexing In the male the posterior edge of the posterior part of the dorsal and the caudal fin are edged with blue.
Breeding This fish spawns in plant thickets and lays adhesive eggs so it can be bred like Characins (see above, Characins) on fine-leaved plants or on nylon mops except of course that hard water as described above is used. These fish are not too difficult to spawn. About 200 eggs are laid and the parents usually leave them alone. They hatch in 12 hours and become free-swimming on the 3rd day. The fry are minute and very difficult to rear. Unless a fairly fresh infusoria culture containing very fine organisms is available, the chances of success are slender. Continental breeders recommend *Cyclops* nauplii as first food. Mild aeration is also recommended so as to keep the food swirling around the fry who, like their parents, do not hunt actively for food, but grab what passes by.

TOXOTIDAE
(Archerfishes)

This is a small family containing five species, renowned for their ability as marksmen. This weird talent is used to supplement their diet by shooting down with drops of water insects resting on plants growing above the water surface. How this is accomplished is not entirely clear but it is believed that drops of water are forced by gill-cover pressure along a tube formed by the tongue and a groove on the palate. When it is performing this peculiar feat the mouth sticks out of the water but the eyes are submerged; thus the fish must not only judge distance but also compensate for refraction if it is to hit its target. It is said that they can aim accurately for a distance of about five feet. As a matter of fact the first shot frequently misses the target but several others follow in rapid succession and the insect is quickly brought down into the water. The amusing part of it is that in an aquarium housing these fishes the marksman's victim is usually swallowed by another fish, but no fights break out on this account.

Toxotes jaculator   Pallas 1766

Popular name   Archerfish.
Origin   Widely distributed from South-East Asia to North Australia, living in brackish water.
Size   Up to 10 inches in the wild. Aquarium specimens usually about 4 to 5 inches.
Appearance   Long, strongly compressed silvery body with black oval spots or bands.
Behavior, Feeding   Peaceful, can be kept in company with other large fishes. However, in order to watch them shooting it is essential to set up a large tank containing 3, 4, or more fishes. The tank should be half filled with water and provided with plants which grow out of the water. Bluebottle flies (obtained by hatching maggots sold as bait), cockroaches, and other insects introduced into the top half of the tank will be rapidly shot down. In my experience fishes which have been fed for a long time on maggots, bits of meat, small fishes, and other similar foods either lose this ability or do not bother to shoot down insects. Best shooting is seen when the fish have not been fed for a day or two.
Water conditions   Add 1 teaspoonful of salt per gallon of aquarium water. Temperature 80°F.
Sexing, Breeding   Not known.

NANDIDAE

This family contains many predatory species with voracious appetites. They come from India, Burma, West Africa, and northern parts of South America. These stockily built fishes of robust appearance have large mouths. Some species can eat fishes half their own size.

The Nandids do best in dimly lit tanks with plenty of hiding places, which are best provided by suitably arranged rockwork to produce caves and arches.

Badis badis Hamilton-Buchanan 1822

Popular name Badis.
Origin India.
Size 2½ inches.
Appearance The coloration of this fish changes rapidly and frequently. The flank has a mosaic pattern, the usual colors being brown interspersed with patterns of red and black. From this the fish can change to patterns of greenish blue or pale pink.
Behavior Does well in community tanks with fishes its own size. This is not only the prettiest but also the best behaved Nandid with a not too large mouth. Aggressive toward its own kind, particularly at breeding time. This fish takes up queer attitudes in the aquarium.
Feeding Mainly live foods. May take some dried food.
Water conditions Neutral to alkaline, moderately hard to hard water.
Sexing Males hollow bellied, females slightly plumper.
Breeding Fairly easy. The fishes spawn Cichlid fashion (see below, Cichlidae) on the underside of a stone arch or flowerpot. The female is removed just after spawning, the male just after the fry become free-swimming. Usually a hundred or so fry are produced, which start squabbling and eating each other at an early age. Hence they must be graded for size, and plenty of shelter provided.

Monocirrhus polyacanthus Heckel 1840

Popular name Leaffish.
Origin Amazon Basin, Guinea.
Size 3 inches.
Appearance The deep, strongly compressed body with serrated fins gives this fish the appearance of a leaf. This mimicry is further enhanced by its clay-colored sides surmounted by irregular black markings and a small fingerlike projection from the lower lip, which resembles a leaf stalk. This camouflage no doubt helps this slowly drifting predatory fish to capture its prey. The highly protrusile mouth opens out like a trumpet to an amazing size.
Behavior This is a species best kept with others of its own kind, in a well-planted tank.
Feeding This fish accepts little else besides live fishes about 1 to 1½ inches long. Since it can eat its own weight in food daily, the mag-

nitude of the feeding problem can be easily imagined. Water Tigers and Water Boatmen are also accepted.

Water conditions   Soft, slightly acid water suits it best.

Sexing   Not possible from external features.

Breeding   This fish spawns Cichlid fashion (see below, Cichlidae) on flat stones, flowerpots, and broad-leaved plants. Eggs are fanned and looked after by the male. Young hatch in 3 to 4 days and are colorless at birth. Later they go through a stage when they are peppered with small spots resembling white spot disease, but this is a normal color pattern and disappears as the fish grow up.

ALBERT KLEE

A typical spawning sequence of the Cichlid. (Left) The prenuptial "dance." (Top right) After laying their eggs on a flat surface, either or both of the parent fish care for the eggs, fanning them with the pectoral fins to aerate them and to keep dirt away. (Bottom) After hatching, the fry are moved to another site by the parents who still guard their youngsters (p. 226).

CICHLIDAE

This family contains perchlike fishes that come almost entirely from Africa, Madagascar, South and Central America; only two species come from Southern India and Ceylon. The Cichlids differ from the Perches, among other things, in the fact that they have one instead of two nostrils on each side of the head.

For convenience of description it is best to divide these fishes into four arbitrary groups. (1) The large Cichlids, e.g., *Aequidens (latifrons) pulcher* and *Astronotus ocellatus*; (2) Dwarf Cichlids, e.g., *Apistogramma ramirezi* and *Pelmatochromis kribensis;* (3) Mouth breeders, e.g., *Haplochromis multicolor*; and (4) The laterally flattened disclike Cichlids, e.g., *Pterophyllum* sp. and *Symphysodon* sp.

The large Cichlids are extremely interesting fishes but are unsuitable for the usual community aquarium. The dwarf Cichlids are reasonably peaceful and can be kept with other species of similar size. However, both have rather similar breeding habits so we will consider them together.

Large and Dwarf Cichlids

These highly evolved fishes show an elaborate premating behavior and care of the young. Any male will not as a rule mate readily with any female; an elaborate courtship is engaged in for the selection of a mate. It is, therefore, best to rear a group of them in a tank and let them select their own mates.

Most Cichlid males have longer and more pointed fins than the females. This is most marked in the dorsal fin. In older fishes this distinction tends to be blurred for some females too sport pointed rather than rounded fins.

Fish belonging to this group deposit their spawn on some hard, firm support. The actual type of support used varies with different species. Some like to spawn on the leaf of a broad-leaved plant such as giant Sagittaria or Amazon Sword, others prefer a flat piece of stone or glass wall of the aquarium, or they clear the gravel from an area on the bottom of the aquarium and spawn on the slate or glass bottom; yet others like to spawn under tunnels or arches (a convenient way of providing these is by placing a flowerpot on its side or arranging rockwork to form an arch) or artificially prepared supports such as strips of plastic, slate, vitrolite (opaque colored glass) etc., set in some firm base. Sometimes they will even spawn on thermometers, thermostats, and other such objects in the aquarium. The type of object used as a rule varies not only with the species but also with the likes and dislikes of the particular pair in question, while some pairs will use different types of objects, almost at each successive spawning.

Thus it will be observed that no hard and fast rules can be laid down; it is best to place in the tank two or three varieties of objects and let the fish choose the one they like. On the whole, dwarf Cichlids prefer to spawn under arches; the large Cichlids prefer flat stones.

Most of the Cichlids have been spawned in waters of widely different pH and hardness values. The spawning tank may therefore be filled with fresh tap water and the thermostat adjusted to 80°F. Allow to stand for about 24 hours and then introduce the pair into the tank.

Spawning

At first both the parents clean the selected spawning site with their mouths, augmented in some instances by "sand blasting" achieved by shooting mouthfuls of gravel at the chosen site. Close observation of the pair will now show the formation of a translucent tubelike structure, usually longer and broader in the female and more pointed in the male, just behind the anal fins. When the tubes are fully developed it is a sure sign that spawning is soon to commence. The female circles around the prepared spot and then traverses it, laying series of eggs close to one another but with a little space between them. The male follows and sprays the eggs with his sperm, thus fertilizing them. This process is repeated at intervals till hundreds of eggs are laid and fertilized.

When the spawning is completed there are three courses open to the aquarist. (1) He can let the fishes carry on looking after the eggs; (2) He can remove the object bearing the eggs; (3) He can remove the fishes. For the commercial breeder interested only in raising fish, one of the latter two methods is best; for the amateur the first one offers a chance to study the interesting behavior of his fish, which he would be ill advised to miss.

When spawning is completed the fish fan the eggs with their pectoral fins, causing fresh water to circulate over the eggs. This probably helps in the gaseous exchange, for eggs too respire, like fishes; it also prevents the accumulation of dirt and bacteria on the eggs. Maximum benefit is derived from these currents as eggs are laid separately, not touching one another, thus exposing a larger surface to the water for gaseous exchange.

Fertile eggs usually have a clear, slightly amber tint but infertile eggs and those going bad for other reasons soon turn chalky white and if left for any length of time would become covered with fungus.

The parents, however, rapidly remove such eggs.

It is particularly important at this stage to disturb the fish as little as possible. Even a trifling thing such as switching lights on and off, jarring the cover glass, observing the fish too long at too close quarters may upset them and result in the fish devouring the eggs. However, pairs vary considerably in the amount of interference they will tolerate.

After a variable time, usually about 3 to 4 days, the eggs hatch and the young are transferred to a pit dug in the gravel by the parents. They take turns at standing guard; while one is on duty the other either rests, searches for food, or digs fresh pits in the gravel. This vigil is maintained day and night. Every now and again the parents transfer the young to new pits. This they do by picking up the young in their mouths and, after performing some chewing movements, expel them with some force into the new pit. It is believed that this action has a hygienic significance, for it cleanses the babies. The transfer to the new pit also helps, for any waste products are left behind in the old pit. The frequent change of the position of the nest may also have a strategic significance in the wild state where the parents would have to defend the young from other fish.

At this stage the fry lying in the pit resemble a mass of vibrating jelly. This illusion is produced by the fry lying huddled together: some lying on their heads, others on their backs, vibrating their tails at a fairly rapid pace. This again creates a current of water, which probably serves the same purpose as the fanning currents produced by the parents earlier. At this stage the fish derive their nutrition from the large yolk sac which can easily be seen on closer inspection. Neither the mouth nor the gills have developed to a functional state. Gaseous exchange occurs through the skin.

As development advances the yolk sac is absorbed, the swim bladder begins to develop, and the fry become free-swimming. This as a rule occurs about the 8th to the 10th day. If at this stage the safety of the youngsters is of paramount importance, the adults should be removed; for though in the wild they would still have an important role to play in defending the young, in the aquarium their presence serves no useful purpose from this stage onward, and as a matter of fact constitutes a continual threat to the life of the young. However, as already mentioned, it is interesting to watch the breeding behavior of these fish and the aquarist is advised to take this risk, small with some species but very great with others.

When the fry become free-swimming they swim among the parents in a tightly knit group, the integrity of which is maintained by a system of signals from parents to fry. This is one of the most intriguing behavior patterns to study; actions of the mouth and tail fin in certain ways produce water currents to which the fry respond by becoming virtually motionless, or coming together in a tight group. Any fry that wanders too far is picked up and shot back into the swarming school.

A few hours after the fry become free-swimming the aquarist should begin to provide food for them. Since they are fairly large they do not need infusoria; they can consume large quantities of newly hatched brine shrimps and microworms. A few days later, sifted *Daphnia* and Grindal worms may be given. If from now on sufficient amounts of live and fresh foods of gradually increasing size are available growth will be rapid. Meaty foods such as chopped earthworms and maggots, whiteworms, *Tubifex*, etc., should form a large part of the diet.

Hatching Cichlid Eggs Away from the Parents

Although this procedure deprives us of the opportunity to study our fishes. it is justifiable to do this if the fish repeatedly destroy their spawn or if we are interested only in rearing fry for commercial purposes.

The best procedure then is to remove the egg-laid stone or leaf to a small aquarium containing water similar to that in the spawning tank. It is advisable to set up gentle aeration around the eggs. The aerator stone should be so placed that the rising air bubbles draw a current of water over the surface of the eggs. It is neither necessary nor desirable to remove eggs that turn chalky white; any such attempt usually injures neighboring eggs. It is far better to add a few drops of methylene blue to the water so that these dead eggs do not get covered with fungus. The amount added is not critical. The water should be a fairly deep blue color. If too little is added, some fungus will develop and the dose can be stepped up. When the fry hatch out they collect in little groups resembling vibrating masses of jelly. These may be broken up now and again by sucking up and rejecting with a large-bore pipette with a rubber bulb.

Once the fry become free-swimming they are fed and looked after as described in Chapter VIII. The methylene blue will have almost disappeared by now; partial changes of water will remove the remainder. It is important to do this for brine shrimp will not live long with the dye in the water.

Finally, it remains to point out that none of the above mentioned adjuncts such as aeration or methylene blue is obligatory. Eggs have been hatched by just unceremoniously dumping them in a quantity of water (even a jam jar) without any further attention. This, however, does not detract from the advice given earlier: chances of success are better in the majority of cases when methylene blue is added and aeration employed.

Apistogramma ramirezi – Ramirez' Dwarf Cichlid, or Ramirezi, with fry. (Male above – female below.) (P. 230.)

Apistogramma ramirezi   Myers and Harry 1948

Popular names   Ramirez' Dwarf Cichlid, or Ramirezi.
Origin   Venezuela.
Size   2 inches.
Appearance   Strongly compressed, thick-set body with a tall spiked (2nd spine) dorsal. Color difficult to describe. All tints of the rainbow can be discerned: rose, violet, blue, green, etc.; striking black band through head and eye and also in dorsal fin.
Behavior   Very peaceful. Can be kept in ordinary community aquaria. Rather delicate. Rarely lives over 2½ years.
Feeding   Accepts most of the usual foods.
Water conditions   Best in moderately soft, slightly acid water. Temperature 78°F.-80°F. Some claim better results at 80°F.-82°F.
Sexing   Difficult until they are mature, when it will be noticed that the male is more brilliantly colored, has a more pointed anal fin, and a longer black spike in the dorsal fin.
Breeding   Typical Dwarf Cichlid. Lays eggs in pits, under arches, or occasionally even on flat stones. They hatch out in 3 days. Fry are free-swimming in about a week. Parents are unreliable, hence it is best to remove eggs and hatch elsewhere. Fry, rather small for Cichlids, may need a few infusoria to begin with.
cardinalis.
Astronotus ocellatus – Oscar, or Velvet Cichlid.

Astronotus ocellatus   Cuvier 1829

Popular names   Oscar, or Velvet Cichlid.
Origin   Amazon, Guianas, Venezuela.
Size   12.5 inches.
Appearance   Very variable, depending on strain, age, and condition. Skin matt, velvety, not reflectile like other Cichlids. Color, marbled olive brown to black with ivory, orange, and red splashes.
Behavior   Surprisingly good-natured for a large Cichlid. Can be trained to take food from the hand and also stroked and petted.
Feeding   Huge appetite. Likes food in large mouthfuls, e.g., live fish, chunks of beef, and earthworms.
Water conditions   Not critical. Temperature 75°F.-80°F.
Sexing   Difficult. Possible in large specimens when female fills with roe. Some males show three prominent round blotches at the base of the dorsal fin.
Breeding   Specimens have to be over 6″ or so before they can be expected to breed; 500-1000 eggs are laid on flat stone. Large tank (4-6 foot) needed with plenty of gravel and some flat stones but no plants. Good parents; as a rule they will not eat eggs or fry. First food, brine shrimps.

Haplochromis multicolor   Hilgendorf 1903

Popular name   Small or Egyptian Mouth-breeder.
Origin   Eastern Africa, Lower Nile.
Size   3 inches.
Appearance   Yellowish clay-colored body with gold and greenish iridescence in places. Blue spangles on fins.
Behavior   Very peaceful for a Cichlid. Can be kept in community tank with fishes its own size. Becomes more aggressive at breeding time, particularly to its own kind.
Feeding   Insect larvae, *Daphnia*, whiteworms; will take dried foods.
Water conditions   Not critical. Temperature 78°F.
Breeding   Can be bred in small tanks (1 foot or over), when about 1½ inches long; 50 to 100 eggs are deposited in a shallow pit. After spawning, female takes up the eggs in her mouth. Male should now be removed. Mouth of female enlarged, stretched, and thin so that eggs can be seen in mouth. Fry hatch in 10 to 15 days, and emerge from mouth. Both female and fry should be fed now. Young return

A. VAN DEN NIEUWENHUIZEN

Haplochromis multicolor – Small or Egyptian Mouth-breeder. (Above male – female below, with eggs or fry in her mouth.) (P.231.)

to the mouth of the female periodically, particularly at night and if danger threatens. First food for fry, brine shrimps. Female can be removed a day or two after fry start feeding.

Hemichromis bimaculatus   Gill 1862

Popular name   Jewelfish, or Red Cichlid.
Origin   Widely distributed, Central Africa.
Size   5 inches.
Appearance   Compressed elongated body. During breeding season develops a remarkable fiery red color, particularly marked on the head. Numerous blue spangles all over body, particularly well developed on head and fins. Hence the name Jewelfish.

Hemichromis bimaculatus – Jewelfish, or Red Cichlid.

Behavior   It would be difficult to find a more pugnacious or vicious aquarium fish. Adults must be kept singly or in pairs.
Feeding   Earthworms, maggots, bits of meat.
Water conditions   Not critical.
Sexing   More pointed and elongated fins in male, who is also more jeweled, but the female may show a more intense red coloration.
Breeding   As for all large Cichlids; about 300 eggs per spawning.

Pelmatochromis kribensis   Boulenger 1911

Popular name   Dwarf Rainbow Cichlid, or Kribensis.
Origin   West Africa, Congo.
Size   Male 3¾ inches; female 2¾ inches.
Appearance   Moderately compressed elongated body. General color green-gold to olive-brown. Ventral surface in belly region ivory and blue with large blood-red spot. Many color variations occur, even in fish from the same spawnings.
Behavior   Usually peaceful, but aggressive at breeding time to own kind. Best kept in pairs.
Feeding   Will eat all foods.
Water conditions   Not critical. Neutral to slightly alkaline water of moderate hardness.

Pelmatochromis kribensis – Dwarf Rainbow Cichlid or Kribensis. (Male above – female below.) (P. 233.)

Sexing Easy. Female noticeably fatter. White abdomen with larger red spot extending almost to dorsum. Female more colorful than male. In young specimens sex can be distinguished by a crescentic golden-orange line in the upper part of the caudal fin of the male.

Breeding Easily bred typical Dwarf Cichlid. Prefers to spawn under arch; 100–300 eggs are laid, which hatch in 3 days. Young become free-swimming on 7th day and take brine shrimp as first food.

Pterophyllum (Species and Hybrids)

Three species or subspecies are recognized: *P. altum,* Pellegrin, 1903; *P. eimekei,* Ahl, 1929; *P. scalare,* Lichtenstein, 1823. The common aquarium Angel is probably a *P. eimekei* × *P. scalare* hybrid.

Popular name Angelfish, or Scalare.

Origin Amazon.

Size 5 inches.

Appearance Very deep, strongly compressed, almost discoid body with winglike dorsal and anal fins. Silver body with black bands, which become pale when the fish is frightened or kept in pale, unsuitable surroundings. In recent years many new varieties have appeared. These are adequately described and illustrated by Wolfsheimer, 1967. However, only a few are commercially available. Of these the melanotic mutants have proved most popular. These include the Lace Angelfish showing a modest increase of pigmentation and the Black Angelfish showing extreme change in this direction. Mutants with elongated fins called Veiltail Angelfish, either ordinary Lace or Black, are frequently available.

Behavior One of the few Cichlids universally accepted as a community fish. However, only small specimens are really suitable for this purpose. Large specimens are aggressive to their own kind at breeding time.

Feeding All the usual food, including dried foods. Large specimens should have fair amount of live or meaty foods. Pregnant Guppies are commonly kept with Angelfish, for their fry provide continuous supply of live food. Angelfish sometimes go on a hunger strike. This occurs when the fish has been maltreated or is frightened. It can also be a sign of internal disease. With care, choice foods, and frequent partial changes of tank water most fishes recover.

Water conditions Not critical.

Sexing Many minute differences have been described. Most of them are unreliable. A reasonably reliable method is to view the Angelfish from the front. Males are then seen to be thin and concave immediately above and behind the ventral fins, while females are fuller and convex in this region. Just before and during spawning the pointed slim genital tube identifies the male, the fat blunt cylindrical one the female.

Breeding It was once believed that acidic water was essential for success. Nevertheless today Angelfish are bred in both acid and alkaline, hard and soft waters. In order to breed Angelfish it is best to commence with half a dozen fish. When 10 to 15 months old, pairs will form. Each pair is then transferred to a 24 × 15 × 15 inch tank. Fishes will spawn on broad-leaved plants or artificial spawn receptors made of vitriolite (opaque colored glass) or slate strips. Eggs can be left with parents or transferred to a small container for hatching as described above, Hatching Cichlid Eggs Away from the Parents. It has been found that although in some districts Angelfish will spawn freely, the eggs do not hatch, or if they do the

Four types of Angelfish. Upper left, the wild form; upper right, Black Lace Veiltail Angelfish (female above, male below); lower left, Veiltail Angelfish; lower right, Black Angelfish (female left – male right) (p. 234).

fry die before they become free-swimming. I have found this to be so in Sheffield. The remedy is to transfer the eggs to distilled water (with a few drops of methylene blue added) for hatching, immediately after the spawning is completed. A delay of an hour or so can ruin almost every egg present.

When male and female Lace Angelfish are mated, ordinary Angelfish, Lace Angelfish, and Black Angelfish are produced. Mating two perfect blacks is difficult. When accomplished, it is reputed to produce all Black Angelfish. Both black mutations are weaker than ordinary Angelfish and have to be separated at an early age from normal Angelfish or they will not thrive. Do not purchase a poorly pigmented Black Angelfish in the hope that it will turn into a perfect black as it grows older. Good blacks are fully pigmented within a few weeks of birth.

GENUS SYMPHYSODON/ (Discus or Pompadour Fish)

This genus contains strongly compressed, disc-shaped Cichlids of a magnificence and beauty unparalleled by any other aquarium fish. Unfortunately, so far they have proved difficult to keep and breed. However, a detailed and accurate analysis of their needs and care has recently been published (Schneider, 1967) which should assist those interested in this genus. Two species, one of which is subdivided into three subspecies, are recognized. These are listed below but it must be pointed out that much criticism has been levied against this classification.

Symphysodon aequifasciata aequifasciata Schultz 1960 Green Discus
S. aequifasciata axelrodi Schultz 1960 Brown Discus
S. aequifasciata haraldi Schultz 1960 Blue Discus
S. discus Heckel 1840 Red Discus

Many records of successful breeding of Discus can be found in aquarium journals. As with other Cichlids, it is best to bring up a batch of youngsters and let them select their own mates. The spawning act is similar to that of *Pterophyllum* sp. Eggs are laid on a broad-leaved plant or flat stone. One or both parents fan and look after the eggs. The young hatch out and hang on mucoid threads. It is generally accepted that it is necessary to leave the brood with the parents, for once the yolk sac is absorbed the young feed off the mucous secretion from the bodies of the parents. Nevertheless, on one or two occasions fry resulting from eggs hatched away from the parents have been reared on fine, sifted, newly hatched brine shrimps.

Once this critical phase is over the young are quickly reared on usual foods.

Symphysodon aequifasciata haraldi   Schultz 1960

Popular name   Blue Discus.
Origin   Amazon.
Size   6 inches.
Appearance   Considered to be the most beautiful Discus. Body color brownish, traversed by dark blue vertical bars. The purplish head and body, particularly adjacent to the fins, is covered by numerous interrupted blue streaks.

GENE WOLFSHEIMER

A pair of Brown Discus spawning. The female (upper fish) is laying the eggs while the male, following closely behind, fertilizes them (p. 238).

Upper left, *Symphysodon discus* – Pompadour Fish, or Discus; lower left, *Symphysodon aequifasciata haraldi* – Blue Discus; upper right, *Symphysodon aequifasciata axelrodi* – Brown Discus; lower right, *Symphysodon aequifasciata aequifasciata* – Green Discus (p. 238.)

The true Gobies (Gobiidae) are bottom-dwelling fishes in which the ventral fins are partially or completely fused to form a sucking disc by which the fish can adhere to solid objects. Gobiidae are closely related to the Eleotridae (Sleeper Gobies) but in these the ventral fins are not fused. Both these families belong to the sub-order Gobiidae which has a world-wide distribution. All fishes belonging to this suborder are rightly called Gobies.

This suborder has provided very few truly popular species for the aquarist. Some grow too large, most sulk or hide all day long, others bury themselves under the gravel. Almost all come from brackish water or sea water. Some need a high degree of salinity, which is injurious to plant life. In their favor one can say that they are peaceful, and since little is known about them this could be a rewarding field of study for the advanced aquarist. We shall deal simultaneously with three species which popularly pass under the name of Bumblebee Fish.

Brachygobius xanthozona   Bleeker 1849

Brachygobius nunus   Hamilton-Buchanan 1822

Brachygobius aggregatus   Herre 1940

Popular name   Bumblebee Fish.
Origin   *B. xanthozona*   Sumatra, Borneo, Java.
   B. nunus   Thailand, Malaya.
   B. aggregatus   N. Borneo and Philippines.
Size   All species 1¾ inches.
Appearance   Identification of living fishes is difficult because of extreme variation of color pattern. All species have a tubby, cylindrical shape and are covered by a variable number of complete or incomplete dark brown or black bands on a sunshine-yellow background. The width of bands also varies and almost completely black specimens occur. Dead fishes can be identified by scale counts.
Behavior   In a community tank these fishes have a habit of disappearing for long periods. When given up for dead they may reappear for a brief moment, and disappear again. These interesting

Brachygobius nunus – Bumblebee Fish.

fishes are best given a tank to themselves provided with plenty of
hiding places.

Feeding   Small live foods.

Water conditions   Needs one to two teaspoons of salt per 3 gallons
of aquarium water. Temperature 75°F.-80°F.

Sexing, Breeding   By shape and the fact that females are less in-
tensely colored. It is also said that yellow bands in the male take on a
reddish hue when in breeding condition. About 100 to 150 eggs are
laid under stone arches or flowerpots in Cichlid fashion. The male
guards the eggs; young hatch in 4 or 5 days.

The Anabantidae or Labyrinth Fishes come from Asia and Africa. Only the Asiatic ones have so far made popular aquarium fishes. This family contains old favorites such as the Fighting Fish and the Gouramies.

The special feature of this family is the labyrinth organ, which enables these fishes to use atmospheric oxygen. This organ, located in a diverticulum dorsal to the gill chamber, is composed of lamellae covered by a vascular epithelium. Atmospheric air taken in via the mouth is forced into the labyrinth, where it gives up O_2 and receives CO_2 from the blood stream. The spent air is discharged, usually via the gill chamber. This auxiliary breathing apparatus allows these fish to survive in polluted waters that would prove fatal to other fish and also to stand overcrowding and life in small containers such as jam jars. If these fishes are prevented from coming to the surface they can still carry on respiration via the gills, but this is usually inadequate to maintain life. That these fish are very highly evolved is apparent not only from the presence of the labyrinth organ but also from their elaborate breeding habits. Eggs are not scattered haphazardly and devoured if opportunity to do so is available, but they are usually hatched and reared in a bubble nest built at the surface of the water. Some of the Anabantidae are mouth-breeders, e.g., *Betta pictum*. The parental care of the Anabantidae, however, is a limited one and as a rule ends shortly after the young become free-swimming and leave the nest.

As a general rule, fights are likely to develop among the males at breeding time. This instinct is very highly developed in the Siamese Fighter, where it is virtually impossible to keep two males together in the same tank. Females also at times engage in mild skirmishes.

Nest Building

As already mentioned, these fish build a bubble nest at the surface of the water. Some, such as the Dwarf Gourami, incorporate filaments of algae or bits of plants among the bubbles to hold the nest together. The nest may be a compact structure composed of thousands of bubbles piled high, or it may be no more than one or two layers of bubbles scattered haphazardly over the surface of the water. The nest is usually built by the male but in some species the females may assist in the process. The actual building of the nest is accomplished by the male standing just under the surface of the water and blowing bubbles. Each is covered with a film of saliva, which prevents the bubbles from bursting when they reach the surface. The mass of bubbles is sometimes piled up to 2 inches high over the surface of the water.

Spawning

The description that follows relates mainly to fighters; any differences between these and other Anabantidae will be noted as we go along.

In between spells of nest-building the male chases the female and engages in much fin-spreading and showing off of colors. At first the female retreats from these advances and seeks shelter among the rockwork or plants. But if she is ready to spawn she ultimately accompanies him to the nest. After a few such visits the actual spawning commences. The pair now take up a position just under the nest, the male curls himself around the female, and both begin to fall through the water, when a number of eggs are released by the female and fertilized by the male. The male now releases the female from the embrace. Somewhat dazed, she reels around seeking her balance while the male rushes to the falling eggs, gathers them up in his mouth, and shoots them into the nest. This process is repeated numerous times until hundreds of eggs are placed in the nest. The spawning over, the male takes charge of the nest and its contents and usually drives the female away. She is liable to be hurt or even killed if she does not heed the warning and ventures too close to the nest. At this stage it is best to remove her and let the male look after the nest. Most Anabantidae males make good fathers and rarely eat the eggs. In some species, e.g., *Trichogaster leeri*, the eggs and fry float; in these the male can be removed if so desired. In others the eggs and fry drop to the bottom and the male continually returns them to the nest. In such species the male has to be employed to look after the nest, for any that fall to the bottom usually perish. Here the male must be kept in till the fry become free-swimming. However, if the male continually destroys eggs and young, these can be saved and reared by transferring to very shallow water (1 to 2 inches deep) and using mild aeration. Anabantidae fry are usually very small and difficult to rear.

Betta splendens   Regan 1909

Popular name   Siamese Fighting Fish.
Origin   Malay, Thailand.
Size   2½ inches.
Appearance   The wild species has been replaced by many aquarium-bred strains, some with long fins and others with short fins. In the long-finned varieties, pure colors are highly prized. These are blue, green and red, although blends of these colors will also produce very beautiful fishes. A short-finned variety with a cream body and short rounded fins is referred to as the Cambodia Fighter. Other short-finned varieties are lavender opalines, where the body is a lavender color and the fins a deep sapphire blue. Similarly we have green opalines and multicolored opalines. Females are usually short-finned, rather drab creatures compared with the males.
Behavior   The Fighting Fish derives its name from the fact that two males will fight each other as soon as they are brought together, tearing each other's fins but rarely if ever causing death. This is as far as their aggression goes. They do not fight other fishes, and are frequently kept in community tanks. The only snag here is that the fish hangs about in a corner and rarely shows its full beauty. If one or two females are introduced, the male shows himself more often. Fully to appreciate this fish, one must have a number of male *Bettas* housed side by side in separate small glass tanks or jars. The display they then put on is something that no aquarist is likely to forget.
Feeding   Accepts all foods but must have a fair amount of live and fresh foods.
Sexing   Females more drab, short-finned, and plumper. The vent is everted, giving rise to an appearance suggesting that an egg is hanging out of the vent.
Breeding   This is one of the easiest fishes to spawn. The only requirement is that both fishes should be really ready for breeding. The male indicates this by building a bubble nest. The female must be very plump. Aquarists describe this by saying "as if she has swal-

Betta splendens – Siamese Fighting Fish. In this remarkable picture by Gene Wolfsheimer, the male is embracing the female in the mating act. The bubbles against the glass are part of the bubble nest. The eggs are clearly visible, slowly sinking through the water below the fish.

lowed a marble." The breeding behavior and details have already been discussed (see immediately above, Anabantidae). The number of eggs laid in a spawning appears to be very variable: some accounts rate it as low as 100 to 200 eggs. I have obtained 250 to 400 fry per spawning on many occasions. The record number has been 960 fry reared from a single spawning. Important points to note are: (1) The male should not be removed until the fry become free-swimming (this takes about a week at 80°F.), for most fry that fall to the bottom perish; (2) Copious supply of fine infusoria, for Fighter fry are one of the tiniest the aquarist encounters; (3) Keep glass cover on for fry are sensitive to cold draughts during the first 2 or 3 weeks of life; (4) Hold temperature steadily between 78°F. and 80°F. Large numbers will perish if temperature drops; (5) Separate fishes at an early stage for large numbers of good quality males can be reared only by intensive individual care and feeding. One-pound jam jars are adequate for this purpose; larger containers do not materially assist in this. (Ghadially, 1963).

Colisa lalia   Hamilton-Buchanan 1822

Popular name   Dwarf Gourami.
Origin   India.
Size   2 inches.
Appearance   Strongly compressed oval body adorned with rows of blue and green spots on a red background.
Behavior   A very peaceful species, but unfortunately of a rather shy and retiring nature, and very prone to dropsy and other ailments such as velvet disease.
Feeding   Takes all foods, including dried foods.
Water conditions   Not critical. Near neutral, moderately soft water.
Sexing   The more brilliant coloring of the male makes sexing easy. The dorsal fin is elongated and pointed in the male, short and rounded in the female.
Breeding   As described in family description; small compact nest containing bits of plants built by male; 200 to 300 eggs are laid, which hatch in 2 or 3 days. Fry become free-swimming on the 5th or 6th day. Fry are very small and difficult to rear. Even with abundant food and expert treatment, one cannot always raise large numbers from a spawning.

Trichogaster leeri – Pearl or Mosaic Gourami. (Male in foreground.)

Trichogaster leeri Bleeker 1852

Popular names   Pearl, or Mosaic Gourami.
Origin   Malaya, Sumatra, Borneo.
Size   4½ inches.
Appearance   Probably the most beautiful of all the Gouramies. It has a long, strongly compressed, silvery iridescent body covered with numerous spots. Diffuse red coloration on ventral surface.
Behavior   A very peaceful fish, ideal for community tanks.
Feeding   All conventional foods, including dried foods.
Water conditions   Not critical. Neutral to slightly alkaline, moderately hard water.
Sexing   The dorsal and anal fins of the male are decidedly longer and more pointed than of the female. This can be detected in small specimens (2 inches). In large breeding-size fish (3 inches and over) the red "throat" of the male and the slightly fuller appearance of the female make sexing very easy. In the author's experience, adult males are usually difficult to come by. It is estimated that females outnumber males by about ten to one.
Breeding   This fish is late in maturing. Success is usually possible

only with fairly large adult specimens. However, once a suitable pair is obtained, breeding large numbers of these fish is very easy. A large tank is set up in the usual way and a few floating plants should be provided. A large, rather diffuse bubble nest is built by this species; 500 eggs are laid which, being light, float to the surface. The fry hatch out in 2 days. Both male and female can be removed after spawning, since fry do not fall to the bottom. However, if you wish to observe the parental care, the male can be left in the tank until fry become free-swimming, on the 5th day. Fry need infusoria as first food. They grow at a very rapid rate if fed well.

References

Ghadially, F. N. *The Fighting Fish of Siam.* Buckley Press Ltd., Brentford, Middlesex, England, 1963.

Jacobs, D. L. (1954). "Use of Acriflavine in Aquarium Management,"*Aquarium, 23,* 123-132.

Jacobs, D. L. (1954). "The Glowlight Tetra. Its Display and Propagation," *Aquarium, 23,* 167-170.

McInery, D., and Gevard, G. (1966). *All About Tropical Fish,* pp. 252-254. G. G. Harrop & Co. Ltd., London.

Rosen, D. E., and Bailey, R. M. (1963). "The Poecilid Fishes (Cyprinodontiformes), Their Structure, Zoogeography and Systematics," *Bulletin of the American Museum of Natural History, 126,* pp. 1-176.

Schneider, Earl (1967). *Enjoy Your Discus.* The Pet Library Ltd., New York, pp. 1-32.

Wolfsheimer, G. (1967). *Enjoy Your Angelfish.* The Pet Library Ltd., New York, pp. 1-32.

XIV Diseases

General Considerations

At first sight it appears that there would be no difficulty in defining what we mean by disease, but the more closely we examine the term the more perplexing it becomes if for no reason than that the boundary between health and disease is very vague indeed. In health the animal is in harmony with the environment (at ease). In disease this harmony is broken and the animal suffers discomfort (dis-ease).

A closed colony of properly maintained aquarium fishes suffers from remarkably few ailments. Trouble usually starts when new specimens carrying some infectious agent are introduced. This can be largely avoided by proper quarantine procedure as detailed later on. We all know that prevention is better than cure, but at times our carelessness or uncurbed enthusiasm leads us to take chances with new arrivals, and this can sometimes lead to trouble. Fortunately most of the infectious ailments can be successfully tackled by a variety of treatments, but to do this effectively we must have some knowledge of disease processes and how drugs act. This we shall examine later.

Although infectious diseases are our major concern, we must not forget that much ill health is either directly produced or secondarily encouraged by such unsuitable environmental conditions as overcrowding, pollution, chilling, toxic substances in the water, and downright poor feeding. Let us then examine briefly the factors involved in the production of diseases.

Etiological Factors

The discovery of the etiology or cause of any particular disease is important, for once we know the cause we can probably devise the means to eliminate it and thus restore the animal to health. True though this is, it is not always as simple as that. Long experience of diseases in animals, including man, has shown that although we can find a cause or the primary factor involved in the production of a disease, there are also many secondary factors that can materially affect the issue.

Thus parasitic and bacterial infections are more likely to gain a foothold and produce clinically detectable disease and/or death in poorly fed, overcrowded fish, or fish that have been chilled by a drop in temperature, than in healthy, well-kept specimens. This shows that besides the infectious factor we also have some environmental factors to reckon with. Again we observe that certain species are virtually immune to attack by certain parasites, some are moderately susceptible, while others fall ready victims. Obviously, then, a species factor is in operation here. We also know that certain strains and certain individuals can be more resistant than others. This indicates that a genetic factor may be involved. This by no means completes the list, for in some instances there are also age and hormonal factors to reckon with, the virulence of the infecting organism, and any acquired or other immunity of the host animal.

These concepts apply not only to infectious diseases but to many others. Nutritional diseases are rarely due to the absence of one single item of diet and are frequently further complicated by secondary infection. Mechanical injuries (trauma) can kill directly or as a result of bacterial and fungal infections that follow in their wake. The same applies to such debilitating chronic diseases as tuberculosis, where death is often not due directly to the primary cause but to secondary infections that follow. Even in tumors we find that genetic, hormonal, viral, chemical carcinogenic, and nutritional factors are involved in their production. Multiple factors are involved in the production of most diseases and for proper therapy one should intelligently assess the importance of each factor and act accordingly.

Classification of Fish Diseases

Diseases can be grouped together in many ways according to their main cause, the signs they produce, the organs they affect, and type of pathological change they produce.

Detailed analysis of every known disease classified in multiple ways for easy reference is really outside the scope of this brief chapter. Only a few diseases are commonly encountered by the aquarist and exhaustive lists of ailments can be found in numerous publications, so we will examine the commoner diseases caused by infectious agents and also (1) diseases produced by unsuitable chemical and physical environment, (2) diseases caused by faulty diet, and (3) genetically produced abnormalities and diseases.

Lack of O₂ and Excess of CO₂

How this state arises has been discussed in detail earlier (Chapter II). Briefly, this condition usually results from overcrowding or from pollution due to overfeeding. It can also arise from not cleaning the filter often enough. The water may or may not show gross turbidity. In mild cases the fish swim about listlessly and lose their appetites; in more severe cases they swim about at the surface, apparently snapping at air. An odd fish in a tank swimming at the surface is quite normal, but if almost all of them are at the surface, then prompt action should be taken.

The first thing to do is partially to change the water (replace 1/3 or even 2/3 if necessary). Aeration should also be started. Next, investigate the cause of the trouble and eliminate it. Look for dead fish, black gravel (overfeeding usually), state of the filter box. Check heating equipment also, for a sudden rise in temperature can also lead to oxygen lack.

Toxic Effect of Excess Acid or Alkali (pH Changes)

As we have already seen (Chapter III), pH and carbonate hardness of the aquarium water show diurnal variations resulting from the photosynthetic activity of plants, and variations if excessive can kill the fishes. The danger of shifting pH too rapidly by excessive additions of acids and alkali is that this can also cause discomfort or death (Chapter II). Thus the recent vogue for soft acid peat water, if carried to excess, can also prove lethal for both fishes and plants.

Both excess acid and excess alkali in the water produce similar signs. The irritant action leads to respiratory distress and excess mucus production, which at times makes the skin look cloudy. In more severe cases the fins will become ragged and begin to disintegrate. This is followed by darting convulsive movements and death. The cure is, of course, obvious, the aim being to restore the pH to a more sensible level, but not too suddenly. As a rule this is better achieved by partial changes of water than addition of chemicals.

Nitrogenous Waste Products

These substances, when they occur in small amounts, are harmless;

but if the concentration rises then they can become dangerous (see Chapter IV). Of all these, ammonia is probably the most toxic, even at concentrations as low as 0.2 to 0.5 mg./liter. This state arises from bad aquarium management: too many fish, too few growing plants, pollution, etc. It is dealt with by partial changes of water and eradicating the cause or causes. Indeed, the condition need never arise if a third of the water is changed every week. A further point to bear in mind is that fish can gradually acclimatize themselves to a fairly high concentration of these substances, but a newly acquired specimen coming from healthier conditions, if introduced to such a tank, may become ill and perish in a day or two.

Metal and Metallic Compounds

Most heavy metals are toxic to fish life, and ideally one should never introduce metallic objects in the aquarium. If for some reason metal has to be used, a good quality (high chromium content) of stainless steel is generally considered permissible.

First on the list of toxic metals should be placed copper, for this metal has probably killed more fish than any other. It is highly poisonous even in minute amounts. Thus a concentration of 1 part copper sulphate in 5 million parts of water will kill many species of fish (Van Duijn 1956).

Copper salts may build up in the tank insidiously in places where water is drawn through new copper pipes or from copper hot-water storage cylinders. Where copper plumbing is used, water should be taken from the main's cold tap after it has been allowed to run to waste for a few minutes.

Copper gauze, coins, or copper sulphate has at times been recommended for the cure or prevention of certain fish diseases and also for the elimination of pests such as *Hydra* in the aquarium. The efficacy of copper in killing these noxious organisms cannot be doubted but the margin between the dose lethal for the pests and that injurious to fish is so small that copper can hardly be considered a safe therapeutic agent.

A further danger with copper is that once it is introduced into the tank it is likely to stay there indefinitely, for it attaches itself to debris, rockwork, and even to the aquarium cement. As long as it stays attached it is harmless, but changes in water chemistry, particularly changes in pH, may once more release the copper, to the detriment of the fish. I speak here from personal experience. A tank in which heavy doses of copper sulphate had been used regularly killed fishes in spite of many thorough cleanouts. Only reglazing the tank rendered it safe.

Zinc salts are also poisonous to fishes and deaths have been reported when fishes have been kept in galvanized tanks. Strip lead or wire is sometimes used to weigh down plants in an aquarium. This is an ancient practice, which seems to be harmless. Nevertheless, theoretically at least, this is bad practice. The toxicity of lead, acute and chronic, is well established and the possibility of mild toxic effects under such circumstances cannot be excluded.

The manner in which salts of heavy metal act is not difficult to understand. These substances are protein precipitants. The first to suffer will be the delicate membranes of the gills; respiratory distress as evidenced by an increased rate of gill cover movements is seen when a fish is suddenly transferred to water containing toxic amounts of heavy metals. In chronic intoxication, inflammation of the gills and other organs is likely to occur.

The fact that fish do well in iron-framed tanks with crumbling top frames that shower quantities of rust and rusty scales demonstrate that iron is not a very toxic metal. However, in areas where the water is charged with iron oxide this is liable to deposit on the gills and cause respiratory distress and even death.

Other Miscellaneous Toxic Agents

Various toxic hazards are known to aquarists. Paint fumes from certain types of paint are dangerous. When redecorating the room the tank should be well covered and the aerator switched off. Rubber tubing of the black variety is reported to give off toxic substances. Most natural rubber products do not appear to be deleterious. Some plastics, such as celluloid, are considered toxic. Perspex (lucite) has proved to be very safe and innocuous and is the best material for making a variety of aquarium gadgets. About various epoxy resins there is much doubt at the moment. Some recently made and poorly cured varieties can be toxic.

Excess of tannins can kill fish not only by the pH changes they engender but also directly, for they, like the heavy metals, are protein precipitants. The signs produced are similar: respiratory distress owing to "tanning" of gill surface, followed by a stage of excitement and then stupor and death. There have been reports blaming insecticides for the death of fishes in natural waters and in aquaria. The danger to aquarium fish is small; however, it is best to keep such substances away from the tank.

Tobacco smoke is considered toxic. However, since it rapidly decomposes in the water the danger is small. If you hold a party in a room containing a fish tank, see to it that the tank is well covered and the aerator switched off. Danger arises only when the air is heavily laden with smoke. There is no danger from a few persons smoking in a room with a fish tank.

The dangers of free chlorine are well known to aquarists. Tap water contains 0.1 to 0.5 mg./liter of chlorine. This substance is an irritant; once more the delicate gill tissues suffer. Fishes should never be placed in freshly drawn tap water. There is, however, no objection to using water directly from the tap for topping up established aquaria or for giving partial changes of water. The chlorine is rapidly diluted and attaches to proteinaceous material in the tank, thus sparing the fishes.

It is now well established that coarse grades of glass wool when used in filters can break up, reach the tank, and injure fishes (Sterba, 1967). Such injured fishes develop secondary bacterial and fungal infections, and often aquarists do not suspect the glass wool. Here is an example of the importance of keeping one's eyes open for the factors involved in producing disease. It is so easy to write off the condition as "bacterial infection." With the advent of nylon wool this danger should now be over.

Disease Due to Improper Feeding

The principles of adequate feeding and nutrition are dealt with elsewhere. If the advice given there is followed, no trouble should be experienced. A brief review of the hazards is as follows: never feed exclusively or even largely on one item of diet however good it might be. Thus feeding large quantities of *Daphnia* leads to poor growth and lean fish because of the high roughage content of the food and its resultant laxative action. A monotonous diet of whiteworm is constipating and has a fattening effect. Dried food alone stunts growth and also probably leads to nutritional deficiencies and wasting. In all such instances the animal and its gastrointestinal tract become prone to infection and inflammation. The outward signs are vague and varied and can be summed up by saying that the fish is literally and figuratively off color.

In some cases putrefaction of unsuitable food in the gut leads to the production of gas. This in turn makes the fish lighter and the fish behaves as if it has swim bladder trouble. Some fancy Goldfish fed on dried food rapidly develop this condition. It subsides in a few days after proper feeding is commenced.

Diseases Produced by Infectious Agents

Diseases caused by large infectious organisms such as worms, crustaceans, and protozoans are spoken of as *parasitic infections or infestations*. Those caused by small organisms such as bacteria and viruses are not referred to in this manner even though, strictly speaking, these organisms are also parasites. All these organisms, large or small, are collectively referred to as pathogens, i.e., capable of producing pathological or abnormal changes in tissues.

White Spot Disease (Ich)

This disease is produced by an infestation of the skin of the fish by a protozoan parasite called *Ichthyophthirius multifiliis*. The parasite resides in the deeper part of the skin (dermis) just under the epidermis. The tissues of the fish react by pouring out a small quantity of fluid, which surrounds the parasite. In this cavity, vesicle or vacuole, sometimes inaccurately called cyst, the parasite feeds on the tissue juices and increases in size. At this stage (adult form) the organism is rather large, measuring 0.2-1 mm. in size. Microscopic examination shows it to be a single-celled organism covered with cilia and containing a large horseshoe-shaped nucleus which at times is difficult to visualize because of numerous opaque food granules that the organism stores for future development.

On the fish the lesion appears as a small (1 to 2 mm.) raised white spot which gets gradually larger and then bursts, leaving behind a small ulcer which as a rule rapidly heals. The plump, well-nourished parasite is now released into the tank (p. 263). It soon attaches itself to some such static object as a plant, gravel, or rockwork, and proceeds to divide and multiply till some 500 to 2000 young parasites are formed, lying in a cyst (cystic stage). The cyst ultimately ruptures, releasing these young pear-shaped organisms (free-swim-

W. TOMEY

A group of Bleeding Heart Tetras, showing clearly the white spots characteristic of Ich, or White Spot disease. In the latter stages of the infection, the fish is so debilitated that it loses strength and hangs listlessly just below the surface.

ming form) covered with cilia and capable of swimming freely and rapidly. These creatures are, however, much smaller than the adult parasite and their food stores are small. Hence they must find a fish before their food and energy run out, or perish. In an aquarium many of them will have no difficulty in finding a fish. On making contact they burrow into the skin and start feeding, until they are transformed into adult parasites. Thus the life cycle is completed.

Certain time intervals in the development of this disease are of importance for correct treatment. It has been estimated that the incubation period (time taken from moment of entry of the parasite in the host to the appearance of the first characteristic signs of the disease) at 80°F. varies between two and four days. Only very rarely is this period prolonged over a week at a temperature of 80°F. Thus it follows that if a newly acquired fish does not show any spots in 4 to 8 days the chances are that it is free from infection.

The parasite stays in the fish for 3 to 6 days (80°F.). The ulcer left behind by the release of the parasite heals quickly in a day or two except in debilitated fish, in which fungus grows over the raw area.

The time taken for the adult parasite released from the fish to form a cyst and for the cyst to rupture and liberate the young parasites has been the subject of much debate. Experiments suggest that all this takes much less than a week. This is borne out by a well-tried-out fact (and personal experience) that if all fishes are re- the temperature maintained at 82° F. for eight days, then it is safe to put healthy fish in, for all the parasites are dead. The cysts have ruptured, and the free-swimming forms, which have been shown to have a life expectancy of only 55 to 60 hours at 68° F., have died. The life expectancy of the parasite would of course be much shorter at 82° F. but the exact time has not been worked out. The eight days wait at 82° F. may show over-caution, but insures safety (Ghadially, 1956; 1964).

Mode of Spread of Infection

Any wet object can transfer the parasite. Thus fish, plants, snails, wet hands, wet nets, etc., can carry the disease organisms. A perfectly dry net is no hazard for none of the stages of the parasite can stand dehydration. *Tubifex* are safe, for the waters they live in are too polluted for fish life and, as we have seen, this parasite cannot last long without its host. It must, however, be borne in mind that after collection the water they are in may become contaminated and help spread the disease. It will be obvious from the above statements that quarantining fishes and plants and practicing hygienic methods should help. In fact, in capable hands this disease is seen only on new arrivals in quarantine tanks, never in established aquaria. Details of quarantine procedure are dealt with later.

Treatments

The main principle behind the treatment of white spot is to introduce a suitable chemical into the water that will kill the free-swimming forms of the parasite and not adversely affect fish or plants.

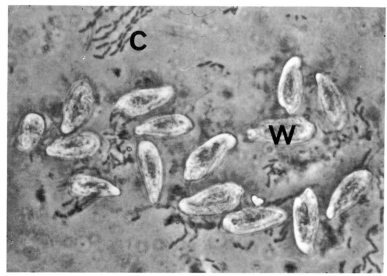

A phase contrast photomicrograph of the free-swimming forms of the White Spot or Ich parasite (W) and chains of bacteria (C). These were collected from the water in a tank containing infected fishes.

No attempt is made to kill the parasites within the skin of the fish, where they are tucked away out of harm's way. Since the spots on the fish and the cysts rupture over a period of time it is important that *not only must a lethal concentration of the drug be produced in the water but that it must be maintained over the entire period of treatment.* It is best to view this as a screen or chemical barrier imposed between the parasite and the fish. Even a brief lifting of the barrier during treatment (produced by a fall in concentration of the drug) may allow a few organisms to break through the chemical barrier, and reinfect the fish, thus restarting the whole cycle.

The chosen treatment must be started immediately the disease is diagnosed; any delay means further spread of infection and heavy peppering of the fish with white spots, which may well kill them.

Methylene Blue Treatment

I shall first describe the method I usually adopt. Carried out properly, one can virtually guarantee to cure the fish in 8 to 10 days. Remove all infected fish to an unplanted tank. Raise the temperature of the infected tank (from which the fish were removed) to 82°F.-85°F. so as to render it safe at the end of the week. Make sure that the temperature in the bare tank containing fish stays fairly high (78°F.-80°F.) throughout the treatment.

Now add a solution of methylene blue to the water. The dye is so harmless to fish that experienced aquarists do not bother to measure the amount. The idea is to add enough to turn the water a very deep blue, even inky blue (approximately 1.5 to 2 ml. (30 to 40 drops) of a 5% solution is adequate for a $2 \times 1 \times 1$ foot aquarium). An equally important point is to see that it stays that way for a week. If after a few days the color fades add enough to restore the original color.

ter is no good; results will be unreliable. Do not complicate matters by raising temperature, or filtering. There is no need for any of this. By the 6th or 7th day all spots will have disappeared; on the 10th day net the fish out and return them to the planted tank they came from.

Although methylene blue is so harmless to fish, it is harmful to plants and as such this drug is not very suitable for use in planted decorative aquaria. Some such as twisted *Vallisneria* are killed outright and many others do not grow too well for a long time afterward. It is said that plants crumble because of lack of light. This is almost certainly a factor but not the whole story.

You will find in some books that in order to spare the plants a much smaller dose of methylene blue is recommended, but in my experience such therapy has proved unreliable.

Treatment of White Spot in Planted Tank

I know of no safe, hundred per cent effective way of treating fishes for white spot in a planted tank. One must accept the possibility of some loss of plants and perhaps of some fish also. Quinine, commonly recommended. suffers from many defects; 1 part per 100,000 of water will not kill the cystic stage and is only partially effective against the free-swimming forms of the parasite. Three parts per 100,000 kills both forms but also destroys several species of plants; 5 to 6 parts per 100,000 is lethal to many fishes and will play havoc with plants. Thus the therapeutic index (safety margin) is rather small. Further, this drug is rapidly destroyed in the water and as it is colorless it is difficult to maintain a predetermined concentration over the entire period of treatment. Chloramine, which is colorless, suffers from similar defects with the added disadvantage that its toxicity varies with pH.

Acriflavine alone is hopelessly unreliable, but at a dose of 10 to 20 mg./gallon (i.e., 10 to 20 ml. of an 0.1 per cent solution) with temperature raised to 85°F.-90°F. is usually effective for fishes that can stand such temperatures. The lower dose is not toxic to fish or plants but at the higher dose some plants will suffer; fish can tolerate twice that amount. An eye should be kept on the color of the water. It is usually necessary to add a further small dose (2 mg. per gallon) on one or two occasions during the course of the treatment, to maintain the concentration.

Mercurochrome is perhaps more reliable than most but it is rather toxic to fishes; sterility and delayed toxicity are sometimes encountered. 4 drops per gallon of a 2 per cent solution is considered adequate. Once again, watch the color: if on the 2nd or 3rd day it fades a little, another drop per gallon is usually needed.

Velvet or Rust Disease

This disease is produced by a dinoflagellate organism called *Oodinium limneticum* (also called *O. pillularis*). The infected fishes have a dusty appearance, as if a fine yellowish brown powder was sprinkled on them. Each grain of the "powder" is in fact a small pear-shaped protozoan parasite measuring approximately $13\mu \times 5\mu$ ($\mu = 0.001$ mm.) riding attached to the surface of the skin. The gills are also frequently infected.

The life cycle is similar to that of the white spot parasite. The free-swimming dinoflagellate form attaches itself to the fish first by the flagellum and later by rootlike processes, which extract nutrition from the host. It grows and becomes the adult pear-shaped form, then drops off and forms a cyst. A series of divisions occur within the cyst and on rupture some 200 or more young dinoflagellate parasites are liberated into the water.

Treatment is on the same lines as that for white spot except that here the parasite is on the surface of the fish and can be easily attacked. Single fishes have been cured in minutes by dipping into a fairly strong solution of salt or copper sulphate. But usually this is

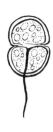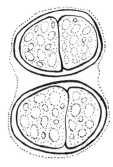

Stages in the life cycle of the parasite causing Velvet. (Left) – free-swimming dinoflagellate form. (Center) – adult parasitic form found on fish. (Right) – parasites dividing in cyst.

of little practical use for when the fish is put back in the tank it will become infected again.

Both methylene blue and acriflavine have been successfully used to treat velvet in planted tanks. Of these two I prefer the latter because acriflavine is apparently less toxic to plants. The method I have successfully employed on numerous occasions is as follows: add 2 mg. of acriflavine per gallon of water (i.e., 2 ml. or 40 drops of a 1 : 1000 or 0.1 per cent solution of acriflavine) in the tank on the first day and the same dose again on the 3rd day. Leave for 7 to 10 days. The fish will be cured within the first few days (2 to 3 days) and most of the drug will have disappeared during the later part of the treatment. Partial changes of water will remove the rest. Some persons recommend that the treatment should be repeated after a week to ten days, for it is argued that such low concentrations may not kill the cystic stage of the parasite. Hence the need to let them hatch out and kill them during the repeat treatment. In recent years I have given only one course of treatment (lasting 10 to 15 days) and the fish have not been reinfected. Plants and fish are not adversely affected. In fact, algae are destroyed to some extent so that the plants look and thrive better after this treatment.

Copper and copper salts are highly effective for killing velvet parasites but because of the risks involved one cannot (wholeheartedly) recommend them, particularly when other safe and effective ways of treating this condition are available.

Neon Disease

This common disease of Neon Tetras was at one time believed to be restricted to this single species. Unfortunately this is no longer true; the disease is known to affect many others such as *Hyphessobrycon gracilis, H. flammeus, H. rosaceus, H. heterorhabdus, Hemigrammus ocellifer* and even a fish as different as *Brachydanio rerio*.

This disease is caused by a sporozoan parasite called *Plistophora hyphessobryconis*. It has a complex life cycle. Groups of these organisms, which at this stage are called pansporoblasts, occur in the tissues of the fish. These in turn produce minute spores, which are liberated when the fish dies or the affected part sloughs off. The spores hatch and produce amoeboid organisms, which then infect other fish. Parasites have been found in very young fry and also in the ovaries of Neons suggesting that the eggs could be infected.

In Neons the disease starts as a grayish white discoloration of the blue-green iridescent part of the fish. Usually the disease runs a slow chronic course over a period of many months, the blemish increasing in size and extent. Finally the fish begins to waste away and dies. Histological sections show necrosis (death) of the affected tissues and many parasites.

So far there is no known cure for this condition. It has been claimed that prolonged treatment with methylene blue in the manner described for white spot may be effective. The disease is believed to halt and even regress if detected early and treated with formaldehyde; one drop for every five gallons is the dose recommended.

One cannot vouch for these treatments; wherever possible it is best to destroy the infected fish.

Fungus Attack

Tropical fish are rarely affected by this complaint unless maintained at low temperatures. Classically, this is the disease of cold-water fish, particularly those kept in ponds.

The condition is characterized by patches or tufts of grayish-white hairy or fluffy growth arising from one or more foci on the skin of the fish. In advanced cases the fins may become ragged and the flesh eaten away.

The hairy appearance is due to the filaments of molds belonging to the genera *Saprolegnia* and *Achlya*, the spores of which are commonly found in the water. These organisms are primarily saprophytes, that is to say they live on dead organic matter but at times they also act as pathogens of low virulence.

A tetra showing mouth fungus.

Hence this organism attacks only debilitated fish or debilitated tissues. Any raw surface such as a wound, abrasion, or ulcer is likely to be invaded by this fungus, which also attacks infertile fish eggs. If too many infertile fungus-attacked eggs are present, the pollution created injures the neighboring fertile eggs and the fungus spreads to them also. Hence the advisability of adding a few drops of methylene blue when such a situation is likely to arise.

The treatment of affected fish falls into two categories: treatment for the fungus and a general check to find out what went wrong to weaken the fish in this manner, paying particular attention to pH changes and pollution or any other situation that might have a bad effect on the fishes' skin.

The fungus-covered area is treated by painting with 0.5 to 1% solution of Mercurochrome, after which the fish is placed in a tank containing potassium dichromate in a strength of 1 : 20,000. Treatment should be continued for 7 to 10 days. Another popular method is to wipe the fungus-covered area with a strong solution of salt and then place the fish in salt water for a few days (strength depends on what the species can tolerate – add a small quantity at a time till some 1 to 2 ounces per gallon has been added over a period of 4 days or so).

Mouth Fungus, Slime Disease, Body Rot (Chondrococcus Infection)

A highly infectious disease which used to wipe out entire shipments of fish. The sequence of events was as follows. In transit, fish (Black Mollies usually) bruised their mouths and fins against the tin cans in which they were transported in those days. These areas became infected with *Chondrococcus columnaris* (also called *Bacillus columnaris*). A fluffy whitish funguslike appearance developed around the mouth. On affected parts of the fins and body slimy grayish-white patches developed. The mouth and fins were soon eaten away by the gangrenous infection and bits of sloughed-off tissues and mucus dangled from the affected parts.

The disease is less frequently encountered today and is fairly easily controlled provided action is taken before much tissue is damaged by the organism. For this 50 to 100 mg. of terramycin per gallon is added to the tank water. The drug is harmless to fish and plants. Fish recover in 48 hours but must be kept under treatment for at least a week.

All other old treatments such as methylene blue, hydrogen peroxide, malachite green, etc., are of so little use that we shall not consider them here.

Infectious Dropsy (Ascites)

The infectious agent responsible for this condition is a bacterium called *Pseudomonas punctata*. In outdoor ponds this disease can reach epidemic proportions but in tropical aquaria only an occasional old fish develops this complaint. Apparently only fishes weakened by old age or by other ailments such as tuberculosis are gen-

A Rosy Barb affected by a severe case of Dropsy. The lower abdomen is grossly distended, and the scales in that area show a roughened appearance.

F. N. GHADIALLY

erally affected. Some species, such as the Dwarf Gourami (*Colisa lalia*), are very prone to this disease. Next in susceptibility are the Carps, followed by *Bettas* and *Poecilia* (*Mollienesia*).

The signs of this disease are unmistakable and are due to the accumulation of fluid (edema) in the fish. The belly is swollen by fluid accumulating in the peritoneal cavity. The scales protrude and tend to stand on end because of fluid accumulation in and under the skin. This also gives the skin a translucent, gelatinous appearance. In time the fish has difficulty in swimming and rolls about. The edematous skin ruptures and ulcers form. The edema of the retrobulbar (behind the eye) tissues causes exophthalmus (protruding eyes).

There is no chance of curing the fish permanently. Salt baths may prolong life by extracting the fluid osmotically, as also will aspirating the belly with a syringe. Such treatments are in our view cruel. It is best to put the fish out of its misery as soon as scale protrusion is detected.

Bacterial Fin Rot

The disease is adequately described by its name; the fins putrefy and disintegrate. As we have seen, fins may rot secondarily to other diseases but here the fins rot primarily because they are attacked by bacteria. There has been controversy regarding the species of organism involved. However, two rod-shaped organisms belonging to the *Pseudomonas punctata* and *P. fluorescens* group are now believed to be responsible.

At one time this disease caused much concern among fish breeders. Young fish, especially Barbs and even more particularly Tiger Barbs, lost their tails regularly at the infusoria-brine shrimp stage. Some were of the opinion that this was a genetic defect, others that it was an infection. In retrospect it would appear that probably both facors were involved, for: (1) This fin rot ceased if little or no infusoria was used and the water changed frequently; (2) Some strains lost their fins in spite of all precautions and also produced many fishes with other obvious genetic abnormalities such as "telescope eyes," abnormal color markings, and swim-bladder defects.

Be that as it may, it is clear now that this disease occurs in fish living in polluted waters. Mild degrees of infection with slight fraying of the fin margin are easily overlooked. It is of course not con-

Bacterial fin rot! The fins are eroded. Blobs and shreds of mucus can be seen coming away from the body and fins; there is an ulcer on the gill cover.

fined to young fish, and it is common enough in badly cared-for community tanks.

As will be gathered from the above, in most cases if diagnosed early no drugs are needed. Partial changes of water, a slightly raised temperature, good food, and aeration should put matters right. In advanced cases acriflavine treatment is recommended; between 10 and 20 mg. per gallon can be employed. At the higher dose plants will suffer. Most fishes can tolerate up to 50 mg. per gallon but some may suffer from temporary sterility. Temperature should be raised to 82°F.

Quarantine Procedure

Once a healthy population of fish has been built up, it is desirable to quarantine or pretreat newly acquired fish, plants, and all other "wet objects" before introduction to the main collection.

The notion behind quarantine is the complete segregation of an individual suspected of carrying a disease from the healthy population to which it is to be introduced. This must be for a duration longer than the incubation period of the disease, so as to establish definitely whether the individual is free from the disease or not, before introducing it to the main community.

Thus, as already pointed out, the incubation period of white spot is about 4 days, so if a newly acquired fish which has been isolated for more than this period, say eight days, does not show the disease then one can be reasonably certain that this fish if released into our main collection will not give rise to white spot in the community.

At one time aquarists used to do just that, but they found that though this method was highly effective against white spot it did not prevent the outbreak of other parasitic infestations, particularly velvet.

The reason for this is that in early stages of this disease the few parasites riding on the fish are virtually undetectable even to the sharpest eyes. So today many aquarists (including myself) prefer to pretreat the fishes with methylene blue or acriflavine before accepting them as members of the main collection. The manner in which I do this is as follows:

In a room far away from my fish house is maintained a quarantine tank. Normally it contains nothing more than water and a thin layer of gravel at the bottom. When a new fish is acquired it is placed in this tank (2 feet $\times$ 1 foot $\times$ 1 foot) and approximately ½ ml. of a 5 per cent solution of methylene blue is added to the water. This fish is observed and fed daily after the main collection have been attended to, never the other way round. If at the end of a fortnight the fish appears normal it is released into the fish house. This procedure kills any velvet parasites if they are present. If the fish develops white spot, the dose of methylene blue is raised to combat the condition.

It is very difficult to ensure that plants do not carry some fish parasites. One should, however, take reasonable precautions, such as washing them under the tap and keeping them in a quarantine tank without fishes for over a week (temperature 80°F.), so as to insure that at least they will not carry white spot to the community. Some aquarists like to add 2 mg./gallon of acriflavine to the water in the plant quarantine tank in the hope that it will kill off other parasites and spores, and also perhaps some algae. This is a reasonable idea. Others like to give the plants a quick dip or a brief bath in brine or permanganate. Unfortunately, any agent strong enough to kill parasites quickly is almost certain to injure or kill the plants.

Congenital Diseases and Malformations

A disease or deformity seen at birth or shortly after may be due to genetic causes or to the action of some noxious agent such as infection or poison acting on the embryo. Only the former kind is transmitted, according to Mendelian law.

Classic examples of true genetic defects are seen in various types of fancy Goldfish: veiltail, lion head, telescope eyes, and the like. Here the pathological changes are prized and maintained through inbreeding by aquarists.

Similar defects also occur in tropical fish. Fighters are at times born without ventral fins, a defect which can be propagated by breeding. Other such examples are popeyed Tiger Barbs with eyes like telescope-eyed Goldfish, and swim-bladder weakness, a condition in which the swim bladder is too small or too large and the fish has difficulty in swimming.

Hybridization with its attendant mixing of genetic material from two different species or subspecies can produce some interesting abnormalities. These include (1) sterility (the best known example is the mule); (2) hybrid vigor, where the offspring are more robust or better able to cope with some infectious agent; (3) gigantism, where the offspring are much larger than either parent.

Perhaps the most interesting and widely studied of these abnormalities is the production of melanomas (black pigmented tumors) when certain strains of Platyfish are crossed with Swordtails (Gordon, 1937) or Guppies crossed with Mollies (Ghadially and Gordon, 1957). It is for this reason that it is difficult to maintain and propagate hybrid Swords, which have a fair amount of black pigment in them.

Examples of genetic and hence transmissible defects are often difficult to distinguish from injuries in embryonic life, for both produce batches of abnormal youngsters. The following defects fall in this category.

Skeletal defects such as deformed spine giving the fish a humped back or crooked appearance can be either genetic, the results of injury, or lack of essential materials during development. Absent fins are not always a genetic defect. Whole broods of Barbs with absent or deformed tail fins were common until it was realized that in most instances, if not all, this could be remedied by clean conditions in the rearing tanks. Yet another example is yolk-sac dropsy where edema of the yolk-sac and death of large numbers of fry occur. A genetic factor is probably involved but the possibility of an environmental factor cannot be excluded.

Here one can note that a susceptibility to certain diseases is sometimes inherited. This is why certain species or strains are more susceptible to a particular infectious disease. Such a defect does not show up as disease unless the animal meets the noxious agent and is thus put to the test by an unfavorable environment.

References

Ghadially, F. N. (1956). "White Spot Disease," *Aquarist, 20*, 216-218; *20*, 239-242; *21*, 12-13. Republished *Aquarist, 29,* 1964.

Ghadially, F. N., and Gordon, M. (1957). "A Localized Melanoma in a Hybrid Fish *Lebistes* × *Mollienesia.*" *Cancer Res., 17*, 597-599.

Gordon, M. (1937). "The Production of Spontaneous Melanotic Neoplasms in Fishes by Selective Matings." *Amer. J. Cancer, 30,* 362-375.

Sterba, G. (1967). *Aquarium Care,* p. 261. Studio Vista Ltd., London.

Van Duijn, C. (1956). *Diseases of Fishes,* pp. 40-41. Poultry World Ltd., London.

XV Enemies

It is customary to list under this heading certain undesirable creatures which sometimes gain access to the aquarium with plants or live foods collected from ponds. This list of proved rogues is rather small, and the aquarist should learn to identify them on sight.

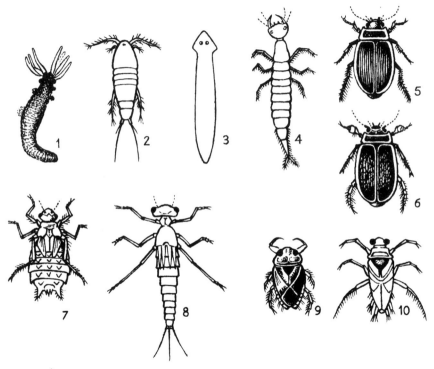

MICHAEL YOUENS

Fish enemies (not drawn to scale):
(1) *Hydra*. (2) *Cyclops*. (3) Planarian. (4), (5) and (6) Larva, adult male and adult female of the Great Diving Beetle (*Dytiscus marginalis*). (7) Larva of the Dragonfly (*Epitheca bimaculata*). (8) Larva of the Dragonfly (*Erythromma najas*). (9) Water Boatman (*Corixa geoffroyi*). (10) Backswimmer (*Notonecta glauca*). (11) Fish Louse (*Argulus* sp.).

Hydra

These lowly evolved animals (phylum Coelenterata), measuring approximately ¼ inch to ½ inch in length, look like fine hairs hanging from plants and glass wall of the tank. These creatures may be white (e.g., *Hydra americana*), gray, brown (e.g., *Hydra vulgaris*), or green (e.g., *Chlorohydra viridissima*), depending on species. They have a short tubular body surmounted by a mouth and radiating tentacles on which are lodged numerous sting cells or nematocysts. These cells can harpoon a small crustacean (e.g., *Daphnia* or *Cyclops*) or fry and inject it with poison. The victim is then maneuvered into the mouth, after which the *Hydra* shrinks in size and sometimes turns into a small gelatinous globule.

Hydra are rather particular about water conditions and temperature, and can hence be destroyed in many ways: (1) Raising temperature to 105°F. for 15 minutes after removal of fishes; (2) Ammonium nitrate method. I have frequently employed this in planted tanks containing fry 1/3 to 1/2 inch in size at the *Daphnia* stage. Add 300 mg. per gallon and repeat the same dose after four days if all *Hydra* are not destroyed by then. It is said that the pH should not be above 7.5. Plants may benefit from this treatment for this compound is a well-known fertilizer; (3) Quinine, chlorine, formaldehyde, and many other agents have been employed to destroy *Hydra*, but these in my view are needlessly drastic. Copper and copper sulphate are highly effective but the use of copper cannot be recommended (see Chapter XIV); (4) Some Gouramies, Paradise Fish, and the pond snail *Lymnaea stagnalis* are reported to eat *Hydra*.

Planarians

These flat worms (Platyhelminthes) (see illustration) usually infest tanks where the feeding is too generous. They crawl along the glass and are unsightly in decorative aquaria. It is generally accepted that they will devour fish eggs but some aquarists are reluctant to believe that these slow-moving creatures can attack fry. I have once witnessed a full-scale battle between planarians and fry in a spawning tank and can confirm that they can play havoc with fry. (The technique seems to be to drop down on resting fry just after the lights are turned out)

There is no easy, certain way of eliminating these pests. Treatments similar to those described for *Hydra* occasionally work. Some aquarists advise baiting them with cooked meat. This is done by putting a small piece of meat in the tank in the evening and collecting the meat covered with planarians next morning.

Water Tiger

This is the popular name for the larval stage of the common water beetle *(Dytiscus marginalis)* (see page 272). Both the larva and the beetle have a bad reputation. The former is to be particularly feared, as it can be small and difficult to detect. I have frequently used the latter to feed Goldfish and larger Cichlids but it should not be allowed in a tank with small fishes. The larva (Water Tiger) has hollow pincers by which it attaches itself to somewhat large fish (up to 2″) and sucks out the tissue juices and blood.

Dragon Fly Larvae (See page 272)

These operate in a manner similar to Water Tigers and as in the case of the former, eternal vigilance is the only solution.

Water Boatmen and Backswimmers (See page 272)

These are commonly regarded as members of the rogue's gallery but their guilt is not clearly established. My experience agrees with that of Innes, who also finds them harmless. I use these to feed the larger fishes (see illustration).

Other Insects and Insect Larvae

These are too numerous to list. The best course is to remove all suspicious beetles or larvae from tanks, particularly those housing fry or small fishes.

Fish Lice   (See page 272)

Not a louse but a crustacean *(Argulus foliaceus)* measuring about 1/16 of an inch. A pest that infests goldfish ponds, it is rarely seen in the aquarium. It can be scraped or plucked off larger fishes, but if many are found, the fish should be removed and the tank cleaned thoroughly.

XVI Snails

It is universally accepted that snails eat fish eggs and as such they should be rigorously excluded from spawning tanks, but the value of snails in furnished aquaria is the subject of much dispute. Those who do not favor snails point out that healthy aquaria can be maintained without them and that they frequently attack and destroy such soft-leaved plants as India ferns. Those in favor of introducing snails observe that they dispose of surplus food and keep plants and tank clean by eating algal growth. This is one of those unending controversies that can never be completely resolved.

MICHAEL YOUENS

Snails commonly kept in aquaria (not to scale):
(1) and (2) Great Ramshorn Snail *(Planorbis corneus)*. (3) Acute Bladder Snail *(Physa acuta)*. (4) Horn of Plenty Snail or Cornucopia *(Thiara tuberculata)*. (5) Great Pond Snail *(Lymnaea stagnalis)*. (6) Mystery Snail *(Ampullaria cuprina)*. (7) Wandering Snail *(Lymnaea ovata)*.

Too many snails in a tank are unsightly, and indicate that too liberal feeding is being indulged in. A modest population of the correct sort of snails is in my view both attractive and useful.

A great oldtime favorite is the Great Ramshorn Snail (*Planorbis corneus*). They fare rather poorly in well-populated tanks because fishes continually peck at their "horns" and harass them. Eggs are laid freely but the newly hatched snails are soon devoured by the fishes. The small Acute Bladder Snail (*Physa acuta*) fares a lot better and is worth having in any tank. It is, however, a prolific breeder and can get a bit out of hand. Another very useful snail is *Thiara tuberculata* (popularly called the Malayan Live-bearing Snail or Cornucopia Snail). It burrows under the gravel and keeps the compost sweet and wholesome. Being of nocturnal habit it is rarely seen until the lights are switched off, when scores of them may be seen swarming over the front glass.

Lymnaea stagnalis, another Pond Snail, is not really suitable for the furnished aquarium for it will certainly attack many aquarium plants; however, it has its uses. If *Hydra* appear in a tank containing fry, half a dozen of these will soon wipe them out as long as there is not too much other food for them in the tank.

Another snail of interest to the aquarist is the Mystery Snail, *Ampullaria cuprina.* It is sometimes called the Infusoria Snail. Some aquarists use these in infusoria cultures, where they devour the lettuce and produce feces on which colonies of bacteria and infusoria can thrive. Sooner or later some of the young snails are introduced into the main tanks but it is said that *A. cuprina* does not attack plants; however, other snails belonging to this genus, e.g., *A. canaliculator, A. gigas,* and *A. paludosa,* can play havoc with aquarium plants.

The list of snails given here is by no means complete but we have examined those of importance or interest to the aquarist. It is unwise to introduce unknown snails collected in the wild into fish tanks. Some snails act as intermediate hosts to fish parasites, others devour plants, while one snail at least (*Lymnaea ovata peregra*) produces a poisonous compound, which produces convulsions in fish.

Fish Index

Page numbers in bold type indicate main entry.
Page numbers in italics indicate illustration.

Index of General Subjects

Page numbers in bold type indicate main entry.
Page numbers in italics indicate illustration.